Learning the Left

Popular Culture, Liberal Politics, and Informal Education from 1900 to the Present

Learning the Left

Popular Culture, Liberal Politics, and Informal Education from 1900 to the Present

Edited by

Paul J. Ramsey
Eastern Michigan University

INFORMATION AGE PUBLISHING, INC.
Charlotte, NC • www.infoagepub.com

Library of Congress Cataloging-in-Publication Data

CIP record for this book is available from the Library of Congress
http://www.loc.gov

ISBN: 978-1-68123-053-5 (Paperback)
      978-1-68123-054-2 (Hardcover)
      978-1-68123-055-9 (ebook)

Printed in the United States of America

CONTENTS

INTRODUCTION

Popular Culture, Learning, and the Left

Paul J. Ramsey

Whether we are fully cognizant of it or not, popular culture changes us as individuals and as a society. We learn its overt and covert messages, both positive and negative. Popular culture even has the power to transform our most intimate behaviors. In an article from the February 2012 issue of *GQ*, provocatively titled "Dinner, Movie, and a Dirty Sanchez," a young woman details the ways in which easily accessible online pornography has altered sexual relations in recent years. The generation of men who grew up with the internet *wrongly* assumes that the sexual positions and activities—which, in pornography, are often done in order to get the best camera angle or to capture the "money shot"—that they have watched over and over again as adolescents are what women actually want and enjoy. Cheekily, Siobhan Rosen (2012)—a pseudonym—concludes her essay with advice for future lovers: "If I want you to come in a place that isn't the biologically designated area, I will make it known," perhaps by "singing 'Pour Some Sugar on Me'" (60).

Of course, popular culture's power stretches far beyond the bedroom, although with no less dramatic results. Its power is particularly acute in

Learning the Left: Popular Culture, Liberal Politics, and Informal Education from 1900 to the Present, pp. vii–xvi
Copyright © 2015 by Information Age Publishing
All rights of reproduction in any form reserved.

the political realm, a force that carries with it the potential for mobilizing
young people for social action, in both destructive and progressive ways.
In the aftermath of the 2012 massacre at a Sikh temple in Wisconsin, the
popular press and scholars had much to say about the ways in which white-
power music and literature served both to recruit and radicalize neo-Nazis
in the United States (Futrell and Simi 2012; Dao and Kovaleski 2012).
In addition to promoting hate and extremism, popular culture also can
rally Americans around progressive causes, even in times of heightened
conservatism. The iconic symbol of popular culture's power to challenge
conservative and ultra-Right tendencies is the folk singer Woody Guthrie's acoustic guitar, which—on the homemade emblem stuck to the body
of the instrument—reads "THIS MACHINE KILLS FASCISTS" (Cohen
2012); perhaps a more accurate pronouncement would have been "THIS
MACHINE KILLS FASCISM."

It is easy to forget what a profound educative role popular culture plays
in the lives of young people (as well as adults). Yet, as Donna Gaines (1998,
177) has noted in her study of suburban teenagers in the 1980s, "Music
… [has become] the kids' religion." Adults do not always fully understand
the ways in which young people interpret their forms of popular culture.
In the 1950s, for example, the older generation of intellectuals often dismissed the liberating aspects of the neo-Bohemians and the Beats (Pells
1989). Similarly, many adults, especially those associated with the Parents'
Music Resource Center, misunderstood the meaning of American hardcore
music in the 1980s. The band names, lyrics, and symbolism were disturbing and violent, but they oozed irony. What was misinterpreted was that
America's punk bands often took the perspective of the social oppressors
to demonstrate the absurdity of their actions and worldview; the kids, for
their part, used "zines" and album inserts (and networks of fellow travelers)
as primers to grasp the "true" meaning of these forms of art. Discussing
a different context, the philosopher Slavoj Žižek (2008) has noted that
cultural symbols are learned and, ultimately, move people to action. As
such, it is partially through music and other forms of mass culture and
media that many young people form their identities and *learn* political
ideals (Blush 2010; Gaines 1998; Giroux 2004; Luschen and Bogad 2010).
Popular culture, therefore, is an educational arena. It is an institution in
which the "political becomes pedagogical," as Henry Giroux (2004) has
argued; thus, popular culture is one of many sites through which a "public
pedagogy" take place (62–63).

Yet, "popular culture" is a slightly nebulous term. LeRoy Ashby (2006,
vii), a leading historian of American popular culture, has noted that
popular culture is a form of "entertainment" that receives "broad support
from ordinary people" and is "accessible to them." Moreover, the "creators
and/or disseminators" of popular culture "seek to profit from it." Such a

definition captures the essence of mass culture's bulk, but not its entirety; both the entertainment and the for-profit aspects can be slightly problematic. For example, the profit motive is ever present on social media sites (such as Facebook), which pull in enormous sums of money through advertising, but the creators of those pages—often non-profit organizations and individuals—do not necessarily see their work as entertainment. The Occupy Wall Street community's Facebook page, which as of May 2014 had over 540,000 "lik s," is more informational than entertaining. Similarly, the profit aspect   popular culture does not necessarily capture some of its forms. Not unlike the do-it-yourself" sensibility of outlaw filmmakers, American punk rock bands in the 1980s were often both the creators and disseminators of their art. Rejecting the consumerism of the music industry, they merely hoped to recover the costs incurred while recording their EPs and LPs (Blush 2010; Kaufman 2003). Therefore, in order to get a glimpse at a broader swath of popular culture in the United States (and its impact on other parts of the world), this book defines popular culture as media, art, and entertainment that is accessible to the masses and that may or may not be part of America's for-profit consumer culture.

In addition to its imprecise nature, the concept of popular culture— particularly the impact on its audiences—is an ideologically contentious issue. Some of the early Frankfurt School social theorists, notably Theordor Adorno, Max Horkheimer, and Herbert Marcuse, vehemently rejected that popular culture had any sort of emancipatory worth. In their view, popular culture was akin to the vacuous pleasures and entertainment that merely distracted the masses in Aldous Huxley's ([1932] 2006) *Brave New World*, a critique that was common among public intellectuals during the mid-twentieth century (Baugh 1990; Pells 1989). Horkheimer and Adorno ([1944] 2002, 137) argued, "Amusement under late capitalism is the prolongation of work. It is sought after as an escape from the mechanized work process, and to recruit strength in order to be able to cope with it again." As such, "No independent thinking must be expected from the audience: the product prescribes every reaction." Of course, Horkheimer and Adorno were largely correct with regard to the uses of mass culture; escapist pleasure and having "fun" are still primary motivations for the consumers of popular culture (Joseph 2013).

Yet, through their "left-wing elitism," Horkheimer and Adorno ([1944] 2002) neither fully took into account the potential for the liberating value or critical thought within what they consider low-brow culture (Baugh 1990), nor did they consider the ways in which ordinary citizens might co-opt and redefine popular culture for their own ends (Jenkins 2006; Mueller 2013). Bruce Baugh (1990), for instance, has challenged Adorno's elitist view of culture, which suggested that popular art had little liberating worth, by noting that "one could produce art that appealed directly to the masses and x P. J. RAMSEY

which helped them to emancipate themselves" (76). During certain periods of time (notably the 1960s) revolutionary art "encouraged ... [Americans] to revolt. It did so by speaking to their everyday reality, in their idiom" (77). In addition to utilizing the language of the masses, the forms of popular culture also matter because the various social classes in the United States often do not share the same cultural spaces; they read different newspapers and appreciate different forms of art (Aronowitz 2003). The Birmingham cultural studies scholars, such as Stuart Hall, also refused to simply dismiss the educative power of the popular, and rejected in turn the high/low-brow dualism by devoting serious study to mass culture (Luschen and Bogad 2010). Hall (1993) pointed to the ways in which popular messages are "negotiated." That is, not all people are merely passive consumers of mass culture; they sometimes transform the intended aims of the consumer industry to form their own subcultures, such as the "geek culture" that has arisen out of popular science fiction films (Mueller 2013). While some forms of popular culture can include emancipatory or politically radical elements, and while Americans often become active rather than passive consumers of mass media and art, it is important, as Giroux and Roger Simon (1989) have pointed out, not to overly romanticize all aspects of popular culture. Even popular films, novels, music, and other forms of art with liberating elements cannot be untangled easily from the capitalist "culture industry" in which they are situated.

As convoluted and disputed as popular culture is, the concept of the "Left" is perhaps even more so. The political terminology took root in revolutionary France when those who opposed the *ancien régime* sat on the left side of the general assembly; the Left-Right dualism held even after the seating arrangements were changed later in the 1790s (Bienfait and van Beek 2001). As a European term, the notion of the Left often conjures up images of revolution in the American mind, the sort of radicalism found in the Marxist-Leninist tradition (Lenin 1917/1994; Marx and Engels 1846/1997; Wolff and Cullenberg 1986). While the Left certainly does encompass various shades of socialism and communism, it also includes a whole range of other political visions, from those of liberals and progressives to those of some communitarians and civil libertarians (especially with regard to personal freedoms). What unites these diverse groups on the Left is a "belief in equality," as well a focus on "freedom and justice" (Fine and Shulman 2003, 12; Mills 2001, 357). In order to capture a variety of leftist views and activities within popular culture, this book, drawing on the Italian political philosopher Norberto Bobbio (1996), uses the term in its broadest sense: the political groupings that challenge the oppression of the status quo, advocate for peace, and work toward social justice (Ramsey 2009b). To ameliorate inequality, the Left openly "connect[s] up cultural with political criticism" in order to "expose lies" and to "insist upon the truth" (Mills 2001, 357; Chomsky 2001, 407, 413).

Utilizing these relatively expanded notions of popular culture and the Left, this collection of essays examines the ways in which young people and adults learned (and continue to learn) the tenets of liberal politics in the United States through the popular media and the arts during the twentieth century. This focus on the history of the civic function of mass culture, it is hoped, will begin a much needed conversation among a variety of scholars, notably historians of education. By the early 1960s, historians became increasingly critical of educational history's parochial focus on schooling (Gaither 2003; Lauzon 2010). Bernard Bailyn (1972, 14, 53), a leading critic, challenged the field to adopt a "broader definition of education," a definition that included "the entire process by which a culture transmits itself across the generations." Lawrence Cremin (1970, xiii), rising to Bailyn's challenge, argued that education was "the deliberate, systematic, and sustained effort to transmit or evoke knowledge, attitudes, values, skills, and sensibilities." In his three-volume history, *American Education*, Cremin examined education writ large from the colonial period to the 1980s. Utilizing his broadened definition of education, Cremin (1988) did not neglect popular culture as an educational site; he examined the publishing industry, radio, and television, although the bulk of his analysis focused on mainstream cultural production and formal institutions, including schools, libraries, clubs, and chautauquas, to name only a few.

Despite the calls for a more-encompassing notion of education—one that includes informal learning sites, such as popular culture—educational history, by and large, has ignored those appeals. That is, most of the leading books and articles in the field continue to examine traditional educational institutions and the figures who shaped those institutions (Gaither 2003; Ramsey 2007), although there certainly are many notable exceptions (e.g., Fass 2007; Kaestle 1988; Lauzon 2011; Warren 2005). Although the history of education has been slow to examine informal educational sites, other fields have been on the cutting edge of such research. Perhaps the most exciting work on popular culture is occurring in curriculum studies (e.g., Ashcraft 2006; Belcher and Stephenson 2011; Beyer 2000; Dolby 2003; Dyson 2003), cultural history (e.g., Ashby 2006; Buhle 1987; Cullen 2001), culture and media studies (e.g., Alvermann et al. 1999; During 1993; Fisherkeller 2002; Frith 1996; Giroux and Simon 1989; Grossberg 1992; Jenkins 1998; Steinberg and Kincheloe 2004), literature (e.g., Stephens 1992; Zipes 2002), and the history of childhood (e.g., Mickenberg 2006; Mintz 2004). Naturally, the multitude of scholars involved with organizations such as the Popular Culture Association and the American Culture Association have published seminal studies on mass culture, particularly through their organs the *Journal of Popular Culture* and the *Journal of American Culture*.

While there have been many notable contributions to the study of mass culture, the bulk of this scholarship does not necessarily (or exclusively) focus its attention on the leftist messages that are embedded within the more progressive forms of popular culture, messages that often called on the young (and the old) to take action (Mickenberg 2006; Mishler 1999; Ramsey 2009a. Nor does it necessarily (or exclusively) share educational history's focus on what was actually learned through these media. This collection of essays is an attempt to correct parts of that scholarly void in the history of education by foregrounding mass culture as an educational site. That is, this book brings together historians of education and scholars in other fields to begin a conversation about the ways in which young people and adults *learned*—or potentially learned—about the political Left through popular culture during the twentieth century, a scholarly conversation that is long overdue.

The various chapters in this volume begin that much-needed discussion by examining the often overlooked aspects of leftist popular culture that served educational functions. Jacob Hardesty analyzes the rise of the phonograph during the early-twentieth century and the ways in which that new technology challenged cultural norms by bringing recognizably black genres of music—notably ragtime and jazz—into white homes. While, in the same period, Daniel Dethrow's essay explores the periodicals, books, pamphlets, and songbooks of the Industrial Workers of the World. Hani Morgan's chapter examines the leftist children's literature, often written by Communist and Socialist Party members, which was widely disseminated during the interwar years. For the Cold War period, both Peter W. Lee and Paul J. Ramsey delve into the popular culture that railed against the conservative consensus of the era; Lee explores progressive film, while Ramsey examines leftist historical fiction. Khuram Hussain explores the educational agenda of the radical black press in the 1960s and 1970s, and Marek Tesar analyzes the ways in which the American counterculture of the same decades inspired a liberating underground scene in Czechoslovakia. Concluding this volume, Richard Ognibene explores the contemporary war over educational reform—a war often fought through the popular press and bestselling books—and argues that some liberal factions are beginning to see small, but notable, victories.

The breadth of the volume highlights both the stability and shifting nature of popular culture and the Left. From the turn of the twentieth century to the present, the leftist media and arts have sought to build a more just and humane society, but the development of new technologies have certainly changed the ways in which those media have connected with audiences, a point that is evident in Lee's examination of film and Ognibene's analysis of authors' blogs. While today it is commonplace for white youngsters to listen to music created by black artists, the generational divide regarding specific genres—especially hip hop, as opposed to the "hot" jazz of the early 1900s that Hardesty discusses—persists. As with popular culture, the specific agenda points of the Left have both remained the same and evolved: the call for strong worker's unions that Dethrow discusses is still with us. What was once progressive, such as the culturally relevant children's books of the interwar era, are now mainstream, but some of the other leftist themes in Morgan's analysis have been discarded or replaced. For example, as the realistic tales of workers (what the Communist Party labeled "Socialist realism") became the new orthodoxy in children's literature, leftists fighting the totalitarianism of the Soviet Union, as Tesar notes, began to use fairy tales and fantasy as educational materials to resist the party's censorship and repression. The fluctuations and consistencies within popular culture and the Left reveal the importance of historical context for a fuller understanding of these issues and demonstrate the need for historians of education to enter into this exciting scholarly dialogue.

REFERENCES

Alvermann, Donna E., Jennifer S. Moon, and Margaret C. Hagood. 1999. *Popular Culture in the Classroom: Teaching and Researching Critical Media Literacy*. Newark, DE: International Reading Association.

Aronowitz, Stanley. 2003. *How Class Works: Power and Social Movement*. New Haven, CT: Yale University Press.

Ashby, LeRoy. 2006. *With Amusement for All: A History of American Popular Culture Since 1830*. Lexington: University Press of Kentucky.

Ashcraft, Catherine. 2006. " 'Girl, You Better Go Get You a Condom:' Popular Culture and Teen Sexuality as Resources for Critical Multicultural Curriculum." *Teachers College Record* 108 (10): 2145–2186.

Baugh, Bruce. 1990. "Left-Wing Elitism: Adorno on Popular Culture." *Philosophy and Literature* 14 (1): 65–78.

Bailyn, Bernard. 1972. *Education and the Forming of American Society: Needs and Opportunities for Study*. New York: W. W. Norton.

Belcher, Catherine L., and Becky Herr Stephenson. 2011. *Teaching Harry Potter: The Power of Imagination in Multicultural Classrooms*. New York: Palgrave Macmillan.

Beyer, Landon E. 2000. *The Arts, Popular Culture, and Social Change*. New York: Peter Lang.

Bienfait, H. F., and W. E. A. van Beek. 2001. "Right and Left as Political Categories: An Exercise in 'Not-So-Primitive' Classification." *Anthropos* 96 (1): 169–178.

Bobbio, Norberto. 1996. *Left and Right: The Significance of a Political Distinction*. Translated by A. Cameron. Chicago: University of Chicago Press.

Blush, Steven. 2010. *American Hardcore: A Tribal History*. 2nd ed. Port Townsend, WA: Feral House.

Buhle, Paul, ed. 1987. *Popular Culture in America*. Minneapolis: University of Minnesota Press.

Chomsky, Noam. 2001. "The Responsibility of Intellectuals." In *The American Intellectual Tradition*, edited by David A. Hollinger and Charles Capper, 406–415. New York: Oxford University Press.

Cohen, Ronald D. 2012. *Woody Guthrie: Writing America's Songs*. New York: Routledge.

Cremin, Lawrence A. 1970. *American Education: The Colonial Experience, 1607–1783*. New York: Harper & Row.

———.1988. *American Education: The Metropolitan Experience, 1876–1980*. New York: Harper & Row.

Cullen, Jim, ed. 2001. *Popular Culture in American History*. Malden, MA: Blackwell Publishers.

Dao, James, and Serge F. Kovaleski. 2012. "Music Style Is Called Supremacist Recruiting Tool." *New York Times*, August 7.

Dolby, Nadine. 2003. "Popular Culture and Democratic Practice." *Harvard Educational Review* 73, (3): 258–284.

During, Simon, ed. 1993. *The Cultural Studies Reader*. New York: Routledge.

Dyson, Anne Haas. 2003. " 'Welcome to the Jam': Popular Culture, School Literacy, and the Making of Childhoods." *Harvard Educational Review* 73 (3): 328–361.

Fass, Paula S. 2007. *Children of a New World: Society, Culture, and Globalization*. New York: New York University Press.

Fine, Gary Alan, and David Shulman. 2003. *Talking Sociology*. Boston: Allyn & Bacon.

Fisherkeller, JoEllen. 2002. *Growing up with Television: Everyday Learning among Adolescents*. Philadelphia: Temple University Press.

Frith, Simon. 1996. *Performing Rites: On the Value of Popular Music*. Cambridge, MA: Harvard University Press.

Futrell, Robert, and Pete Simi. 2012. "The Sound of Hate." *New York Times*, August 8.

Gaines, Donna. 1998. *Teenage Wasteland: Suburbia's Dead End Kids*. Chicago: University of Chicago Press.

Gaither, Milton. 2003. *American Educational History Revisited: A Critique of Progress*. New York: Teachers College.

Giroux, Henry A. 2004. "Cultural Studies, Public Pedagogy, and the Responsibility of Intellectuals." *Communication and Critical/Cultural Studies* 1 (1): 59–79.

Giroux, Henry A., Roger I. Simon, and Contributors. 1989. *Popular Culture, Schooling, and Everyday Life*. New York: Bergin & Garvey.

Grossberg, Lawrence. 1992. *We Gotta Get Out of This Place: Popular Conservatism and Postmodern Culture*. New York: Routledge.

Hall, Stuart. 1993. "Encoding, Decoding." In *The Cultural Studies Reader*, edited by Simon During, 90–103. New York: Routledge.

Horkheimer, Max, and Theodor W. Adorno. (1944) 2002. *Dialectic of Enlightenment*. New York: Continuum.

Huxley, Aldous. (1932) 2006. *Brave New World*. New York: Harper Perennial.

Jenkins, Henry, ed. 1998. *The Children's Culture Reader*. New York: New York University Press.

Jenkins, Henry. 2006. *Convergence Culture: Where Old and New Media Collide.* New York: New York University Press.

Joseph, Manu. 2013. "Let the Poor Have Fun." *New York Times*, September 16.

Kaestle, Carl F. 1988. "Literacy and Diversity: Themes from a Social History of the American Reading Public." *History of Education Quarterly* 28 (4): 523–549.

Kaufman, Lloyd, with Adam Jahnke and Trent Haaga. 2003. *Make Your Own Damn Movie: Secrets of a Renegade Director.* New York: St. Martin's Griffin.

Lauzon, Glenn P. 2010. "Civic Learning through County Fairs: Promoting the Useful and the Good in Nineteenth-Century Indiana." *American Educational History Journal* 37: 387–405.

————.2011. *Civic Learning through Agricultural Improvement: Bringing "the Loom and the Anvil into Proximity with the Plow."* Charlotte, NC: Information Age.

Lenin, V. I. 1994. *State and Revolution.* New York: International Publishers. (Original work published 1917)

Luschen, Kristen, and Lesley Bogad. 2010. "Youth, New Media and Education: An Introduction." *Educational Studies* 46 (5): 450–456.

Marx, Karl, and Frederick Engels. 1997. *The Communist Manifesto.* New York: International. (Original work published 1848)

Mickenberg, Julia L. 2006. *Learning from the Left: Children's Literature, the Cold War, and Radical Politics in the United States.* New York: Oxford University Press.

Mills, C. Wright. 2001. "Letter to the New Left." In *The American Intellectual Tradition,* edited by David A. Hollinger and Charles Capper, 353–361. New York: Oxford University Press.

Mintz, Steven. 2004. *Huck's Raft: A History of American Childhood.* Cambridge, MA: Belknap.

Mishler, Paul C. 1999. *Raising Reds: The Young Pioneers, Radical Summer Camps, and Communist Political Culture in the United States.* New York: Columbia University Press.

Mueller, Gavin. 2013. "Revenge of the Nerds." *Jacobin*, September 26.

Pells, Richard H. 1989. *The Liberal Mind in a Conservative Age: American Intellectuals in the 1940s and 1950s.* Hanover, NH: Wesleyan University Press.

Ramsey, Paul J. 2007. "Histories Taking Root: The Contexts and Patterns of Educational Historiography during the Twentieth Century." *American Educational History Journal* 34 (2): 347–363.

————. 2009a. "The Dark Ages Haven't Ended Yet: Kurt Vonnegut and the Cold War." *American Educational History Journal* 36 (1): 99–114.

————. 2009b. "Plato and the Modern American 'Right': Agendas, Assumptions, and the Culture of Fear." *Educational Studies* 45: 572–588

Rosen, Siobhan. 2012, February. "Dinner, Movie, and a Dirty Sanchez." *GQ*: 58, 60.

Steinberg, Shirley R., and Joe L. Kincheloe, eds. 2004. *Kinderculture: The Corporate Construction of Childhood.* Boulder, CO: Westview.

Stephens, John. 1992. *Language and Ideology in Children's Fiction.* New York: Longman.

Warren, Donald. 2005. "Slavery as an American Educational Institution: Historiographical Inquiries." *Journal of Thought* 40 (4): 41–54.

Wolff, Richard D., and Stephen Cullenberg. 1986. "Marxism and Post-Marxism." *Social Text* 15: 126–135.

Zipes, Jack. 2002. *Sticks and Stones: The Troublesome Success of Children's Literature from Slovenly Peter to Harry Potter*. New York: Routledge.
Žižek, Slavoj. 2008. *Violence*. New York: Picador.

ABOUT THE AUTHOR

Paul J. Ramsey is an associate professor in the Department of Teacher Education at Eastern Michigan University. "Joe" Ramsey completed his doctoral degree in the history of education at Indiana University and is the author of *Bilingual Public Schooling in the United States: A History of America's "Polyglot Boardinghouse"* (Palgrave Macmillan, 2010) and editor of *The Bilingual School in the United States: A Documentary History* (Information Age Publishing, 2012). His historical interests include bilingual education, immigration, childhood, popular culture, and globalization. Ramsey would like to thank his colleagues at Eastern Michigan University, especially Joe Bishop, Kaia-Marie Bishop, John Field, and Christopher G. Robbins, for their support, assistance, and thoughtful feedback.

CHAPTER 1

LEARNING TO LISTEN

Conflicts between Youth and Adults Regarding the Phonograph in the Early-Twentieth Century

Jacob Hardesty

Reminiscent of Richard Storr's 1961 call for an inductive approach to educational history as well as Lawrence Cremin's more famous appeal for a history of education focusing on learning, music historians have convincingly argued that the introduction of recorded music in the late 1800s reframed listening and the surrounding social protocols as an educative activity (Storr 1961; Cremin 1965). Among them, William Howland Kenney (1999, xvii) has pointed to the "learned expectations" of recorded music, while Mark Katz (2012, 14) has contended the public had to "learn to listen" to emergent technologies. Yet how this educative process played out differently for adults and the increasingly recognizable "youth culture" of the early-twentieth century remains unexplored.

This essay introduces age as a sort of independent variable to extend the listening-as-educative-process theme. I argue young people saw the phonograph as a medium to expand opportunities for popular dance. For them, the machine meant the Charleston, black bottom, and various "animal

Learning the Left: Popular Culture, Liberal Politics, and Informal Education from 1900 to the Present, pp. 1–18
Copyright © 2015 by Information Age Publishing
All rights of reproduction in any form reserved.

dances" need not be confined to dance halls or require live musicians to provide accompaniment. In contrast, adults largely sought to maintain (as much as possible) listening practices as they had existed prior to the instrument's invention and diffusion. Like at the town band concert or light opera, where listening required a measure of restrained observation. That is, the development and increasing availability of listening technologies was for adults, at its heart, continuity with the past. For young people, however, learning to listen took a different, more physically active and engaged form.

Three general assumptions ground this essay. First, I focus almost exclusively on the history of the phonograph and give less space to the development of the radio. Certainly, this does not mean that the public listened the same way to both the radio and phonograph. Yet much of the debate about learning to listen—the decoupling of musical performance and consumption—revolved around the novelty of recorded music that the phonograph provided. Second, this essay makes little attempt to distinguish between ragtime and jazz. Certainly, musical and dance differences existed between the two genres. The focus here lies more on how emergent technologies affected the diffusion of both genres. Thus, for the purposes of this essay, I view jazz as a sort of musical evolution of ragtime, and I emphasize continuity over aesthetic distinctions. Finally, while ragtime and jazz were favorites of many on the political Left, I frame the music as anticonservative on primarily generational terms. For the first time, a genre developed by black musicians was enjoying increasingly wide popular appeal, particularly among young people. Among concerned white adults, the interest among youth in ragtime and jazz dance was synonymous with a similar embrace of uncontrollable black sexuality. With the aide of the phonograph, this music made its way into perhaps the most conservative institution, the home.

RAGTIME AND JAZZ DANCING

Throughout much of the nineteenth century, dancing was dominated by comparatively cautious and adult-sanctioned steps. Yet by the turn of the century, the waltz, gig, and other dances appeared, as one dance historian has written, "staid and conservative," especially to young people (Wagner 1997, 302). An emergent assortment of "animal dances" (including the grizzly bear and fox trot) both shocked a generation brought up dancing the waltz and Virginia reel, while also building a new generation of dance enthusiasts. Looking at the demand for dance space, many entrepreneurs saw a viable business opportunity and began opening dance halls to help satisfy a nation that had become "dance mad." In 1895, 130 dance halls existed in Manhattan; by 1910 the number had risen to 195. In Kansas City, 49 dance halls catered to some 16,500 dancers. Young people were especially drawn to the dance halls and the social freedoms therein. One estimate suggests 32,000 high-school age students attended movies daily in 1910, while some 86,000 frequented dance halls. This youth-driven interest in dancing was not shared equally between males and females. One survey of some 1,000 high-school girls and boys, also from 1910, found that nine out of 10 girls knew how to dance, while only three out of 10 boys made such a claim (Peiss 1986, 88, 93; Nasaw 1993, 110; Wagner 1997, 294).

To be sure, both ragtime and jazz were plainly understood as *dance* music. In dance halls, cabarets, and some private homes, bands provided the background music for the turkey trot and cake walk in the 1910s, just as they did the shimmy and Charleston in the 1920s. This unmistakable appeal for movement that ragtime and jazz engendered could cut across class lines. Reviewing a 1912 fund-raising Carnegie Hall concert by early black ragtime band leader James Reese Europe, one *New York Age* author recalled, "White men and women looked at each other and smiled, while one lady seated in a prominent box began to beat time industriously with her right hand, which was covered with many costly gems" (Walton 1912, 6). This common understanding of music-for-movement-sake strengthened as the genre took on more jazz-like characteristics in the late 1910s. Burton Peretti has pointed out that the relationship between jazz and dancing was symbiotic: "The dance hall, the major venue for jazz in New Orleans, retained its role in the North as the incubator for the most rhythmic jazz" (Peretti 1992, 50). And language further revealed the connection between music and dance. In many quarters, "dance band" was synonymous with "jazz band." Kathy Ogren has noted, perhaps the highest praise—and marketing ploy—possible to bestow on a jazz record was that it was "dance-tested" (Ogren 1989, 87–110).

These popular ragtime and jazz dances did have adult adherents throughout the 1910s and 1920s; many danced relatively more cultivated versions of the steps young people were dancing. *Life* magazine aptly claimed in 1912 that the new ragtime dances "spread up and down and far and wide through our metropolitan society...The dancing set in our town must be a half million strong." In New York City, Vernon and Irene Castle, a married couple both from respectable white middle-class stock, sought to "tame" the animal dances. They taught more restrained versions of the bear hop and turkey trot, which one magazine described as "[spiritualizing] the dances thought to be hopelessly fleshy" (Nasaw 1993, 104–106). Dancing for adults remained an attractive recreational activity through the 1920s, though with a different set of meanings attached to it. One 1924 article in *Sunset* magazine extolled the virtues of dancing as "one of the most healthful and joyous of diversions if properly indulged in ..."

reclaimed from the public dance hall and returned to the home through the accessibility of good music. An informal dancing party can be given with no preparation more difficult that rolling up the rugs and calling in the neighbors." Such descriptions, which could read as much like advertisements as journalism, extolled popular dancing as an enjoyable form of exercise, though did not address the discussions about morality that swirled around dancing. The *Sunset* article also alluded to a certain generational divide in musical preferences and the phonograph's ability to satisfy each side. The author wrote, "The older generation prefers the songs of its youth, and it is easy to slip back across the years with the notes of the old-time songs on the modern instruments" (Partridge 1924, 75–76). Indeed, sanctioning such dances among adults was not synonymous with approving of young people attempting the same steps, even the sanitized versions taught by the Castles. And the critics of the new dance steps, those who looked at the new dances with disgust, overwhelmingly came from generations brought up on the waltz and quadrilles, while young people proved to be the new dances' most loyal fans (Hasse 1981, 275–280).

The new dances had detractors, ragtime and jazz dance opponents who focused most of their ire toward high-school-age students, while certainly concerned about the perceived lewd dances taking place on college campuses. Such critics voiced multiple and often overlapping concerns: the degradation of girls, the increasingly sexualized nature of the steps themselves, and the influence of jazz as a black aesthetic on white youth. Underlying much of this opposition were the plainly sexualized allure of the new steps, distinctly absent in the prior century. The "tough dances" not only permitted physical contact, a distinct change from more conservative nineteenth century dances, they celebrated it—an open embrace of corporeal pleasure (Carney 2009, 129). Prominent critics spoke out about the dangers that awaited young people on the dance floor. Chicago superintendent Peter A. Mortenson sounded such an alarm. Addressing the city's board of education, Mortenson warned that popular dancing "has done much to break down the respect for womanhood." The superintendent went on to call out high-school girls for "dress extremes" and questioned why their mothers would allow such "immodesty" (Wilk 1922). To help with implementation, the superintendent suggested, and the board approved, that some 45,000 fliers be made up and taken home for students and parents to review and that 500 additional posters be placed in secondary schools (Forbes 1922). Similarly, a 1913 *Harper's Weekly* article, "Is Modern Dancing Indecent?" warned of debutantes dancing to ragtime music late at night with "darkies" (Giordano 2008, 24).Other reformers took action to educate the public in hopes of minimizing young peoples' ability to engage in such lewd behavior on the public dance floor. In large cities, "vice monitors" patrolled dance halls, carefully documenting iniquitous behaviors of young people in these newly popular public spaces. Congregationalist Rev. Phillip Yarrow, the man the *Chicago Tribune* referred to as the leading "field superintendent" of various vigilance associations, made it his mission to educate the public about the "dance evil" ("Vice Vigilants Open Drive to Purify Illinois" 1922). He scoured public dance halls, writing detailed (if not sensationalized) reports of the various dance and extramusical activities he saw. One such report, designed to "Rouse Public Conscience" and quoted at length in the *Chicago Tribune,* found that nearly 1,000 girls had "fallen" into a life of prostitution after consuming too much "pathological, nerve irritating, sex exciting music of a jazz orchestra" ("Fall of 1,000 Girls Charged to Jazz Music" 1921). He further expanded this line of argument in his book, *Fighting the Debauchery of Our Boys and Girls*: "Dancing which is characterized by movements above the waist rather than from the waist down, or which consist of suggestive movements, is not to be allowed. These rulings would eliminate vulgar Jazz music which influences dancers to use jerky half steps and immoral variations" (Yarrow 1923, 256).

Such accounts, though certainly sensationalized, were not wholly inaccurate. Young men saw newly popular public dance halls as ideal sites for extramusical enjoyment. While he was a student at the University of Chicago, a young Saul Alinsky, along with coauthor Constance Weinberger, studied Chicago's public dance halls and the clientele they attracted. Alinsky, like other jazz opponents, saw jazz dancing as a recognizable catalyst for various social ills, especially regarding the young and impressionable; he made no effort to disguise the dancing he witnessed, simply calling it "immoral." Yet the high-school students Alinsky spoke to saw little problem with the jazz dancing taking place. One boy told Alinsky they just came to "dance and monkey around, that's all." Upon further questioning, the boy explained that he and his high-school friend each hoped to "just take a good-looking woman out on the floor and squeeze a little, like they're dancing over there at the side." Another boy bragged to Alinksy that there would be "no virgins left in Chicago" if he had a car (Alinsky 1928).

Such instances also worked their way into fiction, as writers like Percy Marks, F. Scott Fitzgerald, and Ben Hecht sought to recreate the newly identifiable world of young people. As Kevin White has suggested, the focus on sexuality in many such works characterized a sort of literary primitivism, a revealed emphasis on base sexual desires absent a generation earlier (and still absent from more conservative authors such as Zane Grey). Describing the title character's disproportionately sexualized view of women in Hecht's book *Erik Dorn,* White writes, "He describes a girl he meets in a dance hall by writing that, 'She's not a woman. …She's a lust. No brain. No heart. A stark unhuman piece of flesh.'…This kind of comment would hardly have been acceptable in Victorian America" (White 1993, 48). Though fictionalized, such accounts faithfully represented the general atmosphere

of many public dance halls.Critics of such public dance halls and the iniquitous dances therein extended across the country. One Oregon evangelist
warned "dancing is the first step and easiest step toward hell . . . the first
time a girl allows a man to swing her around the dance floor her instinct
tells her she has lost something she should have treasured" (Giordano
2008, xii). In New York City, the Committee on Amusements and Vacation
Resources for Working Girls announced in 1912 it would even begin moni-
toring Fifth Avenue hotels in addition to the less costly dance halls. This
public acknowledgement that the dance craze existed among young people
across social classes (a *New York Times* headline read "JUNIOR COTIL-
LION WARNING") further indicated the dance craze could cut across
socioeconomic boundaries (Nasaw 1993, 106). Also in New York City, the
Rev. John Straton, from the city's conspicuous First Baptist Church, used a
similar approach as Chicago's Yarrow to speak out again what he termed
the "dance of death" (Straton 1920). In one 1920 sermon, which got the
attention of the *New York Times,* Straton complained that while inspecting
various dance halls, "We saw tipsy girls, as well as men, in all of the halls
visited; and in one place, we saw young women who were raving drunk,
some of them surging out of the hall on to the street outside, with their
loud talking." While Yarrow opted for long tomes about his city's moral
depravity, Straton preferred a more direct approach to educate the public
of the "dance of death" as well as other moral sins of the city. With the help
of his son and various parishioners, Straton outfitted a Model-T Ford with
a "specially built pulpit" and took to the streets of Manhattan. The pastor
would stand on this custom platform, preaching about the sins of dance
and the city's increasing depravity of young people as the car crisscrossed
Manhattan. Occasionally, a cornet player rode along and played as a way to
get the crowd's attention, in case the sight of a man standing and preaching from a pulpit in a car was not attention grabbing enough (Giordano
2008, 31, 203–204).

Underlying such opposition among Straton and others to the relatively
sexualized steps of the turkey trot and, later, the shimmy, was concern
among critics about what they saw as unrestrained black sensuality and
sexuality. White critics used the emergent genre as evidence to justify their
views of African Americans as both culturally and intellectually inferior,
seeking to separate young people from the music on those grounds. Such
opponents not only condemned jazz's supposed inferior musical quality,
but also connected the music to a certain type of unrefined stereotyped
blackness. In ragtime and jazz, the stereotyped sexually charged,
unintelligent, and aggressive black man—what Michele Faith Wallace
terms the "black brute"—had a recognizable musical manifestation, an old
idea with a new medium for re-presentation (Wallace 2003). White critics
regularly attached terms like "primitive" and "sexualized" to the music as

recognizable indicators of supposed extramusical ends, while working to separate young people from such acts.

Yet critics may well have found some comfort in *where* these popular dances were largely taking place. Such steps were in visible public spaces, removed from the inner sanctum of the home. With the introduction of the mass-produced phonograph and subsequent production of dance records, that dynamic began to shift in the late 1910s, gaining force in the following decade. The phonograph allowed an entry into the home for controversial dance halls steps, along with subsequent adult fears that those dances helped create in young people an unacceptable level of sexual interest.

THE PHONOGRAPH

Parallel to the development and diffusion of ragtime and jazz dancing were inventions in listening technology that affected the diffusion of those new steps. Prior to the advent and mass availability of recorded sound, music consumption had been a requisitely live phenomenon. Hearing music required either the ability to perform or being in presence of those who could, and attending concerts was primarily a public event. Among other ensembles, town band performances were held not solely for their musical offerings, but also as a civic opportunity for bringing citizens together (Keene 1987, 316–323). Such groups also played perhaps the most significant role in shaping musical tastes, as "bands were important dispensers of popular music" (Crawford 2001, 468). Performance of such music took place in settings ranging from department stores to formal recitals to home social events (Hasse 1981, 251). With the advent of the phonograph and later the radio, this previously requisite connection between performance and listening was eliminated. That is, listening to music no longer necessarily required the presence of musicians; listeners could enjoy the music they preferred when they desired it.

Various musicologists have noted the impact on musical consumption this decoupling of performance and listening had, particularly in its nascent stages. Among them, William Howland Kenney argues, "the phonograph changed the context in which musical messages were sent and received, lifting them out of ritualized social contexts and transforming them into commercialized memories" (Kenney 1999, 29). David Suisman notes, "As the new musical culture took shape ... it altered the way music was made and heard, bought and sold, as well as affecting more changes that were broader and more subtle" (Suisman 2009, 11). A more singular and humorous example, Mark Katz writes of the bewildered response the composer Arthur Sullivan (of Gilbert and Sullivan fame) had to hearing an early Edison "talking machine" prototype in 1888. According to Katz

(2012, 11), the composer was profoundly disturbed by the experience, later writing he was "astonished and somewhat terrified." And while such technologies were greeted with a combination of enthusiasm and skepticism, the paradigm shift in listening they created was unavoidable. Listening to music became less of a singular *event*. Instead, listening became commodified, something that could be produced, bought, and sold.

The phonograph's origins stretch back into the late nineteenth century. As it came to be developed and mass produced, the phonograph was essentially a hybrid of models developed independently by Thomas Edison and Emile Berliner. In his mid-century history of the phonograph, David Aldridge (1964, 10) notes the significant improvements Berliner brought over Edison's initial design: "A record groove which formed track to guide the sound box across the record... .; Ease and economy in making a large number of duplicate records; .... Better musical results from the lateral process of recording; .... Ease and economy in shipment and storage." Importantly, Berliner's device suggested a clearer pathway to mass production and distribution. Edison's earlier model could only make a single recording of a given sound event. His wax or tinfoil records provided no means for multiple physical records. On the other hand, Berliner's version created in essence a master version, a flat metal disc that coated with a "waxy, petroleum-based solution which was then processed like an etching: dipped in acid to make a 'negative' from which numerous 'positive' reproductions could be pressed" (Suisman 2009, 4). Thus, listeners could hear the same renditions of one performance if two physical records came from the same original negative.

Prior to the invention and mass distribution of the phonograph, the idea of listening to *recorded* sound and not *live* sound was little more than a vision among a handful of inventors. Yet once phonographs became publicly available, the previously requisite connection between audience and performer ceased to exist. More specifically, learning to listen to the phonograph actually developed different social spaces: one necessarily public and the other more private. Public coin-operated phonographs allowed for many the first recreational ability to listen to music on command, while domestic phonographs further redefined accessibility to recorded performance (Nasaw 1993). In each, music consumption lost a degree of the previously necessary public nature of music consumption.

Coin-operated listening salons afforded the public their first experiences and interactions with recorded music. Such instruments were placed in public places such as train stations and resorts, and were displayed at various state, local, and world fairs. Popular throughout the 1890s and early 1900s, coin-operated phonographs were the first technological development to reframe the relationship between music listener and performer. For the first time, listeners could hear music without the necessity of physical presence of an artist. These coin-operated phonographs created a new sort of public-private music consumption hybrid. While listeners still had to visit public coin-operated stations to hear various performances, they each could listen individually, a distinct break with the concert audience listening collectively to the live performance. And the physical act of listening was similarly affected. Instead of sitting in a seat in an auditorium, listeners often stood. Instead of hearing music performed without the assistance of sound amplification, listeners heard music through an ancestor of the headphone. Instead of watching performers, listeners looked at non-musical options such as train schedules. Yet for the first time, listeners could hear what they wished based solely on their individual preferences (Nasaw 1993, 120-125; Kenney 1999, 23-27).

In 1896 the Edison Phonograph Company released the first home phonograph. A decade after Edison released his company's domestic model, the Victor Company released its first home phonograph, the first with a concealed horn. Both companies offered models at various price points, ranging from $250 for the "Official Laboratory Model" to the $6,000 "French Gothic." The *New York Tribune* commented how one home phonograph was "a part of the furniture of the ordinary drawing room" (Thompson 1995, 131, 146). Sales for the Victor's talking machine, the "Victrola," increased rapidly in the first decade of public availability. In 1907, its first full year of manufacture, the company produced roughly 100,000 models. By 1915, Victor produced about 380,000 phonographs designed exclusively for home use (Aldridge 1964, 109). The company also increased its assets from some $13 million to $23 million between 1913 and 1915 (Wagner 1997, 268). The home phonograph easily overtook public coin-operated model as the primary means of musical consumption, redefining listening in that private space and engendering conversations about possible unforeseen consequences.

The increasing popularity of home phonographs was met with some opposition by musicians. In his famous and oft-cited 1906 essay, "The Menace of Mechanical Music," John Philip Sousa (278) wrote, "Sweeping across the country with the speed of a transient fashion in slang or Panama hats, political war cries or popular novels, comes now the mechanical device to sing for us a song or play for us a piano, in substitute for human skill, intelligence, and soul." As Sousa very likely realized, the major thrust of his attack was less than accurate. Phonograph records were not *replacing* "human skill, intelligence, and soul," they *substituted* live "human skill, intelligence, and soul." His 1906 diatribe went on to predict various consequences of "canned music": students would not practice their instruments anymore, musicians would be unemployed, and there would follow a decline in "domestic music." Cognizant of the often symbiotic relationship between music and dancing, Sousa referenced the redefined and even harmful social interaction of dancing to recorded music: "The country-dance orchestra of violin, guitar and melodeon had to rest at times. …Now a tireless mechanism can keep everlastingly at it, and much of what made the dance a wholesome recreation is eliminated." Ever the traditionalist, Sousa would later join a number of lawsuits and testify before Congress to protest the new manifestation of musical creation and consumption. Yet, whether he realized it or not, Sousa was fighting a losing battle about the spread of the phonograph. The proverbial genie of recorded music could not be put back in the bottle (Suisman 2009, 161–168).

LEARNING TO LISTEN AND THE GENERATIONAL DIVIDE

Phonograph and record companies made sure adults learned the appropriate social protocols for listening to recorded music in the home. As early as 1899, many such businesses were offering instruction about creating and listening to recorded music in the home. This advice was meant to counterbalance the natural sense of nervousness that came with the still-new listening and recording device, with an eye toward increasing sales. One early such publication, written by the National Phonograph Company, an early competitor to Berliner's Gramophone business, published a fictionalized account of a domestic "phonograph party." Recounting their guests' initial curiosity about the instrument, the unnamed authors recounted, "Every one of our guests came on Wednesday evening; every one of them as curious as an original Eve (or Adam) and every one of them delighted on learning what was in prospect." The writer suggested having two phonographs on hand for the social gathering, one to record and another one to listen. Such a suggestion may belie the nature of this industry-published instruction manual, since the potential of customers purchasing two phonographs would certainly increase the potential for profit in the still-new world of phonograph sales. Regardless, the anonymous National Phonograph Company author offered rather detailed directions on how such a social gathering should progress. Each guest should take turns performing a short excerpt on the instrument they were instructed to bring. Because of variability in volume, a banjo performer should stand closer to the machine than a clarinet player. Guests were also invited to give short speeches, though the author implied those may be less interesting to hear. After each guest had an opportunity to record, each newly recorded record would be played back to the full group. The hostess had the responsibility for making sure guests understood they should clap after each recording was played back, just as they would in a live performance at the opera or symphony hall (National Phonograph Company 1899).

Victor, the leading phonograph company, based its advertising around a narrative of accessibility to classical music royalty. One 1903 Victor advertisement extolled the number of prominent figures from the classical music world that recorded for that company exclusively. The list included the Italian tenor Enrico Caruso, Spanish coloratura soprano Adelina Patti (who had previously recorded for the European branch of Gramophone), and American soprano Suzanne Adams. Under the headline "The Living Voices of International Celebrities," the Victor Company informed readers, "At the cost of a half-million dollars we have induced the greatest artists known on two continents, to sing or play for the *Victor Talking Machine.*" The advertisement then cited testimonials of other classical music figures who were impressed with the fidelity of Victor records. The noted French actress Sara Bernhardt was quoted, "Yesterday, while listening to the Habanera of 'Carmen,' I thought I was listening, not to the echo of the voice of Calvé, but Calvé herself—the marvelous and only Calvé." An advertisement from 1913 showed Caruso—easily the most prominent artist on Victor's roster—in full opera costume. Pictured next to him was a Victor record. The caption read, "Both are Caruso." Another Victor advertisement, also from 1913 with the bold caption "Victor Exclusive Talent," showed a man and a women sitting staring at the phonograph while it played a record. Surrounding them were miniature musicians, perhaps a foot tall, in opera costume or playing their instrument, meant to convey a message of accessibility to the world's greatest musicians from the comfort of home (Katz 1998, 156). Other companies, most notably Columbia, mirrored this advertising strategy, though could not point to a similar roster of artists that Victor had acquired (Suisman 2009, 125–149).By the early 1910s, record companies slowly but increasingly recognized the earning potential of marketing to young people and their interest in dance. A 1913/1914 advertisement that appeared in *Garden and Home Builder, The Saturday Evening Post,* and *Colliers,* among other publications, extolled the ease with which the Victrola could aid in adult social gatherings, while also acknowledging the increasingly recognizable interest young people had in dance music. The advertisement (Figure 1.1) read in bold at the top "The best friend of a hostess is the Victrola." It continued, "The hostess who has a Victrola never need worry about how the evening will 'go' before mentioning 'Do the young people get tired of general conversation? A Victrola will furnish the latest dance music and set their feet to sliding' " (Katz 2012, 17). The Victor advertisement shows a group of adults sitting around the Victrola, as the hostess greets incoming guests. The Victrola is clearly the center of attention. Guests are seated in such a way that they can easily see the phonograph while it plays, a holdover from attending live performances (see below). The advertisement also belies the continued popular interest in dance and its most fervent adherents. This adult/youth marketing divide continued through the end of the decade and into the 1920s. A 1922 column in the trade journal *Printers Ink* recommended, "Don't forget that father may pay for the phonograph, but sons and daughters are the ones who seem to spend the money most freely for the latest records" (Schrum 2004, 103).

Figure 1.1.   Victor advertisement (Victor Corporation 1914).

The *Printer's Ink* article points to an increasingly evident reality of the introduction of recorded music into the home: young people and adults were learning to use the phonograph in increasingly divergent ways. Whereas adults were teaching each other how to maintain restrained listening practices, young people were learning the ease with which the phonograph brought their favorite dance music into the home. Recognizing the earning potential possible with young people and their disposable income, Victor and other record companies began releasing recognizably jazz records by the late 1910s. The New Jersey-based company is credited with releasing the first jazz record in 1917, performed by the all-white, New Orleans Rhythm Kings, a common practice since recording black or racially integrated ensembles was initially quite rare. For Victor, the move to include the still-controversial music, albeit somewhat tame versions, was likely just one component of a general business expansion that was well underway in the late 1910s. At the time, Victor expanded its Camden plant, increased the line of records produced by the education department, and began releasing first recordings by major orchestras in Boston and Philadelphia (Aldridge 1964, 71–84). Thus, recording the New Orleans Rhythm Kings and other jazz ensembles to follow, may well have been more a business decision than part of some larger company endorsement of jazz as musically valid. The company could maintain adult customers while also expanding to include young people and their interest in jazz dancing.

College students especially had a near insatiable appetite for dance records, and record stores near large universities marketed their wares to the appeal for dancing. In Champaign-Urbana, the G.W. Lawrence Record store supplied students at the University of Illinois with the latest phonograph records. One 1919 advertisement exclaimed: "Dance Records You Can't Be Without!" It noted the records were playable on "any sort of small instrument," though specified Victor and Brunswick phonographs ("Dance Records You Can't Be Without!" 1919). College students eagerly put such purchases to work at Greek house dances, which often had less oversight than the university-sanctioned dances. A joke in the magazine *College Humor* suggested that the Victrola was one of the most essential elements of the fraternity house, an indispensable component of 1920s fraternity life (Boston Beanpot 1925). Alumni of Chi Phi read how the seniors and freshmen from one chapter pooled their money to purchase a "fine Victrola." The device "[improved] the more spacious quarters of the new house"—a clear reference to dance—and would be regularly put to work ("New Victorla" 1926). However, the inability of some fraternities to hold enjoyable and popular dances was a major disappointment. The University of Illinois chapter of Theta Chi complained to its alumni that they only managed to have one "Victrola dance" during the spring 1927 semester, though provided no explanation why ("Active Chapter" 1927).

The accessibility of dance records also provided young people with opportunities to learn and enjoy the bevy of steps that developed during the dance-crazed 1910s and 1920s, often to the frustration of their parents. This shift to increasingly available dance records was not met with any subsequent change in adults' views about the inherent morality (or lack thereof) of popular dances. Instead, many saw recorded music as an unwelcomed invasion of the sacrosanct private home. Still, high-school-age young people took advantage of the increasing availability and repeatability of dance records to teach each other dances, otherwise reserved for public dance halls. Learning to dance the black bottom and shimmy—dances looked at with scorn by traditionalists who continued to harbor Victorian notions of appropriate dance technique—no longer required sneaking out of the home (Hawes 1997, 11). A phonograph, a small collection of records, and a friend with knowledge of the steps provided more than adequate tools to imitate the jazz dances taking place downtown and in makeshift roadside dance halls. Such lessons tended to be more common with girls, who generally enjoyed dancing for its own sake, as opposed to boys who sought extramusical benefits. One high-school student wrote in her diary that she and a friend were dancing to "damn good jazz" until her parents complained. Her mother turned off the dance tune saying, "They call that music!?" Such episodes played out across the country as parents and guardians complained about the "hot" tunes that had extended into their homes (Schrum 2004, 103–104, 117).

By the early 1920s, radio began to supplant the phonograph as the primary tool for distributing dance music, as the popularity of the phonograph began a decade-long decline. The first commercial radio station, KDKA in Pittsburgh, went on air in 1920. Eighteen months later, the number of commercial stations had risen to 220, and by 1930 over 900 stations existed nationwide with over 40% of households owning radios (Giordano 2007, 49). And just as early phonograph companies gave adults instructions on how to hold a successful "phonograph party," early radio manufacturers similarly helped spread the gospel of that emergent technology. The Crosley Radio Company printed invitation cards in the early 1920s that read: "Dear Friends: We have just purchased a new Crosley Radio. In its honor we are giving a radio party _____ evening. We request your presence. Please come, for when the Big Show is on, 'You're *there* with a Crosley'" (Taylor 2012, 243).

Yet the increasing popularity of radio did not usher in an era of détente among adults and young people about what and how they should be listening, especially regarding dangerous "hot" jazz. Young people saw the radio and the dance tunes it could produce as a sort of balance for the less exciting parts of their days, particularly school. One 15-year-old boy suggested students needed jazz music as a corrective for boring algebra lessons. Jazz dancing at the end of the school day provided an adrenalin rush after the drudgery of classes. The boy went on to swear the next day's lessons went much better after "listening to a bass drum beat the rhythm of a popular song." Another boy reported he was "frightened to death" after hearing stations may replace jazz fox trots with speeches and jokes. He said listening to people talk on the radio did not provide any needed dance relief after listening to teachers talk during classes (Forbes 1923).

CONCLUSIONS

In 1877, before the phonograph had become a social reality, an unnamed writer in the *New York Times* perceptively wrote: "It is evident [the phonograph] will lead to important changes in our social customs" ("The Phonograph" 1877). The statement has proven both correct and incorrect. Young people were the most willing to embrace changes in such customs and saw the phonograph as the means to provide the accompaniment to their interest in dance. Yet adults were less likely to embrace such adjustments to "social customs" and instead largely sought to maintain music consumption practices as they had existed when live music monopolized listening. For them, learning to listen was more of a continuation of earlier practices than any distinct break. A 1921 Edison survey of listeners revealed, that while many respondents spoke positively of music that brought about a sense of nostalgia that " 'takes us back to Grandfather days,'" jazz "seemed to trumpet upsetting and bewildering social change" (Kenney 1999, 8, 9). The popularity of ragtime, the genre that first provided the background music for such dances, provided perhaps the most recognizable and worrisome marker for the adult/youth divide through the first two decades of the twentieth century. This increasingly visible youth culture began developing different musical tastes than the previous generations (Hawes 1997; Mintz 2004). Sociologists remind us that music often acts as a sort of social change indicator, a barometer particularly useful in periods of profound change to "social customs" (jagodzinski 2005, Epstein 1995). The phonograph allowed ragtime and jazz, recognizably black genres with sexual overtones, to penetrate the inner sanctum of homes in white America.

REFERENCES

"Active Chapter." 1927. *Tau Topics*, May, 1. University of Illinois Student Life Archives - National Fraternity Reference Files, Box 3.

Aldridge, B. L. 1964. *The Victor Talking Machine Company*. Camden, N.J.: RCA Sales Corporation.

Alinsky, S. D., and Constance Weinberger. 1928. "The Public Dance Hall." University of Chicago Special Collections - Ernest W. Burgess Papers, Box 126, Folder 10.

Boston Beanpot. 1925. "Essential Parts of a Fraternity." *College Humor*, October, 75.

Carney, Court. 2009. *Cuttin' Up: How Early Jazz Got America's Ear*. Lawrence: University of Kansas Press.

Crawford, Richard. 2001. *America's Musical Life: A History*. New York: Norton.

Cremin, Lawrence. 1965. *The Wonderful World of Ellwood Patterson Cubberley: An Essay on the Historiography of American Education*. New York: Teachers College Press.

"Dance Records You Can't Be Without! " 1919. *Daily Illini*, November 15, 7.

Epstein, Jonathan S. 1995. "Introduction: Misplaced Childhood: An Introduction to the Sociology of Youth and Their Music." In *Adolescents and Their Music: If It's Too Loud, You're Too Old*, xiii–xxxiv. New York: Garland Publishing, Inc.

"Fall of 1,000 Girls Charged to Jazz Music." 1921. *Chicago Daily Tribune*, December 19, 3.

Forbes, Genevieve. 1922. "Mortenson Asks Parents to Curb Student Revels." *Chicago Daily Tribune*, January 26, 15.

Forbes, Genevieve. 1923. "Copyright Bar Stirs Radio Fans' Static." *Chicago Daily Tribune*, April 15, 17.

Giordano, Ralph G. 2007. *Social Dancing in America: A History and Reference*. Westport, CT: Greenwood Publishing Group, Inc.

Giordano, Ralph G. 2008. *Satan in the Dance Hall: Rev. John Roach Straton, Social Dancing, and Morality in 1920s New York City*. Lanham, MD: Scarecrow Press.

Hasse, John Edward. 1981. "The Creation and Dissemination of Indianapolis Ragtime, 1897–1930." Ph.D., Ethnomusicology and Folklore, Indiana University.

Hawes, Joseph. 1997. *Children between the Wars: American Childhood, 1920–1940*. New York: Twayne Publishers.

jagodzinski, jan. 2005. *Music in Youth Culture: A Lacanian Approach*. New York: Palgrave Macmillan.

Katz, Mark. 1998. "Making America More Musical through the Phonograph, 1900-1930." *American Music* 16 (4): 448–476.

———. 2012. "Introduction: Sound Recording." In *Music, Sound, and Technology in America: A Documentary History of Early Phonograph, Cinema, and Radio*, edited by Timothy D. Taylor, Mark Katz, and Tony Grajeda, 11–29. Durham: Duke University Press.

Keene, James A. 1987. *A History of Music Education in the United States*. Hanover and London: University Press of New England. Original edition, 1982.

Kenney, William Howland. 1999. *Recorded Music in American Life: The Phonograph and Popular Memory, 1890–1945*. New York: Oxford University Press.

Mintz, Steven. 2004. *Huck's Raft: A History of American Childhood*. Cambridge, MA: Harvard University Press.

Nasaw, David. 1993. *Going Out: The Rise and Fall of Public Amusements*. New York: Basic Books.

National Phonograph Company. 1899. *How We Gave a Phonograph Party*. New York: National Phonograph Company.

"New Victorla." 1926. *The Sigmagram*, April, 2. University of Illinois Student Life Archives - National Fraternity Reference Files, Box 5.

Ogren, Kathy J. 1989. *The Jazz Revolution: Twenties America and the Meaning of Jazz*. New York: Oxford University Press.

Partridge, Pauline. 1924. "The Home Set to Music." *Sunset*, November, 75–76.

Peiss, Kathy Lee. 1986. *Cheap Amusements: Working Women and Leisure in Turn-of-the-Century New York*. Philadelphia: Temple University Press.

Peretti, Burton W. 1992. *The Creation of Jazz: Music, Race, and Culture in Urban America*. Urbana: University of Illinois Press.

"The Phonograph." 1877. *The New York Times*, November 7, 4.

Schrum, Kelly. 2004. *Some Wore Bobby Sox: The Emergence of Teenage Girls' Culture, 1920–1945*. New York: Palgrave MacMillan.

Sousa, John Philip. 1906. "The Menace of Mechanical Music." *Appleton's*, September, 278–284.

Storr, Richard. 1961. "The Education of History: Some Impressions." *Harvard Educational Review* 31 (2): 124–135.

Straton, John Roach. 1920. *The Dance of Death: Should Christians Indulge?* New York: Religious Literature Department, Calvary Baptist Church. Reprint, 1929.

Suisman, David. 2009. *Selling Sounds: The Commercial Revolution in American Music*. Cambridge, MA: Harvard University Press.

Taylor, Timothy D. 2012. "Introduction: Radio." In *Music, Sound, and Technology in America: A Documentary History of Early Phonograph, Cinema, and Radio*, edited by Timothy D. Taylor, Mark Katz, and Tony Grajeda, 239–255. Durham, NC: Duke University Press.

Thompson, Emily. 1995. "Machines, Music, and the Quest for Fidelity: Marketing the Edison Phonograph in America, 1877–1925." *The Musical Quarterly* 79 (1): 131–171.

"Vice Vigilantes Open Drive to Purify Illinois." 1922. *Chicago Daily Tribune*, January 10, 7.

Victor Corporation. 1914. "The Best Friend of the Hostess is the Victrola." *Garden and Home Builder*, December, 166.

Wagner, Anne Louise. 1997. *Adversaries of Dance: From the Puritans to the Present*. Urbana: University of Illinois Press.

Wallace, Michele Faith. 2003. "The Good Lynching and 'The Birth of a Nation': Discourses and Aesthetics of Jim Crow." *Cinema Journal* 43 (1): 85–104.

Walton, Lester A. 1912. "Concert at Carnegie Hall." *New York Age*, May 9, 6.

White, Kevin. 1993. *The First Sexual Revolution: Male Heterosexuality in Modern America*. New York: New York University Press.

Wilk, Louis F. 1922. Board Meeting Minutes of January 25, 1922. Chicago Board of Education Archives.

Yarrow, Rev. Phillip, ed. 1923. *Fighting the Debauchery of Our Girls and Boys*. Chicago: Self-published.

ABOUT THE AUTHOR

Jacob Hardesty is an assistant professor of education at Rockford University, where he teaches courses in educational history and research methods. He completed his doctorate at Indiana University, having previously taught music for four years in public and Catholic schools. His recent work has appeared in *High Ability Studies* and the *American Educational History Journal*. His research interests include the connections between popular culture and schools as well as the achievement of gifted students.

CHAPTER 2

FANNING THE FLAMES OF DISCONTENT

Inciting Teachings of the Wobblies

Daniel Dethrow

In the 1910s, a fiercely ambitious, unapologetically radical union waged war against the industrial capitalist class in America. The stark discrepancies between rich and poor, the widespread practice of inhumane working conditions, and the severe suppression of demonstrations, unions, and strikes at the turn of the twentieth century combined to ignite some of the largest class struggles the United States has known. It was in this harrowing climate that the Industrial Workers of the World was formed. It organized workers, coordinated strikes, held picket lines, battled with police and state militias, and sabotaged with one goal in mind: to abolish the wage system and to turn the power of production over to the hands of the workers. In a word: revolution. But it didn't happen. While the I.W.W. has continued to exist as an organization to this day, its peak membership was reached in the mid 1920s just as most of its organizing leaders were killed, imprisoned, or deported (Renshaw 1967, 195–220; Thompson and Bekken 2006, 105; Dray 2010, 363–367). However, while the long-term goal of squelching the capitalist system and the ruthless industrialists of the early-twentieth

Learning the Left: Popular Culture, Liberal Politics, and Informal Education from 1900 to the Present, pp. 19–30
Copyright © 2015 by Information Age Publishing
19

century may not have come to pass, the union's contributions to U.S. history and the history of "the Left" continues to reverberate.

The I.W.W. (or "Wobblies" as they came to be nicknamed) did win considerable victories: concessions for mill workers in Lawrence, Massachusetts; the eight-hour day for loggers in the Northwest; various labor strikes in South America, Europe, and South Africa; and free speech battles throughout the nation (Renshaw 1967, 221–238; Dray 2010, 285–334). In recent decades, Wobblies lore has enjoyed a revisiting. But one especially fascinating component of Wobblies history has not been given enough attention, and that is their *educational* contributions. The Wobblies' educational tactics were distinct from other unions at the time and laid the foundation for leftist organizing efforts in the decades that followed them. Not only were the educational goals and content more revolutionarily ambitious than other unions, but the I.W.W. was especially adept at using popular media and folk songs to reach large number of workers while branding a distinct image and personality. This chapter explores those educational exploits and considers how the I.W.W. can be integrated into our educational history.

INCITING ACTION: EDUCATION THROUGH PROPAGANDA

In June of 1905 a wide coalition of workers, activists, and labor leaders representing over 34 unions descended upon Chicago to found "the One Big Union." Over 186 delegates were in attendance, including such big-names as Eugene Debs, Mother Jones, Lucy Parsons, Daniel DeLeon, Vincent St. John, and William D. "Big Bill" Haywood. They represented lumberjacks in the Northwest, mill workers in the East, miners in Southwest, and harvest pickers in California. They ambitiously sought to unite ALL workers, including even non-skilled workers and the unemployed regardless of race, creed, color, or sex. Unusual by today's standards, this was especially unprecedented at the time, as nearly all unions previous had been formed to protect skilled artisans and trade workers (i.e., those workers who were specially trained and experienced). Even unions such as the American Federation of Labor (AFL), widespread though it was, was segregated along racial, ethnic, and gender lines.[1] Most unions refused to accept "non-white" members altogether. For the I.W.W., however, such divisions had been the Achilles heel of worker organizing. A solidly united workers' organization would be unstoppable: not only capable of gaining shorter hours and better pay, but of revolutionizing the entire structure of labor and profit, of rich and poor.

The I.W.W. was bold in its defiance of, and outright contempt for, capitalism and the wealthy classes. "Class consciousness" was crucial for the

I.W.W.'s mission, and so it made no effort to water down its revolutionary rhetoric. From its inception, the I.W.W. was intentionally and unapologetically "radical" in its opposition to the emerging new industrial capitalism. Its preamble read:

> The working class and the employing class have nothing in common. There can be no peace so long as hunger and want are found among millions of working people and the few, who make up the employing class, have all the good things in life. Between these two classes a struggle must go on until the workers of the world organize as a class, take possession of the earth and the machinery of production, and abolish the wage system. (*I.W.W. Songs* 1917, 1918, 1968, 1; Renshaw 1967; Bird [1978] 2006; Thompson and Bekken 2006)

Ideologically and rhetorically, the I.W.W. was the most radical industrial labor union in the United States, and this defining characteristic would extend to how it attempted to reach and educate workers. Education within labor unions in the form of classes, speeches, and literature was not unheard of by the early-twentieth century. In fact, several unions enjoyed close ties with various universities, especially in the summer months, using classroom spaces for the education of their members. The practice became so widespread that by 1921 the Worker's Education Bureau (a national agency) was founded in order to coordinate organized labor educational activities for labor leaders. It oversaw efforts between many colleges and labor unions, often in the form of summer training schools or extension classes. In its first year it helped to create the Bryn Mawr Summer School for women workers, the Brookwood Labor College (a full-term residential school for workers) in New York, extension classes for workers at the University of California, and it coordinated the sending of teachers from Amherst College to instruct union members in Springfield and Holyoke (Schneider 1941, 17–18). For decades before the Worker's Educational Bureau, the AFL and several other unions held their own instructional classes for up-and-coming labor leaders. These educational settings allowed unions to train their leaders in strategies of organizing and collective bargaining, as well as the tedious but crucial tasks of collecting dues, recording memberships, accounting, and coordinating the various branches as their union grew. An overarching goal for these educational ventures, then, was the security and longevity of their respective unions.

For the I.W.W. this was not necessarily the case. Education would play a particularly large role for the I.W.W. in a more dispersed way, for not only was it seeking to recruit more workers than any other union, it was also seeking to upset and restructure the entire social and economic structure of labor and production (Dray 2010, 285–287). Education became a necessity not for a few scattered organizing leaders, but for *all* workers in its ranks—and, if possible, all workers it hoped to recruit. Years after its high water mark (during the First World War), I.W.W. member Clifford B. Ellis reflected upon the role that education played for the union:

> The necessity of class education is imposed upon the working class by the facts of industry. That striving toward life—the will to live—which is inherent in every living cell of life, makes it necessary to educate the workers in matters that are deleterious to their health, detrimental to their lives and restrictive of their chances of survival. ... Workers' education is, of necessity, an education in class-consciousness. (Ellis 1988, 368)

The I.W.W. sought to cultivate class consciousness by following the muck-raking methods of the day. Their writings drew workers' attention to the labor injustices of the age in order to recruit and incite action. The membership would need to be knowledgeable not only of the union's creed and stances, but also of the larger historical and social forces behind the I.W.W.'s mission and reason for being. And so the I.W.W. created and distributed thousands of pamphlets, small books, and periodicals—i.e., propaganda (Saposs 1926, 166–167; Peterson 1986, 160). One may define propaganda as information spread with the intent of influencing people in favor of (or against) a doctrine. That the I.W.W.'s educational material and tactics can be viewed as distinctly more propagandist in nature as compared with other unions at the time, is of little dispute. However, one need not impose a bold line between propaganda and education; for if one allows that education consists of instruction and/or training by which people learn to develop their own mental, moral, and physical capabilities, then one should allow that instruction and training consists of subjective values with intent. The I.W.W. was creative with its educational endeavors, and quite insightful about how to incite passionate learning. It utilized popular media such as periodicals, pamphlets, and books; but it also tapped into oral tradition and the use of song in order to educate and rouse workers to action (and thus was able to reach not just literate workers, but illiterate workers as well). The educative propaganda of the I.W.W. created many templates that future leftist organizers would borrow from. And in order to better understand how people "learned the left," then Wobblies' propaganda is a crucial place to begin.

Soon after its formation, the I.W.W. established a headquarters and printing press in Chicago, Eugene, Oregon, and Cincinnati. Their earliest educational tactics came in the form of newspapers. The I.W.W. released *The Industrial Union Bulletin* from March 2, 1907 until March 6, 1909, and then later *Solidarity* and *The Industrial Worker*.[2] These covered national and international news regarding working conditions, strikes, and labor trials. However, these papers also contained explicit educational lessons. Sections of the papers were dedicated to a series of educational lessons that were continued from one week to the next. One such example of these bi-weekly lessons was "Working Class Economics" conducted by James P. Thompson in 1907. Written in a question-and-answer format, a typical passage would read: "Question: 'How does skilled labor count?' Answer: 'As simple labor intensified, or, rather as multiplied simple labor, a given quantity of skilled being considered equal to a greater quantity of simple labor" (*Industrial Union Bulletin* 1907c). These short installments covered a range of topics associated with industry, labor, economics, and political philosophy. The periodicals (and most all I.W.W. publications) encouraged further study and contained suggested reading lists with headings such as:

Learn What It Is—To know what Industrial Unionism is you must read what is said about it by its friends and what it says for itself; only in that way can its present aims and ultimate purposes be understood. The following are recommended to workingmen who desire to learn what Industrial Unionism is:

Handbook of Industrial Unionism........................5c
Constitution of the I.W.W..................................5c
Report of Secretary Trastmann,........................ .5c
"Industrial Unionism," address by E.V. Babe..........5c
"Burning Question of Trades Unionist".................5c
"Address on I.W.W. Preamble"............................5c

(*Industrial Union Bulletin* 1907b)

In addition to news, short lessons, and suggested reading, the periodicals also announced educational meetings. Most common were the Sunday Educational Meetings that would be held in a local hall where various I.W.W. guest speakers would discuss topics similar to the lessons allotted in the paper, such as the history of labor, updates concerning strikes throughout the United States and abroad, organizing tactics, economics, and philosophy (*Industrial Union Bulletin* 1907a).

The dispersal of the periodicals far surpassed their official membership. *Solidarity*, for example, claimed 12,000 sold copies in March 1912, and the circulation of the *Industrial Worker* sold 3,000 to 5,000 copies per issue in its early years (Foner 1965, 150). Much of their readership consisted of migratory workers—a group the I.W.W. was the first to actively recruit—who in turn spread their literature throughout the West by the thousands (Bird [1978] 2006).

From its printing presses in Chicago, Cincinnati, and Eugene the I.W.W. also released dozens of small pamphlets and books. Since many laborers in the early-twentieth century were of foreign origin, it produced dozens of book and pamphlet titles in various languages during the 1910s and 1920s. In concert with respective waves of immigrants, publications were offered in Italian, Hungarian, Russian, Polish, Scandinavian, Spanish, and other languages. In the March 30, 1907 issue of *The Union Bulletin*, I.W.W. leaflets in English sold (per 1,000) for $1.75; in Italian for $3.00; in Finnish for $4.00; and in Swedish, Polish, and Spanish for $5.00. In June of that year, the union added Slavonian, Croatian-Dalmation, German, and Japanese to the list. In the 1928 release of *The I.W.W.: What It Is and What It Is Not*, the I.W.W. boasted "eight publications, in six languages, to make its ideals known to all" (*The I.W.W.* 1928, 3).

A recurring theme in Wobblies' literature was that in addition to capitalism, ignorance was the most dangerous enemy of the working class. It was only through knowledge about their historical conditions and by raising class consciousness that people could recognize and act upon the need for organization and action in order to improve their lives (*The I.W.W.: What It Is and What It Is Not* 1928, 22). Educating workers about the conditions of which they were a part, became the focus of I.W.W. literature, as evident in works such as *An Economic Interpretation of the Job* (1922) and *Education and System: The Basis of Organization* (1924). These books break down concepts such as exchange value, surplus value, source of profit, prices of commodities, price regulation, market law, organizing unions, and coordinating strikes. *An Economic Interpretation of the Job* closely resembles a textbook in that at the end of each chapter a set of review questions appears, such as: "What is labor power?"; "What, roughly, determines wage?"; "What is exchange-value, and use value?"; "Why is capitalism called the 'profit system'?"; "What does Marx call profit?"; "What regulates the price of a commodity?" The printing bureau at 2422 North Halsted in Chicago released roughly 35 books authored by I.W.W. members between 1911 and 1930.[3] As with the periodicals, the last pages of these books also encouraged the reader to send for more literature, reading:

> Those who have read this little booklet through are urged to acquaint themselves with the principles, structure, methods and aim of the I.W.W.... Information and literature can be secured from General Headquarters of the I.W.W., 1001 West Madison Street, Chicago, Ill. (*An Economic Interpretation* 1922, 61)

Other notorious publications outlined the Wobblies' stances on direct action: *Sabotage, Its History, Philosophy & Function* by Walker C. Smith; *With Drops of Blood* by William D. Haywood; and *Cut Down the Hours of Work!*— which aside from educating, also added to the organization's myth making in the national press and gained the attention of the federal government (Renshaw 1967, 195–220; Thompson and Bekken 2006, 105–118; Dray 2010, 363–374).

SONGS TO FAN THE FLAMES OF DISCONTENT

"Oh, how we sang... always singing... the IWW, wherever they congregated, no matter what, or what they faced, there was always song." (Bird [1978] 2006)

Various authors and scholars have noted the use of song by the I.W.W. to bolster bravery and to cement camaraderie. Mixing various emerging song styles of the time—folk song, immigrant folk song, and popular tunes—the Wobblies created hundreds of short, catchy songs for use at gatherings, on the picket line, during strikes, and for memorial. Some were grave, bold, and quite serious. Songs such as: "Hold the Fort" and "The One Big Union" laid out the ideology of the organization while giving courage to the singers amid strikes and demonstrations with lines such as:

> Hold the fort for we are coming
> Union men be strong
> Side by side we'll battle onward
> Victory will come! (Bird [1978] 2006)

Other songs had more of a biting sense of humor, often making fun of figures of authority. Such songs were used during their free speech fights, such as one that mocks the Salvation Army (which was allowed to speak on street corners when the I.W.W. was not):

> Long-haired preachers come out every night
> Try to tell you what's wrong and what's right
> But when asked how 'bout something to eat
> They will answer with voices so sweet
> "You will eat, bye and bye
> In that glorious land above the sky
> Work and pray, live on hay
> You'll get pie in the sky when you die." (*I.W.W. Songs* 1917, 20)

Other songs functioned as memorial or martyr songs, imparting history while simultaneously "fueling the flames of discontent." Violence was very real in the early years of labor strife, and many strikers were beaten, shot, and killed. The most notorious of the I.W.W.'s martyrs was Joe Hill, a labor organizer who was arrested and executed. He was also the author of many of the songs in the I.W.W.'s widely dispersed "Little Red Songbook." The 1917 edition of the songbook was dedicated to the memory of Joe Hill after authorities in Utah executed him in 1915.[4] This edition (and current editions) contained many songs which Joe Hill wrote, such as: "Workers of the World, Awaken!"; "What We Want"; "Scissor Bill"; "The Tramp"; "The Preacher and the Slave"; "Joe Hill's Last Will," and many more (*I.W.W.*

Songs 1919). Accompanying the songs themselves were pictures of martyrs in the booklets, with a caption underneath describing their execution: "Joe Hill– Murdered by the Authorities of the State of Utah November the 19, 1915"; "Wesley Everest: Murdered by the Lumber Trust Centralia, Wash., November 11, 1919"; "To Frank H. Little: Lynched at Butte, Montana, August 1, 1917–Half Indian, Half White Man, All I.W.W.!" (*I.W.W. Songs* 1968). Accompanying the pictures of their martyrs, songs in these booklets covered the history of former strikes, imprisonment of workers, and the execution of workers, such as: "Remember"; "John Golden and the Lawrence Strike"; and "Joe Hill." The power and utility of song was recognized by Joe Hill himself, who once wrote:

> If a person can put a few cold, common sense facts into a song and dress them up in a cloak of humor to take the dryness out of them, he will succeed in reaching a great number of workers who are too unintelligent or too indifferent to read a pamphlet or an editorial on economic science. (Foner 1965, 152)[5]

The songbooks were an especially creative and insightful way for the I.W.W. to reach many workers it would not have otherwise. Not only were so many workers of foreign origin in the early-twentieth century, but also many were illiterate. Songs, then, were able to stand in place of newspapers and books. They taught workers about labor conditions throughout the country, the history of labor, and the ideologies of workers who were opposed to the industrial capitalist system. As for the I.W.W.'s songs in particular, many were written as parodies, adopting the melody of a popular tune and simply replacing the words. For example, "The Preacher and the Slave" was sung to the melody of the popular tune of the day "In the Sweet Bye and Bye," while the song "Dump the Bosses Off Your Back" was sung to the tune "Take It to the Lord in Prayer," "Everybody's Joinin' It" was a reworking of "Everybody's Doin' It," and "John Golden and the Lawrence Strike" was written to the tune of "A Little Talk With Jesus" (*I.W.W. Songs* 1919). Since the tunes were already well known, it was fairly quick and easy to learn the parody songs. The catchy songs stuck well in the minds of those who learned them, as is quite evident in Stewart Bird and Deborah Shaffer's 1978 documentary film about "The Wobblies." There is a wonderful moment in the film when an elderly women being interviewed is asked to recall the 1913 Paterson Strike. Her eyes light up and she sings out:

> Conditions they are bad, and some of you are sad
> You cannot see your enemy, the class that lives in luxury
> The working man are poor, and will be forever more
> as long as you permit the few to guide your destiny! (Bird [1978] 2006)

They were lyrics she had sung 65 years before, but they arose pristinely from her memory. As the film documentary proceeds, this phenomenon occurs over and over as one aging former member of the I.W.W. after another is able to recall songs long preserved in their minds.

LEGACIES AND INFLUENCE

Even though the I.W.W. was dealt a series of devastating blows during the Red Scare of the early 1920s, the ideological teachings of the Wobblies through their periodicals, pamphlets, meetings, and songbooks continued to influence leftist organizers. Two educational sites in particular would infuse their work with ideology and tactics borrowed from the I.W.W. Both Commonwealth College and Highlander Folk School were created in the mid and late 1920s as ventures in labor activism outside the confines of the various mainstream labor unions, envisioning a future that revolutionized the plights of working people. Not all I.W.W. organizers had been rounded up in the raids of the first Red Scare. A few, including former member Covington Hall, helped to found Commonwealth College in 1923.

Commonwealth College was a radical experiment in education that sought to prepare young adults to lead socio-economic reforms through social and political action. In addition to Hall, the initial founders of Commonwealth College came from a variety of academic and labor organizing backgrounds. The director William Edward Zeuch and his secretarial assistant Harold Z. Brown, were academicians, as was F. M. Goodhue who soon joined the faculty with a background in math and engineering. Others, such as Kate Richards O'Hare and W. C. Benton, as well as Hall, had held leadership roles in the Socialist Party, the I.W.W., and trade unions in the 1910s before World War I (Koch 1972, 36). Students (of which there were two dozen or so at any given time) ranged from frustrated college kids, to young organizers in labor, to poor youth in the area. It functioned as a self-sustained community. Students at Commonwealth didn't focus solely on academic studies, but were also expected to help with farming and cooking. Fifty-minute classes were held in the morning and ranged from history, math, economics, and science to how to speak in public, how to write and send out a press release, and how to type and take minutes at meetings. Then students would break for chores (Koch 1972, 10). The college worked to foster connection between their community and labor unrest, and it began to participate more directly in labor struggles beginning in the 1930s, by becoming especially involved in the Kentucky Miners Strike in 1932. In the mid 1930s, Commonwealth created a "Museum to the Class Struggle" made up of newspaper stories and murals. It attempted to educate farmers with a "Farm School on Wheels" in 1934, and held

"Sharecropper School" classes in the mid 1930s in an attempt to raise class consciousness among sharecroppers in the region (Koch 1972, 18, 23).

A few years after the founding of Commonwealth College, Myles Horton founded Highlander Folk School in Tennessee in 1932. Especially famous for its activism in labor and civil rights, the foundational ideologies of Highlander very much mirrored Commonwealth College, and the two activist training centers worked together throughout the 1930s. Former I.W.W. members could often be found at Highlander among the staff, visiting speakers, and as guests. One striking I.W.W. influence in particular was the musical aspect of Highlander. In addition to lectures, visiting speakers, readings, and workshops, Highlander had a music program as part of a wider "cultural program" headed by Zilphia Horton. In his book on Highlander, John M. Glen writes: "Music and folk dancing were forms of entertainment as well as education at HFS [Highlander Folk School]. They instilled a sense of solidarity among students, fostered a feeling of cultural pride" (Glen 1988, 37). Glen goes on to explain that it was the folk music component that really connected the school to the rural community surrounding it, again showing the utility of song as an organizing and educative medium. Highlander Folk School was incorporating songs from the region and often invited their neighbors in Monteagle to attend their plays, sing-alongs, and dances. The songs could serve as a common ground, and by the group-singing nature, taught and imbued a communal sense of togetherness that could not have been otherwise instilled and expressed. In his work, Glen pays close attention to why Zilphia Horton incorporated folk songs into the education program, and writes this of her: "The 'real musical merit' of folk songs, she wrote in 1939, was not their form *but the way they expressed the struggles of working people* " (italics added). As the Industrial Workers of the World had done in the 1910s and as the American Communist Party would do in the later 1930s, Horton and other members of Highlander would also write folk songs by using familiar tunes and simply introducing new lines, turning "hymns, traditional ballads, and popular songs into forceful expressions of protest" (Glen 1988, 54). Examples of this range from "Old MacDonald" becoming "John L. Lewis Had a Plan" (with the refrain "C-I-C-I-O") and "Rock a Bye Baby" becoming "Workers' Lullabye." Perhaps the most famous of Horton's adaptations was changing the gospel tune "I Shall Overcome" to "We Shall Overcome," a now iconic song of the Civil Rights movement. In her work on Highlander, Aimee Isgrig Horton makes the statement that "it was Highlander's labor songs which were most readily and widely shared. Gathered from and inspired by the movement … published in union-sponsored songbooks, they traveled across the South" (Horton 1989, 120). What this statement and the example of "We Shall Overcome" highlights is that in addition to fostering a sense of collectivity, identity, and solidarity, these folk songs travelled on their own by both word of mouth and print educating other groups involved in these movements.

INCITING LESSONS

The educational histories of leftist groups such the Industrial Workers of the World, are exciting ventures both in content and methodology. They offer new realms and arenas for education, challenging us to move beyond organized public schools as the only sites worthy of exploration. Studying groups such as the I.W.W. confronts head-on the relationship of propaganda in education, how ideology functions in our educational history, as well as how people learn and are inspired toward action. The songbooks of the I.W.W. are especially valuable for the educational historian, for they challenge us to consider how education manifested itself in artistic and creative ways—ways that reached even people who were not literate. The implication that song can be educative is especially exciting because it opens a multitude of subjects yet to explore. For those willing to widen their methodological scope, future study in the history of education promises to be enriching, fun, and highly intriguing.

NOTES

1. The Knights of Labor was the first union to recruit members regardless of race or sex—though this practice did not last for the entirety of the union's life.
2. *The Industrial Union Bulletin* was a bi-weekly paper, three to five pages in length. It was discontinued due to low funds within the organization. The Industrial Worker was published from March 18, 1909 to September 4, 1913, and then started again in April 1916 and today remains the English language paper of the I.W.W.
3. *For closer examination of these publications, visit the I.W.W. website: www.iww.org and search under the heading: "I.W.W. Pamphlets and Other Literature."
4. Joe Hill was convicted of murder despite vague evidence. His trial achieved international attention, and President Wilson attempted to intervene twice, pleading for the governor of Utah to re-try the case. Despite this, Joe Hill was shot to death in 1915 (see Foner 1965, 154).
5. First published in *Solidarity* (December 23, 1911).

REFERENCES

Bird, Stewart and Deborah Shaffer (Directors) 1978. *The Wobblies* [Docurama]. 2006.DVD.

Dray, Philip. 2010. *There is Power in a Union: The Epic Story of Labor in America*. New York: Doubleday.

An Economic Interpretation of the Job. 1924. Chicago: I.W.W. Publishing Bureau.

Education and System: The Basis of Organization. 1924. Chicago: I.W.W. Publishing Bureau.

Ellis, Clifford B. [1930] 1988. "Education." In *Rebel Voices: An IWW Anthology*, Edited by Joyce L. Kornbluh, 365–368. Chicago: Charles H. Kerr.

Foner, Philip S. 1965. *History of the Labor Movement in the United States, Volume IV*. New York: International Publishers.

Glen, John M. 1988. *Highlander: No Ordinary School, 1932–1962*. Lexington: University Press of Kentucky.

Horton, Aimee Isgrig. 1989. *The Highlander Folk School: A History of its Major Programs, 1932–1961*. Brooklyn, NY: Carlson Publishing.

I.W.W. Songs: to Fan the Flames of Discontent. 1917. Chicago: I.W.W. Publishing Bureau.

———. 1918. Chicago: I.W.W. Publishing Bureau.

———. 1968. Chicago: I.W.W. Publishing Bureau.

The Industrial Union Bulletin, Official Publication of the Industrial Workers of the World. 1907a. March 26.

———. 1907b. April 6.

———. 1907c.

The I.W.W.: What It Is and What It Is Not. 1928. Chicago: I.W.W. Publishing Bureau.

Koch, Raymond, and Charlotte Koch. 1972. *Educational Commune: the Story of Commonwealth College*. New York: Schocken Books.

Peterson, Larry, 1986. "The Intellectual World of the IWW: an American Worker'sLibrary in the First Half of the 20th Century." *History Workshop* 22 (Autumn): 160.

Renshaw, Patrick, 1967. *The Wobblies: The Story of the IWW and Syndicalism in the United States*. Chicago: Ivan R. Dee.

Saposs, David J. 1926. *Left Wing Unionism: A Study of Radical Policies and Tactics*. New York: International Publishers.

Schneider, Florence Hemley, 1941. *Patterns of Workers' Education: The Story of the Bryn Mawr Summer School*. Bryn Mawr College.

Thompson, Fred W. and Jon Bekken, 2006. *The Industrial Workers of the World: Its First 100 Years*. Cincinnati, OH: Industrial Workers of the World Press.

ABOUT THE AUTHOR

Daniel Dethrow is a doctoral candidate in the history of education at Indiana University, Bloomington, and is working on his dissertation about schools in the coal camps of southern Colorado in the early 1900s. His research interests focus on early-twentieth century topics such as labor history, workers colleges, folk schools, Americanization programs, and U.S.-directed schooling in Puerto Rico.

CHAPTER 3

TEACHING CHILDREN THE "REAL" STORY

Oppositional Children's Literature, 1920–1940

Hani Morgan

Children's literature has, at times, been used to transmit a radical ideology. Historians often consider radical ideology to mean an agenda designed to challenge or oppose the practices of governments, ruling classes, or established organizations. In the first half of the 20th century, various authors wrote books and magazine articles that were critical of the social order and expressed views antithetical to America's cultural and social norms. This literature expressed the values of the working class, immigrants, and other groups in the United States.

These were turbulent decades in the United States, during which leftist groups and ideas were relatively common. Many radicals in America opposed the country's entry into World War I, but other groups espoused an agenda that was threatening to the social order. For example, the Industrial Workers of the World opposed capitalism. In response to these groups, laws were passed and raids conducted to protect the interests of conservatives

Learning the Left: Popular Culture, Liberal Politics, and Informal Education from 1900 to the Present, pp. 31–47
Copyright © 2015 by Information Age Publishing
31

and Western businessmen. In 1917, the Espionage Act was passed, followed one year later by the Sedition Act. These two laws prohibited individuals from supporting enemies of the United States or interfering with the goals of the military. A more powerful show of force occurred in 1920 when the government responded to bomb threats with the Palmer Raids, which was one of the most intensive efforts in U.S. history to subdue the agenda of radicals (Buhle 1998a). Ten thousand people were arrested in a brutal manner. Although these raids and laws were effective in controlling radicalism, they did not eliminate it; it persisted through the late 1920s and into the 1930s.

Radical authors challenged the status quo and taught children the opposite of what they usually learned from their school textbooks (Mickenburg 2006). This leftist literature—which varied considerably in its liberal aims—promoted social justice, exposed children to the real world, and provided ways for understanding and shaping society. Some of the authors who wrote these works were communists and socialists (Mishler 1998, 128). Much of this radical literature originated abroad, but was translated and available in the United States. Because this type of work tended to appeal only to specific groups, its readership was usually limited. In addition, progressive educators such as John Dewey and George Counts popularized a new way of teaching that created a need for children's books that reflected the actual workings of society.

This chapter explores radical children's literature published between 1920 and 1940 and focuses on authors who expressed oppositional views, such as Lucy Sprague Mitchell, Wanda Gág, Alfred Kreymborg, Helen Kay, Arna Bontemps, Mary White Ovington, William Brown, and others. Although the essay draws on the scholarship of prominent researchers in this field to identify radical children's books and to explain what motivated the authors, it analyzes various themes within that literature, offering a unique interpretation of progressive literary categories: oppositional children's literature and the real world, oppositional children's literature and injustice, oppositional children's literature and science, and oppositional children's books and race. The chapter also delves into parts of this radical literature that previous scholars did not fully utilize, and its findings—although partially paralleling those of other researchers—include new details and insights.

REASONS FOR THE PUBLICATION OF RADICAL CHILDREN'S LITERATURE

During the first half of the 20th century, progressive educational philosophy became more popular, and schools increasingly implemented instruction based on progressive ideals, which were designed to prepare children for the real world. Progressive educators like John Dewey believed that rote memorization was inferior for teaching children how to solve real-world problems, and that the latter method was necessary to improve the social order. Dewey and other philosophers, such as George Counts, influenced authors to write children's books with radical themes.

The progressive movement in education developed from the writings of Benjamin Rush and Thomas Jefferson in the 18th century, Henry Barnard and Horace Mann in the 19th century, and John Dewey in the 20th century (Ornstein and Hunkins 2013). Although progressives sometimes disagreed with each other and split into various groups (including activity-centered, child-centered, neo-Freudian, and creative) they all believed that overreliance on textbooks, authoritarian teaching, static goals without consideration for the changing world, memorization of facts, corporal punishment or intimidation, and separation of education from children's experiences were detrimental (Ornstein and Hunkins). Radical children's literature published between 1920 and 1940 reflected many of these goals, especially those that aimed to connect students' education to the real world and to teach them to solve problems related to injustice.

The Communist Party also influenced authors to write oppositional children's books, but in an indirect way. Although the Communist Party's radical ideology promoted beliefs that were harmonious with those of leftist authors, the party did not devote as much effort to organizing programs aimed at producing children's literature as it did to promoting its radical perspective, because its members tended to perceive children's literature as inferior (Mickenburg 2006). The values that communist authors promoted, however, raised awareness of leftist perspectives, which led some authors to write children's books based on this ideology.

Like the communists, socialists held beliefs antithetical to American norms, but the socialists differed somewhat in their approach to influencing children. Socialists created Sunday schools and used literature and other resources to promote their ideology, but unlike the communists, who concentrated on children from working-class families, socialists aimed to reach youth of all backgrounds (Mickenburg 2006). The first socialist Sunday schools emerged shortly after the founding of the Socialist Party in 1901 and continued to expand until 1919–1920 when the party split. However, a few schools continued to operate in the 1920s, and by the 1930s the party grew stronger and organized more schools in New York City. A split in ranks once again weakened the party, and by the end of 1936, socialist Sunday schools no longer existed in the United States.

Socialist Sunday schools aimed to expose the inequalities that capitalism promoted, such as poverty and crime, and were designed to provide alternative perspectives to the individualistic, anti-working class ideology that public schools promoted. Although many staff members had no pedagogical training and relied too much on reading resources intended for adults, the schools used a wide variety of teaching strategies including guest speakers, role playing, field trips, question-and-answer sessions, and socialist and non-socialist reading material (Teitelbaum 1998).

Additionally, African-American children's literature expanded during this period. Early adult fiction often ridiculed people of African descent, and these stereotypes could also be found in children's books (Larrick 1965). However, during the early 1900s, as a consequence of the increasing demands of a growing middle class of African Americans who wanted their children to read books that portrayed their children accurately, more authors wrote texts designed to challenge demeaning perspectives of African Americans (Harris 1990a, 545). The Crisis Publishing Company (an organ of the NAACP) and the Dubois and Dill Publishing Company produced many of these books.

Soviet children's books and the Soviet system of education also influenced many American authors and progressive educators. Both Dewey and Counts visited the Soviet Union and were impressed with the Soviet method of pedagogy, and many educators also approved of Soviet children's literature. Much of this literature emphasized the usefulness of science and machinery, but also focused on the importance of solidarity, organization, and the values of collective and cooperative living. Soviet educational authorities used a highly organized system to spread children's literature to remote areas and studied how children reacted to it (Doniger 1934).

One of the most influential Soviet authors was Mikhail Ilin. A major reason Ilin's books appealed to American authors and educators was their lack of propaganda. Whereas some reviewers criticized American children's books for "lies" aimed to teach children to hate anything that challenged American norms, they often praised Ilin's books for being entertaining and promoting the interests of children (Mickenburg 2006). Although American educators praised much of Ilin's literature for its apolitical perspective, some of his work was extremely critical of America and its capitalist system. For example, in *New Russia's Primer: The Story of the Five-Year Plan* (Illin 1931), a children's book translated by George Counts, Ilin describes America as a region where a few greedy people strive to make a profit while the rest of the population goes hungry.

> Automobile manufacturers spend millions of dollars for the purchase and destruction of used automobiles. Steamship companies wreck hundreds of the latest steamships.

What does this mean? Have people lost their senses, or what is the matter? The burning of corn, the spilling of milk, the destruction of automobiles, the wrecking of steamships — why is this done? Who profits by it?

It is profitable to the Foxes and the Boxes. Mr. Fox burns a few train-loads of grain in order to raise the price of corn. Mr. Box gives orders to spill tens of thousands of bottles of milk into the river in order that milk may not be sold too cheaply. And in the meantime school physicians in New York report that one out of every four children in the city is undernourished. (Ilin 1931, 11–12)

Although in this part of the book Ilin expresses a favorable attitude toward the Soviet economic system, in other parts his intent is to emphasize the importance of machinery.

In addition to Soviet texts, children's books originating in other countries motivated American authors. One of these books, *Fairy Tales for Workers' Children* (Zur Mühlen 1925), was translated from German and was the first one published by the communist press in America. This book was also an inspiration to author Helen Kay, the first American to have a book published by the communist press (Mickenburg 2006).

Fairy Tales for Workers' Children is a collection of short stories that expose children to the inequalities the working class must endure. The first story, "The Rose-Bush," is about a plant that can communicate with people. In the beginning of the story, the bush talks to a man who works for a wealthy lady. He explains to the rose bush that this woman and others who are well off do minimal work, while the rest of the people barely have enough to get by:

The man laughed a little sadly, saying, "Oh, beloved Rose-bush, you don't yet know the world, I can see that. The lady did not lift a finger to earn the money."

"Then how did she get it?"

"She owns a great factory in which countless workers drudge; from there comes her wealth."

The Rose-bush became angry, lifted a bough up high, threatened the man with her thorn-claws, shouting, "I see you enjoy yourself at my expense because I am still young and inexperienced, telling me untruths about the world of men. Still I am not so stupid, I have observed ants and bees, and know that to each belongs the things for which he has worked."

"That may be so among bees and ants," the man sighed deeply, "yet among men it is different. There the people receive just enough to keep them from starving—all else belongs to the master. The master builds splendid mansions, plants lovely gardens, buys flowers."

"Is that really true?"

"Yes." (Zur Mühlen 1925, 5)

Later in the story, the wind speaks to the rose bush and explains that inequalities between the poor and the rich can be controlled. The wind urges the bush to fight and to refrain from blooming. The bush obeys the wind, and after deciding to refrain from drinking water, the bush appears withered and dead to her rich owner. The rich lady then commands for the bush to be thrown out; as the man who spoke to the bush at the start of the story digs her up, she speaks to him again and asks him to take her home where her health is restored, and her roses are broken off and given to the poor.

OPPOSITIONAL CHILDREN'S LITERATURE AND THE REAL WORLD

Lucy Sprague Mitchell was one of the leading authors during this period who wrote progressive books designed to provide children with an impression of the real world. Born on July 2, 1878, she was a shy and withdrawn child, and her childhood was at times harsh because her father used an authoritarian form of discipline that led her to keep her thoughts to herself (Smith 2000). Mitchell's father was a businessman with economic interests in educational and cultural institutions in Chicago. He met with a wide variety of people, including John Dewey and Jane Addams (Smith 2000). Lucy met Dewey when she was a teenager and, by that time, had read all his works. Even though she had done little work with disadvantaged people, she began reading to learn more about this population.

Unlike her father, Lucy became fascinated with the social reform efforts of Dewey and Addams and rejected her father's business standards. Many of her books exalt industrial labor and were designed to challenge social hierarchies. Mitchell believed that texts should emphasize everyday experiences to enable children to gain more control of society. She felt that in addition to using language for communication, children should also enjoy its sound and feared that adults would strip children of this joy of language by requiring them to learn the adult standards of speech and by using stories that were too abstract (Smith 2000). In *The Here and Now Story Book* (Mitchell 1921), her most important work, Mitchell writes in a manner consistent with these beliefs. In a poem entitled "The Subway Car," for example, she focuses on topics involving ordinary city life and uses a rhyming style that promotes enjoyment:

Up on high against the sky
The elevated train goes by.
Above it soars, above it roars
On level with the second floors
Of dirty houses, dirty stores
Who have to see, who have to hear
This noisy ugly monster near.
And as it passes hear it yell,
"I'm the deafening, deadening,
thunderous, hideous,
competent, elegant el." (Mitchell 1921, 241)

Another poem in the same book, "A Locomotive," has a similar theme. Although both of these poems describe industrialization, they also hint at its darker side. In "The Subway Car," the subway is described as "an ugly monster," and in "A Locomotive," modern machinery is compared to a demon that is polluting the environment:

In the daytime, what am I?
In the hubbub, what am I?
A mass of iron and of steel,
Of boiler, piston, throttle, wheel,
A monster smoking up the sky,
A locomotive! That am I!
In the darkness, what am I?
In the stillness, what am I?
Streak of light across the sky,
A clanging bell, a shriek, a cry,
A fiery demon rushing by,
A locomotive
That am I! (Mitchell 1921, 320)

Mitchell hoped this type of literature would not only benefit children but also adults: that by exposing teachers and parents to the language of children, adults would alter the way they communicated with children.

While Mitchell believed her style of writing for children was beneficial, others disagreed, and *The Here and Now Story Book* received mixed reviews. More traditional educators believed that rather than expose children to the real world, educators needed to protect them from it and use fairy tales instead. However, Mitchell believed that fairy tales would confuse children because such tales were not based in the real-world experiences that children readily understood. She believed that fairy tales could be used to develop children's imagination after they gained familiarity with the real world (Mickenburg 2006).

Mitchell applied the progressive, child-centered philosophy of educators such as Dewey not only to her own work, but she also influenced and trained other communist authors: her work as an educator extended far beyond the field of children's literature. Mitchell raised the standards for teachers when she opened the Cooperative School for Teachers (CST) in 1931, and she was also involved with eight experimental schools in an effort to create a more knowledgeable type of teacher who had more experience and could handle a wide variety of teaching situations (Smith 2000). Before the creation of the Cooperative School for Teachers, most teachers needed only high school degrees or were prepared through a strict methodological approach. The CST abolished regimented methods courses and allowed teachers the freedom to use the appropriate pedagogical styles that would best serve the needs of students (Smith 2000, 35).

In addition to Mitchell, other authors wrote children's books with similar themes. *Mike Mulligan and His Steam Shovel* (Burton 1939), for example, is a story that exposes children to machinery, suggesting that these devices and the people who operate them are capable of tremendous accomplishments. While Mitchell's work, at times, expresses a negative attitude toward machinery by suggesting that it is ugly and leads to unpleasant consequences, such as pollution, *Mike Mulligan and His Steam Shovel* leaves the impression that machines are much more benevolent:

> Mike Mulligan had a steam shovel,
> a beautiful red steam shovel.
> Her name was Mary Anne.
> Mike Mulligan was very proud of Mary Anne.
> He always said that she could dig as much in a day
> as a hundred men could dig in a week,
> but he had never been quite sure
> that this was true. (Burton 1939, 3)

This book explains how Mike Mulligan and his steam shovel dig canals and tunnel through mountains in order for boats and trains to pass through. In other similar books—including *How the Derrick Works* (Jones 1930) and *Diggers and Builders* (Lent 1931)—the illustrations suggest that laborers need to be strong and skillful. Two books in this genre—*Diggers and Builders* and *A Steam Shovel for Me!* (Edelstadt 1933)—also feature ethnic or racial minority groups (Mickenburg 2006).

OPPOSITIONAL CHILDREN'S LITERATURE AND INJUSTICE

Although some aspects of Mitchell's *Here and Now Story Book* suggest that machines and industrialization are somewhat sinister, Wanda Gág's most successful 1928 children's book, *Millions of Cats*, suggests that modern society is brutal and leads to inequality. Unlike Mitchell's book, which is designed to expose children to industrialism, *Millions of Cats* is a fictitious story that teaches that the competition and greed of the world are extremely destructive. This story is about an old lonely couple who decide to get a cat. The husband searches and is delighted when he finds an enormous number of cats. He wants to take the prettiest one home, but cannot decide which one to take, so he takes them all. When he arrives home, his wife tells him they can keep only one. The old man tells the cats they need to decide which cat is the prettiest. The cats then destroy each other in a fight over which one is the prettiest, and only one not-so-pretty cat survives:

> They bit and scratched and clawed each other and made such a great noise that the very old man and the very old woman ran into the house as fast as they could. They did not like such quarrelling. But after a while the noise stopped and the very old man and the very old woman peeped out of the window to see what had happened. They could not see a single cat!
>
> "I think they must have eaten each other all up," said the very old woman, "It's too bad!" "But look!" said the very old man, and he pointed to a bunch of high grass. In it sat one little frightened kitten. They went out and picked it up. It was thin and scraggly. (Gág 1928, 13)

The "thin and scraggly" cat is the hero because Gág felt sympathetic for those who have less power in society. Before publishing *Millions of Cats*, Gág produced radical drawings. These drawings caught the attention of Ernestine Evans, an editor who after visiting the Soviet Union became interested in producing children's books with socialist themes and helped Gág publish her book (Mickenburg 2006).

Similar to Gág's *Millions of Cats* is Alfred Kreymborg's work, especially *Funnybone Alley*. One of the factors contributing to Kreymborg's progressive ideas was his exposure to Greenwich Village. Early in his career, Kreymborg worked on a magazine in Ridgefield, New Jersey, but later moved it to the Village. Although he maintained a distance from the more radical villagers and was uncomfortable being associated with them, this new location reflected and encouraged unorthodox thinking, unconventional behavior, and liberated lifestyles. The Village offered inexpensive rooms to single adults who wished to be free of family obligations in order to develop their artistic pursuits (Churchill 1998).

In *Funnybone Alley*, Kreymborg describes a community in New York where people have different values than those in the rest of the city. Community members seem to be anti-capitalist and sympathetic to socialist principles. This is evident when Kreymborg describes their interest in treating others fairly in business affairs:

> The shopkeepers have a failing which is common to one and all. Peter Pringle, the shoemaker, Ben Benjamin, the grocer, Dilly Derrydown, the toy-man, Pa Peppermint, the confectioner, Bartholomew Bang, the barber—these and the rest of them are afflicted with tenderness. And no one is inclined to stop that soft disease from spreading. So they find it hard to charge more for their goods than their goods are worth. And often charge less. (Kreymborg 1927, 26)

The school in *Funnybone Alley* is also different from other schools and is based on similar practices to those that progressive educators urged: it is cooperative, child-centered, egalitarian, noncompetitive, and emphasizes the interests of the students (Mickenburg 2006). The school is also less rigid regarding the hours students need to arrive and leave, and unlike the process in many other schools, the children do some of their most important learning in the real-life environment of the city, outside of the classroom.

Another book designed to teach children how to respond to inequality and the problems of capitalist societies is Helen Kay's *Battle in the Barnyard: Stories and Pictures for Workers' Children*. Published in 1932, this book consists of a series of short stories emphasizing the necessity of resistance to different forms of oppression, often leading to a level of improvement for the oppressed people. Stories of this nature tended to be very radical because communist publications linked the suffering of children to capitalism. In 1934, the literary critic E. A. Schachner argued that books of this nature called for the destruction of capitalism through revolution (Mickenberg 2006).

One story from this book is "The High Hat Ants," which is about two colonies: the Fuscae and the Amazon. The Amazon consists of powerful and strong ants that capture the weaker Fuscae colony and treat them as servants. The Amazon ants capture the Fuscae by seizing their unhatched eggs because they know that adult Fuscae will resist being servants since they have experienced freedom. However, one day they inadvertently capture a Fuscae that was in the process of breaking out of its egg and had already learned to think. This ant begins to wonder why it and the other Fuscae are doing all the work for the Amazon ants. Its questions spread anger, which leads to revolt. The Amazon grow weak because the rebelling Fuscae no longer supply them with food. Most of the Amazon perish; the Fuscae take control and announce that everyone, including the upper classes, must work. The ending is a happy one because justice prevails:

> The Fuscae saw this. And they organized themselves into a strong army. They then took over all they had built, the houses, store rooms, and sun parlors. The leaders announced that everyone, even the aristocrats, must work in order to eat. Some few learned, but most were too spoiled to change, and so they perished.

> Now, the whole ant village lives happily in the large suburban homes at the base of the hemlock tree where the wind whispers wonderful tales as it sails through the dense foliage. (Kay 1932, 18)

Although the theme of this story—that it is possible to revolt and be successful—is obvious, the story is somewhat fanciful for several reasons. First, rather than choose people as characters, Kay chooses ants. Second, in real-life societies, even when conditions resulting from severe oppression improve, discord and conflict often persist and seldom does everyone live happily ever after.

A more realistic account regarding the outcome of resistance to inequalities in society occurs in the first story of Kay's book, entitled "Bread." This story is about Jane, a student who cannot concentrate in school because she has an empty stomach and is thinking about bread and butter. Her teacher becomes annoyed, and asks Jane to leave class because she fails to pay attention. On her way home, Jane meets her classmate Cora, who informs her about a plan the children at their school have to demand better treatment. They return to school and, with the other students, carry signs demanding free food for children who cannot afford it. After a few minutes of picketing, the police arrive and demand that the children stop, but the children continue to protest. The police then get angry and take 20 children away in a wagon, but the children are fearless and happy because they have now learned how to fight for their rights:

> Several of the boys and girls began to sing. Jane looked out of the back of the patrol. She seemed like quite a different little girl. As she gazed through the barred window she could see her schoolmates following the police car. They were running. And in their hands they were carrying signs demanding, "Free Car Fares" and "Free Lunches for Children of Unemployed." (Kay 1932, 13)

Articles and stories exposing youth to injustice also appeared in the *New Pioneer,* a magazine for children. In a 1932 issue, for example, a text written by Jack Hardy explains how school textbooks often mislead readers, because powerful groups wish to leave facts out and provide false information in order to avoid representing the perspective of the working class (Mickenburg 2006).

OPPOSITIONAL CHILDREN'S LITERATURE AND SCIENCE

In 1925, John Scopes was brought up on charges for teaching evolution in Tennessee, leading to what is now known as the Scopes Monkey Trial. This legal case was not the only controversy during this era involving teachings that contradicted religion; some authors published children's books that used science and theories of evolution to achieve the same end. One of the most radical books was *Science and History for Girls and Boys* (1932) by William Brown. Brown's ideas were so controversial that he was tried for heresy by the Episcopal Church's House of Bishops (Buhle 1998b). In *Science and History for Girls and Boys*, he writes that the Bible contains irrational stories and, thus, is not the word of God:

> And now you can understand what the first part of the Bible, the Old Testament, really is, and how foolish it is to call it the Word of God. Even two hundred years ago there were learned men and writers who said that a book that contained so many absurd stories could not possibly be the Word of God. Men whom American children are taught to regard as almost the greatest in American history, such as Franklin, Washington, Jefferson, Adams, Hamilton, Lincoln and many others, did not believe what any church of their time said about the Bible. Today no really learned man, even if he believes in God, admits that there is any revelation or message from Him in the Bible, and even in the churches the best educated people do not believe it. (Brown 1932, 108)

Brown argues that in contrast to the fictitious stories of the Bible, science can help people have an accurate understanding of the world, including the origins of humankind.

> So there is no need to bother about what the Bible says on that subject. Adam and Eve and the Garden of Eden are simply part of a very old story, like Sin-bad or Bluebeard which I will explain later. When the ministers of these religious people pretend to know science and argue about the question as if they did, they are simply foolish. All the professors of science in all universities and all their pupils would tell you that man came from some lower animal; just as we saw, all the land animals came from fishes. (Brown 1932, 108)

Another children's book teaching that humans evolved from lower animals is *Rhymes of Early Jungle Folk* (Marcy 1922). As its title implies, this book consists of a series of rhyming passages that describe an evolutionary process contradicting creationism. The text is less radical than Brown's because the author is less explicit. However, the rhymes obviously express a Darwinian ideology. One of the rhymes, for example, describes a time before humans could speak when they would swing on branches from tree to tree:

> They swung themselves from tree to tree,
> By grasping for a limb,
> And flung themselves
> From very dizzy heights,
> And raised aloft among the boughs,
> With every passing whim;
> And perched on high,
> Perceived the jungle sights.
> They didn't have a language then;
> There wasn't much to say;
> They chattered all,
> In funny little cries,
> To tell of food, fear, or love,
> Or scold their foes away,
> Or warn a reckless youth
> Against surprise. (Marcy 1922, 82)

OPPOSITIONAL CHILDREN'S LITERATURE AND RACE

Arna Bontemps wrote several culturally authentic children's books during this era, one of which was *Popo and Fifina: Children of Haiti*, which he co-authored with Langston Hughes. Although similar books today would be considered mainstream, in the first half of the 20th century the shortage of these types of books and the negative attitudes held by many white Americans toward people of African descent made this book quite progressive. Violet Harris (1990b) notes that *Popo and Fifina* is culturally authentic for several reasons. First, Haiti is not portrayed as a region with uncivilized people, and the characters in the story have many positive characteristics. Popo, for example, is eager to help his mother with the household chores:

> When Popo went inside he found Mamma Anna and Fifina making a bed for Baby Pensia. They had already set up the big bed in which Mamma Anna and Papa Jean were to sleep, and they had fixed a straw pallet on the floor for Popo and Fifina. Now they were stuffing a gunny sack to make a bed for Pensia.
>
> "What can I do?" Popo asked. "I want to help too."

"The beds are about finished." Mamma Anna said. "But we'll need some dry leaves to start the charcoal fire. You can get those for us."

That pleased Popo. He scrambled out of the house and ran across a sandy slope to a place where the brush seemed thickest and driest. (Bontemps and Hughes 1932, 11)

Harris also mentions that Caribbean novels published during the same period often contained exotic, ribald images, and demeaning illustrations. However, this book rejects such content, and the authors resisted the suggestions of influential editors to make it more stereotypical (Harris 1990b).

Mary White Ovington also authored culturally authentic children's books during this period. Ovington was affiliated with the NAACP and wrote books that celebrated the achievements of African Americans, entertained children, and encouraged racial pride, but her books also contained some stereotypes (Harris 1990a). One such book is *Zeke*, the story of an intelligent young man who has to leave home to pursue his education and shows courage in adapting to his new environment. At the start of the story, his family and members of the community are at the train station to wish him good luck on his journey to the Tolliver Institute. They are happy and proud that he is going there because he is the first one to attend from their part of the county. Although the scenery on the way to the institute is pleasant, when Ezekiel arrives, he does not enjoy his new environment and soon becomes miserable. Unfortunately, he cannot return home because by doing so he would let everyone down:

No, he couldn't go home; the disgrace would be too great. Everyone would think that Ezekiel Lee, the best scholar in his school, who won a silver medal last spring and got his name in the Montgomery newspaper, had been unable to enter Tolliver Institute. (Ovington 1931, 6)

This type of literature also appeared in the *Brownies Book,* a magazine created by W.E.B. Du Bois and published in 1920 and 1921. Focusing on prominent black individuals and intended for children from 6 to 16 years old, the *Brownies Book* had an audience consisting mostly of middle-class, urban blacks who were affiliated with the NAACP. The magazine used news stories, poetry, fiction, drama, and biographies to emphasize the contributions of black people. Dubois and editor Jessie R. Fauset also wanted to entertain children and teach them cultural pride and a code of honor (Harris 1990a).

In addition to exposing the inequalities between powerful groups and the working class, the *New Pioneer* magazine also focused on interracial cooperation and issues of racial discrimination. In 1931, for example, the magazine published the story "Pickets and Slippery Slicks" by Myra

Page. In it, two white and two black children become friends and perceive this relationship as natural. But when the two white children's parents find out about the friendship, they punish their children, call the black children derogatory names, and tell them not to come to the white part of town again (Mickenburg 2006). More civil rights content in this magazine appears on the cover of the October 1932 issue, which included an illustration of two children from different racial backgrounds to emphasize the importance of interracial friendship. Also in this image, above the two children, is the statement "Free the Scottsboro Boys." The Scottsboro boys were a group of black teenagers who were wrongly accused of raping a white woman, and the case included many elements of racism (Kelley 1998). The statement "Free the Scottsboro Boys" illustrated the magazine's commitment to racial justice.

CONCLUSION

Different forms of radical children's literature were published between 1920 and 1940 for various reasons. Progressive authors from this era wrote children's literature designed to expose youth to machinery, industrialism, and the real world to prepare them for real-life experiences. Although children's literature designed to expose youth to machinery and industrialism was progressive in several ways, it was less radical than other texts that were published by communists and socialists. The latter were more radical because they often taught children how to oppose the existing social order, and suggested that capitalism was a detrimental economic system.

Another genre of children's literature that challenged American cultural norms between 1920 and 1940 involved material that contradicted the Bible. Children's literature of this nature taught that humans evolved from lower animals long before the story of Adam and Eve was first recorded. One of the most radical authors of this type of literature was William Brown, because he not only exposed children to an alternate way of perceiving the world, but also because he insisted that his unorthodox views were correct.

Although culturally authentic children's literature is today considered mainstream, in the 1920s it was radical because it contradicted the common stereotypical portrayals of minority groups. Culturally authentic children's literature emerged during this period as a result of the growing demands of African Americans who wanted their children to have books that represented their culture more accurately and positively. Other radical authors desired to teach those children who faced injustice how to control inequalities, and to be proud of their cultural heritage. The stories written during this period are just as important today as they were in the first half of the 20th century because social inequalities persist. However, today more forms of this genre of literature are regarded as mainstream rather than oppositional because there is a growing desire in American society to create more opportunities for disadvantaged youth.

REFERENCES

Bontemps, Arna, and Langston Hughes. 1932. *Popo and Fifina: Children of Haiti.* New York: Macmillan.

Brown, William M. 1932. *Science and History for Girls and Boys.* Galion, OH: Bradford-Brown.

Buhle, Paul. 1998a. "Red Scare." In *Encyclopedia of the American Left,* edited by Mari Jo Buhle, Paul Buhle, and Dan Georgakas, 691–692. New York: Oxford University Press.

———. 1998b. "Brown, William Montgomery." In *Encyclopedia of the American Left,* edited by Mari Jo Buhle, Paul Buhle, and Dan Georgakas, 111. New York: Oxford University Press.

Burton, Virginia L. 1939. *Mike Mulligan and His Steam Shovel.* Boston: Houghton Mifflin.

Churchill, Suzanne W. 1998. "Making Space for Others: A History of a Modernist Little Magazine." *Journal of Modern Literature* 22: 47–67.

Doniger, Simon. 1934. "Soviet Education and Children's Literature." *Journal of Educational Sociology* 8 (3): 162–167.

Edelstadt, Vera. 1933. *A Steam Shovel for Me!* Philadelphia: Lippincott.

Gág, Wanda. 1928. *Millions of Cats.* New York: Coward McCann.

Harris, Violet H. 1990a. "African American Children's Literature: The First One Hundred Years." *The Journal of Negro Education* 59: 540–555.

———. 1990b. "From Little Black Sambo to Popo and Fifina: Arna Bontemps and the Creation of African-American Children's Literature." *The Lion and the Unicorn* 14: 108–127.

Ilin, Mikhail. 1931. *New Russia's Primer: The Story of the Five-Year Plan.* New York: Houghton Mifflin.

Jones, Wilfred. 1930. *How the Derrick Works.* New York: Macmillan.

Kay, Helen. 1932. *Battle in the Barnyard: Stories and Pictures for Workers' Children.* New York: Workers Library.

Kelley, Robin D. 1998. "Scottsboro Case." In *Encyclopedia of the American Left,* edited by Mari Jo Buhle, Paul Buhle, and Dan Georgakas, 730–732. New York: Oxford University Press.

Kreymborg, Alfred. 1927. *Funnybone Alley.* New York: Maccaulay.

Larrick, Nancy. 1965. "The All-White World of Children's Books." *Saturday Review* 48: 63–65, 84–85.

Lent, Henry B. 1931. *Diggers and Builders.* New York: Macmillan.

Marcy, Mary E. 1922. *Rhymes of Early Jungle Folk.* Chicago: Charles H. Kerr.

Mickenburg, Julia L. 2006. *Learning from the Left: Children's Literature, the Cold War, and Radical Politics in the United States.* New York: Oxford University Press.

Mishler, Paul C. 1998. "Children's Literature." In *Encyclopedia of the American Left*, edited by Mari Jo Buhle, Paul Buhle, and Dan Georgakas, 127–128. New York: Oxford University Press.

Mitchell, Lucy S. 1921. *The Here and Now Story Book*. New York: E. P. Dutton & Company.

Ornstein, Allan C., and Francis. P. Hunkins. 2013. *Curriculum: Foundations, Principles, and Issues*. New York: Pearson.

Ovington, Mary O. 1931. *Zeke*. Freeport, NH: Books for Libraries.

Smith, Mary K. 2000. "Who Was Lucy Sprague Mitchell ... and Why Should You Know?" *Childhood Education* 77: 33–36.

Teitelbaum, Kenneth. "Socialist Sunday Schools." In *Encyclopedia of the American Left*, edited by Mari Jo Buhle, Paul Buhle, and Dan Georgakas, 774–775. New York: Oxford University Press.

Zur Mühlen, Herminia, 1925. *Fairy Tales for Workers' Children*. Chicago: Daily Worker Publishing Company.

ABOUT THE AUTHOR

Hani Morgan is an associate professor in the Department of Curriculum, Instruction, and Special Education at the University of Southern Mississippi. He completed his doctoral studies at Rutgers University in the social and philosophical foundations of education. Morgan is the author of over 30 published articles and seven entries appearing in *The Dictionary of Modern American Philosophers* (Thoemmes Press, 2005). Morgan's historical research interests include the representation of minority groups in children's literature and progressive education in the United States. He would like to thank the members of the Organization of Educational Historians who attended his presentations on oppositional children's literature and provided valuable feedback on this topic, and Joe Ramsey for his guidance in writing this book chapter.

CHAPTER 4

A GREEN PEACE TINTED RED

Cold War America in
The Boy with Green Hair

Peter W. Lee

"Please don't tell why his hair turned green!" implored the tagline in an advertisement for *The Boy with Green Hair*, a Radio-Keith-Orpheum (RKO) Radio Picture film production released in 1948 ("The Boy with Green Hair" 1948a). The studio ballyhooed the stakes as far greater than any spoiler warning. With industry powerhouse producers Dore Schary and Adrian Scott and first-time director Joseph Losey behind the camera, the ad copy suggested something special about a boy with jade locks. Utilizing eden ahbez's popular *Nature Boy* as a theme song, glorious Technicolor (a requirement, considering the title), a universal message that "war is bad for children," and a solid cast including Pat O'Brien, Barbara Hale, Robert Ryan, and Dean Stockwell billed as "the boy," *The Boy with Green Hair* had the potential to become a moral blockbuster.

RKO lost $420,000 on the picture ("Boy Budgeted"; "$109 Million"; C. J. Trevlin Ledger 1994).[1] Critics pointed to a flawed execution, and industry trade papers exposed backstage bickering. Losey later admitted, "There are certain things in the film that embarrass me terribly because they are

Learning the Left: Popular Culture, Liberal Politics, and Informal Education from 1900 to the Present, pp. 49–69

so blatantly sentimental" (Caute 1994, 88). *The Boy with Green Hair* did not just represent a case of flawed filmmaking, although several commentators pointed to poorly-plotted sequences. The production violated the old showbiz adage: timing is everything, because the film's frosty reception stemmed from the political and social milieu of the early Cold War. A year earlier the Truman Doctrine "scared the hell out of the American people" with warnings of sinister Soviet masterminds hatching plots for world revolutions (Levering 2001, 51). Lest small-town U.S.A. end up a gulag, hyper patriotism separated red-blooded Americans from those who were then, or had been, card-carrying "others." In this atmosphere, the movie's progressive youngster learned that a lone voice in the left failed to combat a socially conservative orthodoxy in which military might makes right.

PLANTING SEEDS

The mobilized "Hollywood Unit" during World War II portrayed the United States as taking the moral high ground in its melting pot rhetoric (Doherty 1999). In war films like *Bataan* in 1943 or *Desperate Journey* in 1942, Uncle Sam's GIs consisted of common Joes from every station in life, rendered on the silver screen in shades of gray, to make the world safe for democracy. Dedicated to the proposition that all men were created equal in the fight against totalitarianism, Hollywood (on the surface) presented American soldiers as one nation and indivisible, even unto death (Bruscino 2010, Wall 2008).[2]

Many of Hollywood's top brass, having served in the war effort at home or on the front lines, returned with a renewed obligation for "message pictures" advocating social reform. *Pride of the Marines* in 1945 and *The Best Years of Our Lives* in 1946 examined the nation's responsibility to servicemen, albeit, as the titles suggested, through a valorized narrative (Bodnar 2003, 87–132, Doherty 2007, 213–243). Progressive filmmakers tackled racism (*Pinky* in 1949), anti-Semitism (*Gentleman's Agreement* and *Crossfire* both in 1947), the mentally ill (*The Snake Pit* in 1948), and alcoholism (*The Lost Weekend* in 1945). When RKO scored with the low-budget whodunit *Crossfire*, producer Dore Schary told columnist Hedda Hopper on June 30, 1947:

> I believe the screen must balance itself between the very lovely gentle films such as *Going My Way* [1944; with Bing Crosby as a crooning priest] and a harder, realistic type of film that presents facts as sometimes they exist. I doubt any art can maintain its integrity by living in a purely fictional world [....] I think it must balance itself constantly to remain alert, alive, and progressive.

Concerning the sordid facts of life, he concluded, "In order to root them out we must expose them to the light of the public's contemplation so that this sordidness can be attended and irradicated [sic]" (Hedda Hopper papers 1947).

After Crossfire's success, RKO producer Adrian Scott bought a short story about a boy whose hair turns green. Scott, who had adopted a war orphan from the London blitz, saw the tale as a political and social allegory and asked screenwriter Ben Barzman to adapt it for the movies. According to Barzman's wife, her husband instantly saw the significance: "If a little boy who is a war orphan suddenly has green hair, it might be for a reason" (Barzman 2003, 84). After World War II, green hair signified ever-lasting peace.

THE GREEN YEARS

The film opens in a police station with a hitchhiking boy, Peter Frye (Dean Stockwell), whose bald pate confuses the cops. Child psychologist and "boy expert" Dr. Evans (Robert Ryan) coaxes the youngster to explain his lack of hair. "It's a long story," the kid says. "You wouldn't believe it." He narrates a happy childhood, one so innocent that on August 27, 1947, Joseph Breen, chief of the Production Code Administration—Hollywood's censorship body—recommended to RKO executive Harold Melniker that Peter's opening dialogue omit "the birds and the bees and the flowers and stuff like that" and references to his parents' divorce (Production Code Administration records). World War II broke up this idealized family as his parents left "for a long, long time" (Losey 1948). In a moment that lives in infamy, a telegram arrives informing that mom and dad will not return. Relatives pass the boy around and he ends up with Gramp (Pat O'Brien), an ex-performer turned singing waiter. Gramp is a good guy; he lets Peter roam the whole house, even if the boy breaks ceramic knick-knacks. Peter is not without inner demons: when Gramp works evenings, Peter, alone in the old, dark house, keeps a baseball bat nearby.

As the story progresses, Peter's boogeymen vanish in the intimate atmosphere of small-town America.[3] Losey directs a close-knit community: everyone from the milkman to the barber ruffles Peter's hair in friendly fashion. With a pretty Miss Brand (Barbara Hale) for a teacher and classmates who accept the new kid, Peter concludes, "Boy, I was really livin'" (Losey 1948). The boy integrates himself, complete with a job delivering groceries and his own bicycle. The dark didn't even faze him: the camera follows his moving the baseball bat from the bedpost to the floor.

The telling moment occurs when the school sponsors a drive for orphaned kids. The camera pans the posters from Peter's perspective; his shadow follows the images of destitute refugees (real-life photos include Wang Xiaoting's 1937 still of a crying baby in Shanghai). Posters ripped from the then-current headlines entitled, "Remember Greece," "United Jewish Welfare Fund," and "United China Relief " call attention to a global effort to aid children, of whom Peter's shadow will shortly join. One class-mate innocently observes one of the pictured youngsters resembles Peter because, well, Peter is a war orphan as well.

Frye resents his classmate's equating him to Europe's tired and poor ref-ugees. As one American World War II orphan, Ann Bennett Mix, recalled about growing up, "World War II newsreels and magazine pictures showed us that war orphans lived overseas, not in the United States, where most of us had enough to eat and a place to live" (Mix 1998, xvii). Frye's identity as a war orphan undermines his American-ness: despite his attempts to fit in, Peter remains an outsider. Gramp confirms the bad news: his parents "could have got out, but they stayed behind and died, trying to save little boys and girls, like yourselves, like them," and he gestures at the wall. The adults leave and Peter angrily rips the poster that started it all. Off screen, a girl loudly inquires if war orphans actually exist. Brand (the teacher) assures her: "If they could speak to you, they themselves would tell you how much these clothes really means to them and they'll tell you 'thank you for remembering us' " (Losey 1948).

Peter remembers Brand's words. At work, he overhears three women gossip over wartime preparedness. The camera tracks Peter gathering foodstuffs while the women provide a running commentary, reflecting the youngster's own thoughts. "Unless we're prepared there's just no way of avoiding it," says one. Another suggests the inevitable: "It seems like it's human nature to want to kill." The logic continues: "If it's human nature to kill, it's all the reason to be ready in case the other fellow wants to start something." They conclude, "War will come, want it or not, the only ques-tion is when" (Losey 1948). An alarmed Peter drops a bottle of milk; the motherly nourishment of all humanity spills over the floor. The busybodies glance down, smile, and walk off, unconcerned about the symbolic destruc-tion of Peter's safe haven.

At dinner, Peter asks Gramp to confirm the women's conversation. Gramp deflects the question by saying he keeps a little green around him, referring to a house plant. The color represents "hope and promise of a new life." Peter also experiences a new direction the next morning when his hair turns green during a bath. An alarmed Gramp optimistically proph-esizes "something grand." The boy disagrees. Planning to run away, Peter sobs himself to sleep in a forest glen and awakes to see the war orphans from the posters, transported from stark black and white posters to real-world Technicolor. Although the picture never states explicitly, director Joseph Losey recalled the other orphans were supposed to be "dead." He directed the child actors to speak in a low monotone to reflect "absolute horror, real terror [...] the dreadful starvation ... the concentration camp feeling" (quoted in Caute 1994, 473–474). While this assembled juvenile United Nations act deadpan, the cinematography undermines the "concentration camp feeling": their man-made destitution contrasts sharply with nature's brilliant green foliage. Life trumps mankind's devastation.

The dead children's spokesman, Michael (Richard Lyon), gives Peter a message of hope:

> There's a reason for your green hair [...] everywhere you go [...] people will ask, "Why does he have green hair?" So you will tell them, "Because I am a war orphan and my green hair is to remind you that war is very bad for children." You must tell *all* the people. The Russians, the Americans, the Chinese, the British, the French, all the people all over the world that there must not ever be another war.

In short, if Peter acts, "there never will be another war, and there never will be any more war orphans" (Losey 1948).

Peter accepts the mission in an about face. He spins around and approaches the camera, breaking the fourth wall as his face fills the screen. Peter addresses the audience: "They think everybody has to get killed. The world doesn't have to be blown up" (Losey 1948). Armed with this revelation, Peter resolves to spread his message to all and sundry, including the milkman; a disbelieving barber; Doctor Knudson, who reaches for some medication; and Miss Brand. Other townsfolk feel less charitable. Gramp succumbs to peer pressure and takes Peter to the barber. The angry neighbors, and the camera, look on as the locks fall past Peter's tear-stained face. The lad recognizes his mission's failure as the pile of hair mounts. He decides to run away and the flashback ends.

After a fade-in to the present, Peter asks Evans if he believes the tale. The boy expert says no and diagnoses the lad doesn't believe it himself. The assertion leaves Peter incredulous, but Evans explains, "If somebody really believed something, they don't get discouraged and run away just because they haven't convinced anybody on the first try." In other words, Evans encourages Peter to stick to his guns while concurrently finding the tale preposterous. Peter opens the door and sees Gramp, Brand, and Knudson waiting in the lobby. Gramp restores the boy's faith with a letter from Peter's late father. Dad Frye tells his son not to mourn, for his parents died "for something fine and worthwhile. It will have been fine and it will have been worthwhile if those who have not died will not forget. If they forget, remind them" (Losey 1948).

With belated adult support, Peter leaves with Gramp and Brand. Knudson asks Evans for his professional opinion. Evans reflects for the audience, "I'm not really concerned whether the boy's hair is really green or not. I believe in what he was trying to say […] that's all that matters, isn't it?" (Losey 1948). The End.

JADED VIEWPOINTS

Peter's green hair mattered to many people at the start of the Cold War. According to RKO's hype, the film was "not just the story of a boy—but the amazing human drama of a strange happening and what it did to people—to their lives, their hate, jealousy, laughter!" ("The Boy With Green Hair" 1948a). Studio publicity proved apt: the green hair did have a "strange happening" on people. Both young Frye's neighbors and the larger public deemed Peter's hair a veiled attack on American normalcy. Initially, the townsfolk, especially the children, don't care about the boy's tinted locks. Early on, one little girl declares it "super" and runs to tell her mom. Peter, however, prefers his original hairstyle and adults come up with some cosmetic solutions that avoid the heart of the issue. Since the case leaves Knudson baffled, Gramp offers to dye it. Peter snaps, "You mean like ladies do? No one's going to paint my hair!" Peter also considers cutting it off out of the question. He insists he "wants to be like everybody else" (Losey 1948).

Peter's early narration underlined his desire to fit into the social establishment. As an outsider who recently fit in, he doesn't want to be an outcast again. Unfortunately, the filmic adults see Peter's jade locks as a threat to their community. As Gramp and green-haired Peter walk down the street, adults do double takes and even a neighborhood dog barks at this deviance in their small town. "It's a little peculiar," one citizen admits, the only explanation the film offered, or needed, to fear the green-haired boy. The grown-ups rub off on Peter's peers and his class turns on him, chanting over, "Peter's got green hair." Another kid forewarns, "How would you like your sister to marry someone with green hair?" (Losey 1948). One exhibitor provided an indirect answer, reporting he "gave it added exploitation" and "curiosity alone brought in about average business." Despite the film's setting, he concluded, "It is not quite the small town's dish [because] the picture is a little too much for our patrons" ("The Exhibitor" 1949a, 3).

As historians have noted, public discourse rendered not only green hair as a source of contamination, but equated communism with disease, resulting in the need for containment to quarantine perverse ideologies and infected people (Smith 1992). The kids soon reject Peter's hair and the enthusiastic girl now backs off, explaining a fear of contagion: "Mother says I shouldn't get too close" (Losey 1948). The adults fret about the water and milk supply, wondering if this contamination is contagious—much to the consternation of city officials and the milkman. The latter frets about his declining revenue: Peter directly challenges their way of life. As a result, the adults gang up on Gramp to convince him to shave the boy. As RKO's story synopsis makes clear, "the townspeople, [Peter] finds, and even Gramps [*sic*], are in a conspiracy against him. They don't like to be reminded of war and they don't like anyone who is 'different' " (Production Code Administration records).

Miss Brand remains sympathetic. As the schoolmarm, she demonstrates a progressivism the townsfolk lack. She inventories her students' hair colors (black, brown, blond, red, and green) to demonstrate that follicle pigmentation is no excuse for discrimination. The sole red head shares a look with Peter, but any shared bond of uniqueness remains unsaid. Unfortunately, the larger community, including Peter's desire to fit in, drowns Brand's efforts. As RKO's story synopsis reads: "despite Miss Brand's sympathy and understanding, Peter is heartbroken. He doesn't want to be different, to be an outcast" (Production Code Administration records). The youngster blames the whole business on his parents. "They didn't care about me," he cries. "They only cared about saving the other children. They didn't care what happened to me" (Losey 1948). He links his green hair with his parents' disappearance: because they aided refugees abroad, they neglected their own American kid, who becomes an orphan himself.

The international war orphans correct Peter's attitude concerning his green hair. His vision establishes a postwar idealism, especially the "one world" movement advocating global government as a step toward universal peace. But the Cold War froze such notions. On April 15, 1948, *The Philadelphia Inquirer* aptly demonstrated through maps showing blood-red ink seeping from the Soviet Union across the globe, the "one world" plan was a "one-sided love affair" on the American side. "For a time we suffered the delusion—which Stalin never did—that Communism and Capitalism could live happily ever after," the newspaper reported. "We wanted 'One World.' So did Stalin." According to the newspaper, after "placating and appeasing Russia, we saw the light. But then the damage had been done." As for the American faith "that the United Nations would bring us everlasting peace," the Soviet presence all but nullified that political body ("Two Worlds Atlas" 1948, 13–14).[4]

Peter's multi-ethnic gang of war orphans band together, but in order to succeed, the Fryes' small town must change. But implementing a world view would prove difficult: *The Philadelphia Inquirer* preferred vigilance, chastising Americans for dismantling the "strongest force in the world" after 1945 ("Two Worlds Atlas" 1948, 14). The women shoppers patronizing Peter's workplace reflect this discussion, resigning themselves to military preparedness. Peter upsets their argument through behavior modification. As Michael alluded, who better to express this view than a green-haired boy whose status as an "orphan" segregates him from the town? Peter embraces his role as the orphans' champion. When Gramp later suggests a haircut, the boy emphatically says no: "I like it the way it is. It's important. It has a meaning" (Losey 1948).

With the adults against him, Peter seeks encouragement from his fellow orphans. But a gang of schoolboys ambush him with scissors. Unlike the international moppets who found Peter's hair a symbol of hope, these American youngsters reflect their community's near sightedness. When the resident nerd loses his glasses in the scuffle, he implores the green-haired kid to find his specs, promising, "I won't hurt ya, I won't do nothing, honest!" Peter trusts him and finds his glasses, but the blinded youngster tries to detain him, justifying his broken promise with the rigors of American masculinity: "Just because I wear glasses you think I'm a sissy." Peter escapes but the confrontation shakes his resolve. Gramp concedes maybe the townsfolk were right. "It's the last thing in the world I want you to do [to cut your hair], but people have been talking." Peter realizes, without Gramp's support, he has lost everything. "Nobody believes me. Nobody listens" (Losey 1948).

Peter's words fell on deaf ears, but the townsfolks' actions spoke louder. When he gives up his green locks, the whole town gathers at the barber shop. Peter's watering eyes affect the townsfolk. Gramp looks away. The townsfolk shuffle out silently, their minds lost in second thoughts. Even the bespectacled boy has guilty feelings, offering Peter an army knife—a symbol of American manhood, but not exactly in accordance with Peter's vision of peace. "Everybody makes fun of me because I wear thick glasses," the boy says, rationalizing his earlier duplicity with a desire to conform (Losey 1948). Young Frye, also no longer a threat to the community, makes nothing of this attempt at peace. Instead, his forced conformity spurs him to run away.

In the final reel, the former boy with green hair returns to the small town. The film suggests the townspeople might change, but doubts remain. The boy expert, Dr. Evans, sees Peter's green locks as a flight of fancy and less important than his message. Should Peter's hair grow back a normal brown, the townsfolk need not confront their prejudices, even if they heed Peter's message of peace. If his hair remains green, which Peter prefers, Michael and the others would not have died in vain, but the tinted locks could jeopardize Peter's fitting in at home among his jaded neighbors. The ambiguous ending indicates Hollywood's own conflicting ideologies of containment and its involvement with the Red Scare. The backstory behind *The Boy with Green Hair*—made public in the press—not only demonstrated the politics of the postwar film industry, but also the impact of cultural containment as Hollywood became the front lines of the Cold War's home front.

BACKSTAGE INTRIGUE

RKO released *Crossfire*, a film about anti-Semitism, a year before *The Boy with Green Hair* lit up the box office. The studio, struggling in the postwar slump, hoped to duplicate its success with *The Boy with Green Hair*. Concurrently, the Supreme Court decision *United States versus Paramount Pictures, Inc.* (334 U.S. 131, 1948) mandated studios to divest themselves of their theater chains, eliminating a guaranteed source of income for their products (Manchel 1990). While studios felt separate but equal pressure from government branches, the industry faced further competition from television at home and from the international troubles abroad as the Iron Curtain cut off half of Europe from their markets. RKO, with its long history of a merry-go-round management, faced a complete reorganization.

Aviator, innovator, and munitions maker Howard Hughes took control of cash-strapped RKO. Hughes promptly shut down the studio to adapt to the changing economic and political milieu. In the interim, McCarthyism caught *Crossfire*'s producer Adrian Scott and director Edward Dymtryk in a different sort of crossfire before the House Committee on Un-American Activities (HUAC) as members of the infamous Hollywood Ten.[5] Dore Schary assured the press, despite the Red Scare and HUAC, that he saw "no signs of a change in screen content to avoid subjects of social significance." Asked if he would have made *Crossfire* in light of Scott's and Dmytryk's blacklisted status, Schary insisted that as a business venture, "It is apparent that such subjects are of interest to audiences" (Brady 1948, X5). Concerning *The Boy with Green Hair*, previously under Scott's purview before his dismissal, Schary declared, "It is a pro-peace picture, and we are going to make it with no change in subject matter." (Brady 1948, X5).

Schary's decision proved risky. David Platt, film critic for The Communist Party USA's newspaper, *The Daily Worker*, proclaimed the Americans' self-perception as championing the free world was actually the reverse. "Unlike the film industries of the Soviet Union, Republic of China, and the People's Democracies, which serve peace and the advancement of humanity, "Hollywood was controlled by the same gang that owns the munitions industry" (quoted in Hoberman 2011, 134). In RKO's case, Platt's heated charge was not off base. As film historian J. Hoberman notes, several "comrades" permeated *The Boy with Green Hair*'s production, much to Howard Hughes's alarm. According to Hoberman, screenwriters Ben Barzman and Alfred Lewis Levitt penetrated the green hair with red ideology, and Joseph Losey ensured the picture would retain this crimson tint throughout filming (Hoberman). That Peter Frye's message echoed *The Daily Worker,* only reinforced the Red Scare's notion of Hollywood as a bastion for Communist contamination of American values.

Hughes took a hard-line against the Soviet Union, regardless of *The Boy with Green Hair*'s plea on behalf of war orphans. According to film scholars Richard B. Jewell and Vernon Harbin, Hughes's takeover generated an exodus as "talent left in droves to escape the curtailment of artistic freedom by RKO's McCarthyist new owner boss." This included Schary, who citing Hughes's interference, left for rival studio Metro-Goldwyn-Mayer (MGM) (Jewell and Harbin 1982, 15; "Dore Schary Resigns" 1948,1, 4; "MGM-Schary" 1948, 1, 4; Berlett and Steele 2004). With Schary gone, *The Hollywood Reporter* divulged Hughes had ordered the script "completely revamped since it was assigned to [blacklisted] Adrian Scott," although it declined to state what had changed ("Ames" 1948, 1). Screenwriter Ben Barzman reminisced that Hughes specifically altered the dialogue between Peter and Michael. When Michael informs Peter, "War is harmful to children and all living things," a fired-up Frye was to shoot back, "And that's why we gotta have the greatest army, the greatest navy, and the greatest air force in the world!" Barzman's wife later speculated that actor Pat O'Brien, as Gramp, would have capitulated, but Stockwell refused with a resolute, "No, sir" (quoted in Caute 1994, 87; Barzman 2003, 105). Decades later, Stockwell recalled his standing up to Hughes: he knew the picture had "an important, universal, and politically loaded antiwar theme, and that the boy with green hair was in reality a symbol that there shouldn't be any more war" (quoted in Moore 1984, 115).

Hughes wasn't one to let a 12 year old stand in the way. The studio chief spent $200,000 in retakes and shelved the film for six months (Caute 1994, Barzman 2003; Spiro 1948).[6] *The Independent Exhibitors Film Bulletin* noted Schary "expertly handled" a "strong and badly needed message." Now, "the picture has been cut and changed so drastically that there is assertedly little of value left to the picture" ("'Boy's Hair' Cut" 1948, 22). As *The New York Times* informed the public, the film "symbolizes the world's war orphans and the picture is one with a pronounced message [because] it stresses the devastating effects of war upon children, and in terms of blighted and suffering youngsters is a poignant plea for peace" (Spiro 1948, X3). In contrast, "those high up" in the studio brass were "less than enthusiastic about the film's implications." The paper did not elaborate, but it reported, "various changes were ordered" (Sprio).

Life magazine summarized the off-camera power play: "Hollywood Titans Wage a Battle over a Modest Little Movie with a Message," the article headlined. And then it asked, "It is part of a permanent controversy: should pictures have messages? What kind of messages? Whose messages?" The magazine flatly stated Hughes "hates messages—his pictures have always been concerned with simple and fundamental things like death (*Hell's Angels* in 1930), crime (*Scarface* in 1932) and sex (*The Outlaw* in 1943)." Here, Hughes rejected the idea "that people should not be discriminated against because of superficial physical differences" and "wars are wrong because they create human suffering." The writer thought Hughes threw a fit over nothing, since the film's morals were, "so bathed in gentle humor and fantasy and pretty Technicolor and cloying music, and the story moves around so haphazardly that no one should be violently affected" ("Green Hair Trouble" 1948, 81, 83–84).[7] But Hughes made certain to divert productions away from green-haired critics. As two biographers contend, the new RKO "became increasingly known for its stable of big-breasted starlets, most of whom never achieved recognition—except with Hughes" (Brown and Broeske 2004, 241).

SEEING RED

Hughes's hostility underscored the mixed reviews. When *The Independent Exhibitors Film Bulletin* reviewed the final film, fears of losing Schary's "expertly handled" moral were assuaged: "It is apparent much overloading of 'message' has been cut, avoiding blatant propaganda and achieving its result through subtlety." The journal admitted the movie "may be almost too subtle now, and its meaning may be lost on some people," but found it better than "hitting audiences on the head with a heavy-handed preachment" ("Finds Cut" 1948, 22). For *The Rotarian,* Jane Lockhart lamented, "Its message somehow comes out vague and unresolved, as if the makers couldn't quite make up their minds as to what they were trying to say." Perhaps that was an indirect observation at the tug-of-war in the studio (Lockhart 1949, 36). The Boy Scouts' *Boys' Life* remained ambivalent over Peter's suitability for its readership: "We won't attempt to predict whether or not you'll like this unusual movie. It has considerable humor and fantasy, a serious side, no romance, no swashbuckling action, but you sit there interested, wondering what will come next" ("Movies of the Month" 1949, 33). *Harrison's Reports* hoped the picture would find a wide audience: "Although the story seems best suited for class audiences, its human appeal should put it over also with the masses" ("Boy" 1948c, 186). *Boxoffice* also had qualms about the bottom line: "Those customers who like this offering will like it a lot, but subject to some question is the possibility that they are to be found in sufficient quantities to make the feature a financial success in average situations." The film was "different" than the usual fare, but the "fantasy whimsy," was "little of dramatic impact to command attention" ("Feature Reviews" 1948, 135). Peter Frye's progressivism had appeal, the trade papers noted, but few wanted to hear it.

The New York Times's Bosley Crowther damned the movie. He acknowledged RKO attempted "a novel and noble endeavor to say something withering against war on behalf of the world's unnumbered children who are the most piteous victims." But he went no further, arguing, "For all its proper intentions, the gesture falls short of its aim" (Crowther 1949b, 26). The paper described the picture's gimmick as "unevenly appealing" and deemed the whole thing a dream sequence. *The Philadelphia Inquirer* claimed the Russians were gobbling the globe while "America was busy dreaming details of the United Nations and the 'One World Movement' that would herald Utopia on Earth" ("Two Worlds Atlas" 1948, 3). Crowther found Peter Frye first to enter this la-la-land of world peace. Deeming the "phenomenal hirsute coloration and the resentment of the townsfolk thereto" a hallucination, Crowther implied Peter was mentally unbalanced as the news of his parents' death, and the following scene of the women lamenting the inevitability of war, overwhelm him. His hair discoloration reflects a runaway imagination sprouting from Peter's overtaxed mind. Thus, the townsfolk, in their efforts to cure him, remove the tell-tale sign and restore the status quo. Crowther considered the picture unworkable "and frankly, it's banal" (Crowther, 26).

Worse than boring, Crowther found the boy's vision of world reform offensive. "But to reason, in adult whimsy, that wars are caused by such a superficial thing as resentment of coloration is absurd and misleading," he commented, his own assertion of a color-blind America a bit of fancy (Crowther 1949b, 26). In a follow-up article, he called the green-haired boy completely artificial. He again faulted that the boy's hair had turned green as a protest against war, as "a symbolic adult conceit." Like Ann Bennett Mix, Crowther doubted whether "an orphaned American boy could so identity himself with the orphans of Europe": a one-world coalition of war refugees was impossible (Crowther 1949a, X1). Like Hughes, Crowther advocated a rewrite. To make the film "more genuine," he again reiterated the whole film as a fantasy, "lost somewhat in the confusion of its own clever metaphors" rather than permeated into America's self-perceptions (Crowther). *Time* magazine didn't waste a second in blasting the picture for trying to "cram its ideas into the mold of 'entertainment' [which comes off] as contrived and insincere as a singing commercial" ("New Pictures" 1949, 84).[8]

Some moviegoers agreed. On February 13, 1949, *The New York Times* published a letter from viewer Constantine Mitchell, who said that the production "did so little with it [the theme], so very little. The tragedy is that a clever idea has been ruined for future use as a good movie" (Mitchell 1949, X4). At the Palace in New York, reviewer Norbert Lusk interviewed some patrons. Many agreed the film generated buzz with an unusual plot, but "the idea with which the boy becomes obsessed is weakly motivated." Another added, "For all its proper intentions, the gesture falls short of its aim." Other moviegoers wanted the green hair resolved as "a boy's hallucination or whether it is intended to be a strictly whimsical device" (Lusk 1949, 18).

Some opinions made a leap of faith and accepted the film in totality. At *The Los Angeles Times*, critic Philip Scheuer described the picture as having a "moving quality far above that which the ordinary movie is able to evoke." Despite the weak plotting, he argued, the picture successfully advocated understanding "in the sequences detailing the consequences to Peter of his being set apart from others, a 'freak' " and his turning mockery into an opportunity (Scheuer 1949, 7). However, even the producers were a bit squeamish with their ideals: they had Stockwell don a green wig and a tight-fitting bald pate rather than alter his genuine hair "for fear of exposing him to ridicule in his private life," one behind-the-scenes report revealed (Berg, 1948, F12).[9] The picture's message for tolerance didn't translate beyond the studio soundstage and certainly not into the public. The critics' attacks on the film read as defensive measures against a social message that hit too close to home.

The Motion Picture Herald suggested showmen played up the film as not a typical product while avoiding the message. "Perhaps it can be best described in a few words as a fantasy with a message, although that's hardly the language to use in advertising it to customers. The language for them is 'a new and different kind of picture, in Technicolor,' " reviewer William R. Weaver mused (Weaver 1948, 4389). He added the preview audience who sat through the picture paid to see a musical comedy, *A Song is Born*, and had reservations. "Following some restiveness in the early passages, the audience settled down into obviously fascinated attention, and there was applause at the conclusion." Despite this apparent audience approval, Weaver sensed the picture did not quite gel. The story "reads somewhat more like a subject Walt Disney might have chosen for the animation medium," although he credited the producers for avoiding cartoon fantasy (Weaver). *The Independent Exhibitors Film Bulletin* found the picture "completely acceptable as enjoyable entertainment, despite the 'message' that has been so painlessly injected." The paper placed a caveat in its box office rating as "good generally, if exploited" (Abrams 1948, 11). *The Hollywood Reporter* also placed an upbeat spin: It found the film "episodic and uncertain in its dramatic direction," which devised it easy to advertise. "There is no denying the piece needs exploitation, but certainly beginning with the title right down the line, there are abundant opportunities for showmanship" ("Green Hair has" 1948, 3).

Boxoffice suggested some selling tips: "In addition to the exploitation possibilities inherent in the title, the film carries a preachment for peace, indicating advisability of tieups with churches, civic service organizations, local veterans' groups and the like. An obvious but effective street ballyhoo stunt would be the use of a youngster with a green wig." Potential taglines suggested the film as an outsider: "You've Never Seen a Picture Like It ... So Completely New ... So Utterly Different ... That You'll Remember It Forever ... And Want to See it Again and Again ... The Story of a Boy Who Underwent an Incredible Adventure ... And Found Himself Alone Against the World." Another suggested, "The Picture That Will Reaffirm Your Faith in Humanity" ("Exploitips" 1948, 136). In the film's first run in big cities, *Boxoffice* reported the picture grossed 20% above average. "While not spectacular, this is solid box office," the paper reported and predicted a stronger run in neighborhood and small town theaters (Sykes 1949, 22).

Despite some good notices, exhibitors had a rough time trying to entice moviegoers. One happy exhibitor approved the "well made story of a war orphan" because "business was 50 percent above normal [...] the largest Saturday business in three months" ("Exhibitor" 1949b, 3). However, this Arkansas showman was the exception. One manager gave a neutral review: "An unusual picture with a different story and bits of humor. Enjoyable" ("What the Picture" 1949d, 38). Others were less subtle. "This picture has been highly advertised, and business was above average, but comments were not too good, as some of my patrons said they didn't like it so much," one small-town Louisiana exhibitor relayed ("What the Picture" 1949a, 41). A Rhode Island counterpart complained his ballyhoo for a two-day screening didn't pay. "This doesn't live up to expectations. Nothing to it. Poor attendance and many disappointments" ("What the Picture" 1949b, 41). An Illinois showman conceded the acting and Technicolor impressed, but griped, "It did very poor business. Some patrons complained that it was too far-fetched and had a very poor title. Don't pay too much for it. You will never miss it if you don't play it. If you do play it, don't give it preferred time" ("Exhibitor" 1949c, 3). One of the optimistic reports stated it was "something different in pictures [with] an intriguing title," but his customers were indifferent: "Those who came were pleased, although they probably did not go out and encourage other people to rush down and see it—or not to miss it. I broke even on it" ("Exhibitor" 1949a, 3). Another vented his frustration: "We had to look carefully to see if green grass was not growing in the aisles on the second day of this opus. We have never had a more disgusted and irritated audience than on this one. Supposed to carry a message but if so the public are getting fed up with messages" ("What the Picture" 1949c, 54). *The Film Daily* optimistically called the film "an understanding drama of child life and a more penetrating study of emotional upheaval, the dawn of purpose and the inner sense of one who is marked by destiny to remind the world of the tragic implications of armed conflict between nations" ("Boy" 1948b, 5). Unfortunately for theaters, the audience, if they bothered to show, found such themes aggravating.

CONCLUSION

From RKO's standpoint, *The Boy with Green Hair* flopped badly. Critics traced the film's mediocre earnings to a poor technical execution, but Peter Frye's failure signified a demise of a different sort. As *The New York Times* noted, out of 644 preview cards from the final release's screening, "none made any reference 'to either Reds or fascism' " (Spiro 1948, X3). But the film dealt with neither: the plot's focus—bigotry at home—did not fit the emerging Red Scare, which was already dominating Hollywood's criticism of American society. Although movies inferred an undercurrent of discontent—science fiction especially highlighted atomic holocausts, alien invaders, and behemoth beasts defying conformity—the industry, struggling against the start of a long postwar slump, was more concerned with dollar signs than ideology (Evans 1999). One exhibitor summarized his comrades' take on *The Boy with Green Hair*: "There is not enough entertainment—especially at RKO's everlasting percentage." The studio's cut of ticket sales, in addition to the print rental, discouraged many exhibitors from booking risky RKO features ("Exhibitor" 1949a, 3). Where it counted most, the film's bottom line, *The Boy with Green Hair* ran in the red.

Red warning lights also blared in the film's ideology, as the Red Scare stifled the industry's brief flirtation with message pictures. Director Joseph Losey, who defended producer Adrian Scott before HUAC, found his services unwanted and went abroad to Italy and England. As film historian Giuliana Muscio notes, Italian filmmakers considered themselves "the self-appointed builders of national-popular culture [and] were strongly anti-American and, most of all, anti-Hollywood" (Muscio 2000, 121). Losey took advantage of Britain's fewer restrictions to attack McCarthyism with *Intimate Stranger* in 1955 and *Blind Date* in 1959. The latter film ran afoul in the United States. *Variety* headlined *Blind Date* made for an uncomfortable bed fellow: "Alleged *Reds*, in partnership with ex-*Nazi* sell *Blind Date* to *Paramount*" (quoted in Shaw 2006, 180–182).[10] *Blind Date* had few evening engagements and Losey failed to sustain a long-term deal with an American distributor, even after signing a repentant anti-Communist oath with Columbia Pictures in 1960.

Hollywood progressivism hibernated during the Cold War (Radosh and Radosh 2006). During the war years, being left was right: when comparing communism to fascism, few were nuts about the Nazis. By 1952, Twentieth Century-Fox head Darryl Zanuck admitted, "I doubt very much whether *Snake Pit*, *Gentleman's Agreement*, and *Grapes of Wrath* would be successful if released today. Like everything else, audience changes." He concluded, "I cannot think of a picture on the market today which deals with a 'thinking problem' and which is also successful" (quoted in Behlmer 1993, 215-216). When Dore Schary encountered anti-Communist fronts who viewed the juvenile delinquents featured in *Blackboard Jungle* as an attack on Americanism, Zanuck sympathized. He wrote to Schary on January 1, 1956: "I made *The Grapes of Wrath* with the best intentions in the world and it was used by the Communists to bolster communism and expose the plight of the American farmer in the dust bowl. *Pinky* was also exploited by the Communists, as was *No Way Out*" (Dore Schary papers 1956).

Schary himself had a social regression as the decade closed. When *Crossfire* scored in ticket sales, he touted message pictures before Hedda Hopper. When he became the production maestro at MGM, he held a press conference, claiming he would unmuzzle company mascot Leo the Lion. One trade paper noted:

> [Schary] made it clear that his program of "progressive" films, introduced at RKO with such pictures as *Crossfire*, *The Farmer's Daughter*, and *The Boy with Green Hair*, will be continued on Leo's lot. The "new regime" will allocate from five to ten features each year to the 'progressive' bracket ("Metro Will Scrap" 1948, 10).

Four years later, the producer recanted. "I'm now convinced that Communists are dedicated to the overthrow of the government by force and violence," he divulged. "I wouldn't hire one and I would fire anyone who was a Communist now" (Hedda Hopper papers 1952). In an interview, Hedda Hopper challenged him with a hypothetical situation concerning one of the most notorious members of the Hollywood Ten: Should Dalton Trumbo submit a script that was "brilliant and there was no propaganda in it," would Schary take the bait? The producer refused to bite: "I would not. The content of the script wouldn't concern me" (Hedda Hopper papers 1952).[11] Nor, apparently, did it concern the movie-going public.

As the Cold War heated up, studios capitulated, leaving behind hot-blooded Atomic Age warriors to safeguard small town America from invading Reds. When RKO's "comrades" penetrated American conformity with a boy advocating a green peace, anti Communists went on a red alert. Moviegoer Constantine Mitchell griped, "Toys are made to sell to dealers and parents and not to children. If we made toys to fit children, we wouldn't sell them." He concluded, "Substitute exhibitors and movies for dealers and toys and you get an idea of a movie industry failing" (Mitchell 1949, X4). The commies' use of a child to undermine American values made the picture more insidious. One showman wrote, "Curiously enough, our children's attendance at our Saturday matinee was above average," confirming the Communist subversion had an effect on the future protectors of the Free World ("What the Picture" 1949b, 41).

"When my hair grows back, it's going to grow back green," Peter tells Dr. Evans in the end (Losey 1948). One hopes for young Frye's eventual triumph as a mascot to rally an end to war. But in 1948, Peter's victory remained doubtful. Critics suggested the boy would have more success if he entered a realm of cartoonish make-believe: "What sets out as a tale with a clear-cut moral, winds up as a confusing hybrid, spotted with a symbolic signposts [sic] that leads to nowhere," one critic groused ("NY Critics" 1949, 6). In the harsh reality outside theaters, weapons of mass destruction proliferated, "just in time to get more youngsters like Peter," as one woman shopper lamented in the film (Losey 1948). Her words proved prophetic: the following year, China went "red," the Soviet Union acquired the bomb, and the United States responded with a mushrooming military industrial complex, all while the classical Hollywood Dream Factory crumbled. With the Iron Curtain closing the European market, HUAC screaming red over the pinko-tainted Hollywood Ten, and increasing competition from television, the only green the industry valued was the almighty dollar. Conformity, not confrontation, became the orthodoxy of the 1950s. Entrapped in an emerging garrison state, the boy with green hair did not stand a chance of finding a ray of sun.

NOTES

1. The studio originally set the budget at $300,000 but the final negative cost pushed the price tag to $800,000. As discussed below, surrounding controversy led to $200,000 worth of additional takes for a total cost of $1.068 million. The additional footage was ultimately not used. The film grossed $1.370 million, mostly in the domestic market, but when the studio factored in distributing costs, publicity, advertising, insurance, copyright fees, 35mm and 16mm prints, and other expenses, the film resulted in a heavy loss.
2. Such egalitarianism belied an undercurrent of long-stemming prejudices. The exclusivity implied by the term the "American Way" prohibited racial and religious "others" from participating.
3. An early screen treatment placed the setting in the appropriately named Centerville, Indiana (Rodell 1947).
4. Specifically, the newspaper lamented the Soviet Union's insistence on turning down membership applications from "free world" nations, such as Austria, Finland, Portugal, Ireland, and Italy, and their refusal to "refer the Greek problem to the General Assembly" ("Two Worlds Atlas" 1948, 14).
5. Film historians Larry Ceplair and Steven Englund contend Scott and Dymytrk were "two of RKO's most dependable artists." One studio head, Peter Rathvon, commented, "Sure hated to lose those boys. Brilliant craftsmen, both of them. It's just that their usefulness to the studio is at an end" (Ceplair and Englund 1983, 335).
6. Sources did not specify on the other story alterations.

7. Dore Schary responded with a David-and-Goliath parallel. He claimed his green haired boy made a mockery of a wannabe Hollywood giant (Schary 1948, 13).

8. The magazine unfavorably compared *The Boy with Green Hair* to *The Search* (1948), an MGM picture about a boy trying to find his mother in postwar Germany and the need for the United States to participate in international affairs. Shot on location, the film garnered critical praise for its neo-realism although audiences, like those of *The Boy with Green Hair,* were lukewarm. Ivan Jandl, who starred in *The Search,* won the Academy Award for Best Juvenile performance. Ironically, Dean Stockwell accepted the award on Jandl's behalf, since Jandl, living in Communist Czechoslovakia, could not attend (Fred Zinnemann papers).

9. Stockwell hated the uncomfortable skull cap and stomped on it after the final shooting (Berg 1948).

10. A former Hitler Youth, Hardy Kruger, had the lead role.

11. Schary's rapport with Hopper didn't last. On August 25, 1955, Schary wrote to Howard Dietz, recalling his relationship with Hopper as "comfortable relationship from late 1948 [the year *The Boy with Green Hair* was released] until sometime in 1952" when he disagreed with her endorsing John Beatty's polemical text *Iron Curtain over America.* "By implication Miss Hopper makes the invidious charge that MGM (and since MGM's production is handled by me) and I are dedicated to destroying America" (Dore Schary papers 1955).

REFERENCES

"$109 Million in TechniPix." 1948. *Daily Variety,* February 13: 1, 12.

Abrams. 1948. "'The Boy with Green Hair' Delightful Fantasy with Heart." *The Independent Exhibitors Film Bulletin,* December 6: 11.

"Ames to Produce 'Boy' in Technicolor at RKO." 1948. *Hollywood Reporter,* January 5: 1.

Barzman, Norma. 2003. *The Red and the Blacklist: The Intimate Memoir of a Hollywood Expatriate.* New York: Nation Books.

Behlmer, Rudy, ed. 1993. *Memo from Darryl F. Zanuck: The Golden Years at Twentieth Century-Fox.* New York: Grove.

Berg, Louis. 1948. "The Boy With Green Hair." *Los Angeles Times,* August 1: F12.

Berlett, Donald L., and James B. Steele. 2004. *Howard Hughes: His Life & Madness.* W. W. Norton, 2004.

Bodnar, John. 2003. *Blue-Collar Hollywood: Liberalism, Democracy, and Working People in American Film.* Baltimore: The Johns Hopkins University Press.

"'Boy' Budgeted at 300G." 1947. *Hollywood Reporter,* September 29: 4.

"The Boy With Green Hair." 1948a. [Advertisement]. *Life,* November 1: 3.

———. 1948b. *The Film Daily,* November 16: 5.

———. 1948c. *Harrison's Reports,* November 20: 186.

"'Boy's Hair' Cut." 1948. *The Independent Exhibitors Films Bulletin,* November 8: 22.

Brady, Thomas F. 1948. "Hollywood Issues." *New York Times,* January 25: X5.

Brown, Peter Harry, and Pat H. Broeske. 2004. *Howard Hughes: The Untold Story*. New York: Da Capo.

Bruscino, Thomas A. 2010. *A Nation Forged in War: How World War II Taught Americans to Get Along*. Knoxville: University of Tennessee Press.

Caute, David. 1994. *Joseph Losey: A Revenge on Life*. New York: Oxford University Press.

Ceplair, Larry, and Steven Englund, 1983. *The Inquisition in Hollywood: Politics and the Film Community, 1930–1960*. Berkeley: University of California Press.

C. J. Trevlin Ledger. 1994. *Historical Journal of Film, Radio, and Television*, 14 (1): Appendix I, microfiche.

Crowther, Bosley. 1949a. "Artificial Coloring." *The New York Times*, January 16: X1.

———. 1949b. " 'Boy with Green Hair,' Starring Dean Stockwell, Pat O'Brien, Opens at the Palace." *New York Times*, January 13: 26.

Doherty, Thomas. 2007. *Hollywood's Censor: Joseph I. Breen and the Production Code Administration*. New York: Columbia University Press.

Doherty, Thomas. 1999. *Projections of War: Hollywood, American Culture, and World War II*. New York: Columbia University Press.

Dore Schary papers. U.S. Mss 37AN. Schary. Blackboard Jungle 1954–1956, Dore Schary papers, 1920–1980, Box 33. Wisconsin Center for Film & Theater Research, University of Wisconsin, Madison.

"Dore Schary Resigns RKO Post." 1948. *Hollywood Reporter*, July 1: 1, 4.

Evans, Joyce A. 1999. *Celluloid Mushroom Clouds: Hollywood and the Atomic Bomb*. Boulder, CO: Westview.

"The Exhibitor Has His Say." 1949a. *Boxoffice BookinGuide*, October 8: 3.

———. 1949b. *Boxoffice BookinGuide*, October 29: 3.

———. 1949c. *Boxoffice BookinGuide*, September 24: 3.

"Exploitips." 1948. *Boxoffice*, November 20: 136.

"Feature Reviews." 1948. *Boxoffice*. November 20: 135.

"Finds Cut Version of 'Boy with Green Hair' Effective." 1948. *The Independent Exhibitors Film Bulletin*, November 22: 22.

Fred Zinnemann papers. "The Search—Jandl, Ivan 1947–1949," production files-produced, 58-f.790, Margaret Herrick Library, Beverly Hills, California, Academy of Motion Picture Arts and Sciences.

" 'Green Hair' has Appeal; 'Dynamite' Nifty Support." 1948. *Hollywood Reporter*, November 16: 3.

"Green Hair Trouble." 1948. *Life*, December 6: 81, 83–84.

Hedda Hopper paper, "Schary, Dore 1947–1955, undatted." 84-f.2891. Margaret herrick Library, Beverly Hills, CA. Academy of Motion Picture Arts and Sciences.

Hoberman, J. 2011. *An Army of Phantoms: American Movies and the Making of the Cold War*. New York: The Free Press.

Jewell, Richard B., and Vernon Harbin. 1982. *The RKO Story*. New York: Arlington House.

Levering, Ralph B., ed. 2001. *Debating the Origins of the Cold War: American and Russian Perspectives*. Lanham, MD: Rowan & Littlefield.

Lockhart, Jane. 1949. "Looking at Movies." *The Rotarian*, April: 36.

Losey, Joseph. 1948. *The Boy with Green Hair*. RKO Radio Pictures. Warner Home Video, 2010, DVD.

Lusk, Norbert. 1949. " 'Boy with Green Hair' Called Unusual Picture." *Los Angeles Times*, January 19: 18.

Manchel, Frank. 1990. *Film Stuldy: An Analytical Bibliography*. Vol. 1. Cranbury, NJ: Associated LUniversity Presses.

"Metro will Scrap 'Safe' Production Policy—Schary." 1948. *Independent Exhibitors Film Bulletin*, August 16: 10.

"MGM-Schary Close Deal Today." 1948. *Hollywood Reporter*, July 14: 1, 4.

Mitchell, Constantine. 1949. [Letter to the editor.] "Wrong Approach." *New York Times*, February 13: X4.

Mix, Ann Bennett. 1998. "Introduction." In *Lost in the Victory: Reflections of American War Orphans of World War II*, edited by Susan Johnson Hadler, Ann Bennett Mix, and Calvin L. Christman, xvii-xxvii. Denton: University of North Texas Press.

Moore, Dick. 1984. *Twinkle, Twinkle, Little Star (But Don't Have Sex or Take the Car)*. New York: Harper & Row.

"Movies of the Month." 1949. *Boys' Life*, February: 33.

Muscio, Giuliana. 2000. "Invasion and Counterattack: Italian and American Film Relations in the Postwar Period." In *Here, There, and Everywhere: the Foreign Politics of American Popular Culture*, edited by Reinhold Wagnleitner and Elaine Tyler May, 116–132. Lebanon, NH: University Press of New England.

"The New Pictures." 1949. *Time*, January 10: 84.

"NY Critics Hail 'Accused,' 'Green Hair' Noble Effort." 1949. *Hollywood Reporter*, January 17: 6.

Production Code Administration records, RKO 1947–1949. "The Boy With Green Hair," Motion Picture Association of America. Margaret Herrick Library, Beverly Hills, CA. The Academy of Motion Pictures Arts and Sciences.

Radsoh, Ronald and Allis Radosh. 2006. *Red Star Over Hollywood: The Film Colony's Long Romance with the Left*. San Francisco: Encounter.

Rodell, John S. " 'The Boy with Green Hair' Treatment," February 29[*sic*], 1947, Box 1290s,

RKO Studio Records, PASC 3, Performing Arts Special Collections, University of California, Los Angeles.

Schary, Dore. 1948. "Modest Titan." *Life*, December 20: 13.

"Schary, Dore 1947–1955, undated," 84-f.2891. Hedda Hopper papers, Margaret Herrick Library, Beverly Hill, CA, Academy of Motion Picture Arts and Sciences.

Scheuer, Philip K. 1949. " 'Boy With Green Hair' Exerts Haunting Spell," *Los Angeles Times*, March 5: 7.

Shaw, Tony. 2006. *British Cinema and the Cold War: The State, Propaganda, and Consensus*. London: I. B. Tauris.

Smith, Geoffrey S. 1992. "National Security and Personal Isolation: Sex, Gender, and Disease in the Cold-War United States." *The International History Review* 14: 307–37.

Spiro, J. D. 1948. "Hollywood Memos." *New York Times*. September 5: X3.

Sykes, Velma West. 1949. "RKO's 'The Boy With Green Hair' Gets February 'Blue Ribbon Award.'" *Boxoffice*, March 12: 22.
"Two Worlds Atlas ... East Vs West." 1948. *Philadelphia Inquirer*, April 15: 13–14. Baskes folio G1035 .P53 1948 (NLO) Herman Dunlap Smith Center for the History of Cartography, Newberry Library, Chicago, IL.
Wall, Wendy L. 2008. *Inventing the 'American Way': The Politics of Consensus from the New Deal to the Civil Rights Movement*. New York: Oxford University Press.
"What the Picture did for Me." 1949a. *The Motion Picture Herald*, April 2: 41.
———. 1949b. *The Motion Picture Herald*, April 9: 41.
———. 1949c. *The Motion Picture Herald*, April 16: 54.
———. 1949d. *The Motion Picture Herald*, May 28: 38.
Weaver, William R. 1948. "The Boy with Green Hair." *The Motion Picture Herald*, November 20: 4389.

ABOUT THE AUTHOR

Peter W. Lee is a history and culture doctoral candidate at Drew University. His dissertation examines the construction of boyhood during the early Cold War as represented in American films. His latest publications include chapters in *The Ages of the Avengers* and *Children in the Films of Alfred Hitchcock*. His historical interests include popular culture, youth culture, and the Middle Ages. Lee thanks Jenny Romero and the Margaret Herrick Library research staff at the Academy of Motion Picture Arts and Sciences, Maxine FlecknerDucey at the Wisconsin Historical Society's Center for Film and Theater Research, James Ackerman at the Newberry Library's Herman Dunlap Smith Center for the History of Cartography, the staff at UCLA Library Special Collections, and MischaHoneck at the German Historical Institute for invaluable assistance.

CHAPTER 5

LEARNING THE POLITICAL LEFT THROUGH POPULAR NOVELS

Howard Fast, Historical Fiction, and the Cold War

Paul J. Ramsey

During the Progressive Era and throughout the interwar period, left-leaning novelists and artists confronted the economic, political, and social issues in America through their work. As such, overtly leftist fiction, even that directed at adolescents and young adults, was not only accepted, it was also remarkably popular (Pells 1989). In addition to vividly portraying the fetid conditions in Chicago's meatpacking industry and in immigrant tenement housing, for example, Upton's Sinclair's *The Jungle* explicitly called for socialism to alleviate America's ills (Sinclair [1906]1986), as did some of Theodore Dreiser's later works (Mookerjee 1974; Dreiser 1931). Sinclair Lewis, the first American writer to win the Nobel Prize in literature, critiqued middle-class culture and conformity in both *Main Street* (Lewis [1920] 1963) and *Babbitt* (Lewis [1922] 2003), while the socialist John Dos

Learning the Left: Popular Culture, Liberal Politics, and Informal Education from 1900 to the Present, pp. 71–88

Passos (1932) bitterly attacked American militarism. Perhaps more than any other leftist writer in the Progressive Era, Jack London, a dedicated socialist, found an eager audience for his work among America's youngsters (London [1908]1957).

After the Second World War, however, liberal thought in the United States was under attack. What emerged in the aftermath of the war, especially between 1947 and 1955, was a conservative consensus—along with the more hysterical McCarthyism—that emphasized American unity to combat the supposed communist threat (Ashby 2006; Pells 1989; Rodgers 2011). This consensus was bolstered by the postwar triumvirate of power, the "power elite," to use C. Wright Mills' ([1956] 2000) term: the corporate, political, and military leaders. For the most part, America's public intellectuals—many of whom had been communists or socialists in the 1930s—acquiesced to the new "conservative age." Believing that America's postwar prosperity had reduced the need for any sort of radical reform and earnestly accepting the imminent threat of the spread of Stalinist-style totalitarianism to the United States, many leading intellectuals agreed with Arthur Schlesinger's political analysis and implored Americans to hold onto the "vital center" (Pells 1989).

With intellectuals moving to the center and many other segments of the society moving to the far Right (under the guidance of the House Un-American Activities Committee and Senator Joseph McCarthy), all things leftist, including progressive education, were perceived as abetting America's new archenemy, the Soviet Union (Pells 1989; Hartman 2008). The print media—taking direction from the new "power elite" (Mills [1956] 2000)—and libraries reinforced this new consensus as publishers consolidated their holdings and as libraries censored their titles; by mid century, historian Carl Kaestle has written, "popular culture had reached the height of cultural homogenization" (Kaestle 1988, 535; Jenkins 2001). Manuscripts that had overt leftist leanings were rejected. "[N]o commercial publisher, due to the political temper of the times," the novelist Howard Fast wrote in the afterward of his 1951 self-published *Spartacus*, "would undertake the publication or distribution of the book" (Fast 1951, 365).

Because of the general anxiety about the Soviet "threat," youngsters were often "protected" from leftist ideas, particularly those regarding socialism. As a result, many high school students in the 1950s had, at best, a tenuous understanding of the communist economic structure against which the United States was waging a war. Seeing the need for some knowledge of the distinctions between the United States and the Soviet Union, educational officials and policymakers in the 1950s began to encourage schools to offer secondary courses that developed students' understanding of communism, but these courses and lessons tended to be superficial and ultra-patriotic and, especially in the South, merely demonized anything that conservative groups perceived as leftist (Scribner 2012; Hartman 2008).

Despite the need for some sort of understanding of the Soviet economic system, teachers (especially during the McCarthy era) often ignored the topic, fearing being branded as sympathizers or, worse, being terminated. Of course, this fear was not unfounded. Many teachers, including those in higher education, lost their jobs and were questioned by the U.S. House of Representatives' Un-American Activities Committee (HUAC), a phenomenon that Fast experienced first-hand and one which he explored through his work (Fast 1994; Hartman 2008; Ohmann 1997; Zinn 1997). In *Silas Timberman*—a book dedicated to the "hundreds of teachers who have fought so valiantly against tyranny"—the title character was a literature professor who was brought up on charges by the HUAC and eventually jailed. In the book, Timberman's attorney summed up the situation quite bluntly: "Thinking becomes dangerous, and one of the most dangerous sources of thought are the schools. You have to control the schools, and that means controlling the teachers and what they teach" (Fast 1954, 263). Like later literature that explored the Cold War era—such as Norman Mailer's (1991) *Harlot's Ghost*—Fast's book about the persecution of teachers highlighted that during the United States' quest to defeat the Soviet Union, America—to a certain degree—adopted and institutionalized the very tyranny it was attempting to fight.

Although largely shunned from the official curriculum out of fear and persecution, the tenants of the political Left did reach young people during the Cold War. That is, despite the new "political temper of the times," as Fast termed it, liberal and leftist ideas made their way into some forms of popular culture, such as comic books. Although rock and roll, bebop jazz, and Beat literature inspired a rebelliousness among many youngsters, fiction that called for political action (although more disguised in the 1950s than in the 1930s) remained in the repertoire of youngsters' reading choices (Fast 1951, 365; Ashby 2006; Mintz 2004; Pells 1989). While a specific literary category for young people did not really coalesce until the 1960s (what is now called young adult literature) the central aspects of that classification—children and young people as protagonists, simplistic prose, and themes that appeal to the young—have long been part of the American literary tradition (Cart 2001), the nineteenth-century work of Horatio Alger (e.g., [1868] 1990) being a particularly salient example. In fact, many leftist writers in the 1950s—as well as musicians—deliberately turned their attention toward younger people both to instill progressive values in the coming generations and to find new audiences for their work, particularly if they had been blacklisted; Fast himself penned a number of books for younger children during the period (Mickenberg 2006; Fast 1954).

In the popular fiction directed at a young audience during the early Cold War period, some authors couched their left-leaning messages within the relatively safe genre of historical fiction, a genre in which liberal messages could be masked somewhat. Although Fast's radicalism was relatively well-known—particularly after the publication of *Citizen Tom Paine* in 1943, the year in which Fast official joined the Communist Party—his fiction used history to illuminate oppression and discrimination, the tyranny of capitalism, and the dangers of militarism (Fast 1943, 1947, 1957; Hicks 1945; Mickenberg 2006; Sorin 2012). After Fast and others were brought up on charges by the House Un-American Activities Committee for their involvement with the Joint Anti-Fascist Refugee Committee—which aided Yugoslavia's Tito in the fight against fascism—their attorney noted, "We are going to show that the House committee, by its own standards, would regard such outstanding Americans as Thomas Jefferson, Tom Paine and Abraham Lincoln as un-American" (Fast 1994, 175). Although Fast and his colleagues were eventually sentenced to prison, Fast's fiction, like his attorney's statement, demonstrated the progressive and humane elements in history, features he hoped would provide alternatives to the future and, thus, challenge the status quo in Cold War America (Mickenberg 2006).

Like historical fiction, science fiction and fantasy also proved to be genres in which writers could disguise leftist agendas without upsetting the new conservative order. While certainly no radical, Ray Bradbury published *Fahrenheit 451* in 1953, a book that—with its condemnation of censorship—was a not-so-subtle attack on McCarthyism (Bradbury [1953] 1991; Leonard 2005; Amis 1960). Kurt Vonnegut, whose career in science fiction began in the 1950s, also rejected censorship and the culture of the Cold War era. In his 1961 short story "Harrison Bergeron," originally published in *Fantasy and Science Fiction Magazine*, Vonnegut described a world in the year 2081 in which "everybody was finally equal." Although a seeming critique of the Soviet Union's goal of creating a classless society, Vonnegut, a socialist, was partially directing his criticism at American conformity (Vonnegut [1968] 2006, 7). In his first novel, *Player Piano*, Vonnegut created a United States in which elite scientists governed the entire nation, while ordinary citizens were simply expected to conform to the scientists' notion of a good society. Because the nation was mechanized, non-scientists had no role in the society except to follow the rules and to "[g]et a little fun out of life," often through consumerism and television (Vonnegut [1952] 2006, 3, 164–165; Ramsey 2009a). Unlike historical novels, science-fiction writers also had the freedom to explore the possibility of a nuclear holocaust, thus challenging the nuclear proliferation that marked the Cold War (Vonnegut 2000; Brians 1984).[1] While science fiction and fantasy will be considered—especially as those genres intersected with historical fiction—the focus of this chapter is on leftist historical novels and their leading author, Howard Fast.

HOWARD FAST, THE RED

Born to Jewish immigrant parents in 1914, Howard Fast grew up poor in New York and, because of his mother's passing in 1923 and his father's long hours at the factory, was primarily raised by his slightly older brother Jerome. Due to the family's poverty, Howard and his brother went to work at ages 10 and 11, respectively, delivering newspapers. "In actuality," Fast remembered, "we had no childhood; it slipped away" through work (Fast 1994, 31). A gifted student with a proclivity for fiction, Fast wrote novels while still in secondary school; he sold his first story to a science-fiction magazine as a teenager. Steeped in the radicalism of 1930s New York City, the young Howard Fast admired leftist writers—Jack London, George Bernard Shaw, and John Reed—and studied the work of Karl Marx (Fast 1994).

By 1942, Fast, only 28 years old, had published four novels, including *The Last Frontier* and *The Unvanquished*, both of which received a fair amount of critical acclaim. Although his career as a novelist was in full swing, so too was the Second World War, and Fast felt compelled to join the fight. Although hoping to become a soldier, he was recruited as a writer for American BBC radio, disseminating news to the Allies. In 1943, Fast's classic *Citizen Tom Paine* was published and became a wildly popular bestseller; in the same year, Fast officially joined the Communist Party, believing that "the Communists ... [were] the bravest and most skillful fighters for man's freedom," and thus held the best chance of defeating fascism (Fast 1957, 13; Fast 1994; Sorin 2012). Fast's historical fiction, like the contemporary young adult genre, has an easy-to-read style with young protagonists (e.g., Fast 1962), or it examines major historical figures (at least partially), during boyhood as in *Citizen Tom Paine* and *The American*. Although entertaining, his fiction, not unlike many contemporary young adult books, is sometimes slightly inaccurate historically and occasionally overly romanticizes his characters' endeavors (Sorin 2012).

While Fast's body of work is quite extensive—over forty novels and several nonfiction pieces—this essay examines only his most popular works between 1945 and 1965, as well as a few earlier works that were either republished in the period or were still in wide circulation. These "classic" novels represent not only the work that reached a mass audience, but also those that truly captured Fast's "real" literary voice. That is, as an active Communist Party member who regularly wrote for *The Daily Worker*, Fast did produce a fair amount of propaganda for the cause, work that was edited and reviewed by leaders to ensure its adherence to the party line. Yet, Fast was not a Communist ideologue; he regularly challenged aspects of the party (Fast 1957; 1994). In 1949, for instance, Fast was selected as a representative of the National Committee of the Communist Party of the United States to charge "the leadership of the Soviet Union with anti-Semitism, the violation of a basic socialist ethic and a grave threat to the world Communist movement"; the Russian representative dismissed the charge, stating only, "There is no anti-Semitism in the Soviet Union" (Fast 1994, 218). Fast's unwillingness to toe the party line was particularly salient when it came to his writing. In 1946, he was charged with "white chauvinism" for using the term "boy" to refer to an African American child; the party officials thought he should have used the word "youth" instead (Fast 1994, 141). His novels also came under intense scrutiny by the party; his use of historically accurate terms demonstrated to the leaders that Fast was not "politically developed," and his *Citizen Tom Paine*, it was said, contained "Trotskyite tendencies" (Fast 1957, 136–138; Sorin 2012). After Fast learned of Nikita Khrushchev's 1956 "secret" speech about Stalin's crimes, he officially severed his ties with the Communist Party; shortly afterward he called the party a "naked god" whose followers refused to see, at least initially, that the god was "ugly in his nakedness" (Fast 1957, 1; Fast 1994). Of course, Khrushchev's speech was, at least partially, a convenient epiphany to excuse his membership. As the philosopher Slavoj Žižek has noted, "one need not know the truth about the Stalinist terror in order to suspect that something was hideously wrong in Stalinism" (Žižek 2008, 49).

TYRANNY AND OPPRESSION

Although Howard Fast was not doctrinaire, his own views and those of the Communist Party overlapped considerably. Both rejected—at least, officially, for the Communist International—tyranny and oppression, injustices Fast witnessed in postwar America, such as Jim Crow racism, the persecution of liberals, and the exploitation of workers (Fast 1994; Mishler 1999). As such, Fast explored freedom fighting in a variety of historical epochs, including in antiquity. While breaking the chains of ancient bondage was the focus of his 1958 *Moses, Prince of Egypt*—a book the public intellectual Reinhold Niebuhr found "impressive" (Niebuhr to Fast 1957)—the topic was taken up seven years earlier in his best-selling (and self-published) *Spartacus*. Fast (1951), somewhat accurately, depicted Rome as an immoral slave society in which the wealthy and powerful lived only to satisfy their hedonistic appetites. As the slaves revolted, however, Spartacus told his fellow gladiators, "We will make an end of Rome, and we will make a world where there are no slaves and no masters" (166). In Fast's portrayal, Spartacus, as a slave and, thus, essentially a tool or pawn of the Romans, became more class conscious as the rebellion wore on, noting, in a message to the Senate:

The world is tired of the wealth and splendor that you have squeezed out of our blood and bone. The world is tired of the song of the whip. It is the only song the noble Romans know. ... You put little children into your mines and work them to death in a few months. And you have built your grandeur by being a thief to the whole world. Tell your Senate that it is all finished. That is the voice of the tool. (215)

As if coming from the pen of Karl Marx, Spartacus summed up his message by stating, "The whole world will hear the voice of the tool—and to the slaves of the world, we will cry out, Rise up and cast off your chains!" (215).

While Fast was perhaps the premier leftist writer of historical fiction during the period, other up-and-coming writers also used that genre (as well as science fiction) to promote a vision of a more progressive future. The young Gore Vidal—whose spectacular entry into historical fiction came in 1962 with the publication of *Julian*—also challenged various forms of oppression by exploring Roman history, but, unlike Fast, focused more on cultural—rather than political or economic—oppression. Vidal ([1962] 1964) detailed the life of the Roman emperor Julian; part of the Constantinian dynasty, Julian eventually rejected his family's Christianity and, as Augustus, worked to re-establish paganism throughout the empire. For Julian—as well as for Vidal, who openly expressed his atheism—early Christianity posed a threat to intellectual freedom and ignored the problems of the present with its focus on the afterlife (Peabody and Ebersole 2005). In *Julian*, Libanius, the emperor's mentor, rejected the implications of Christianity in the empire by stating, "The truth is that for thousands of years we looked to what is living. Now you look to what is dead, you worship a dead man and tell one another that *this* world is not for us, while the next is all that matters. Only there is no next world" (Vidal [1962] 1964, 464).

The narrow focus on class and racial exploitation in many of Fast's historical novels prevented him from examining the oppression of other groups of Americans, such as gays and lesbians, an oppression that did not escape Vidal's critique. If anything, Fast (1951) pandered to Americans' homophobia by portraying ancient Romans as immoral homosexuals; Spartacus and his band—in Fast's depiction—rejected same-sex relations, thus compelling readers to identify with the slaves. Vidal ([1962] 1964), by contrast, offered a more nuanced look at antiquity. Vidal ([1948] 1965), in his 1948 *The City and the Pillar*, also directly illuminated the discrimination against homosexuals in the 1930s and 1940s and defended their civil liberties. As one character noted, "Why should any of us hide? What we do is natural, if not 'normal', whatever that is. In any case, what people do together of their own free will is their own business and no one else's" (93).

Perhaps resonating more with his American readers, Fast explored the themes of tyranny and oppression during the American Revolutionary period as well. Fast examined the colonial and revolutionary eras in a number of his works, including the series of short stories "Old Sam Adams"—which was republished in 1960—and *April Morning* (Fast 1960, 1962), but it was in his classic *Citizen Tom Paine* where his thoughts on injustice in early American history had the most force. In a slightly romanticized way—as in most of his novels—Fast (1943) traced Paine's road to radicalization from his childhood to his involvement in the American Revolution (Sorin 2012). For Fast, it was in 1775 when Paine's ideas on revolutionary action coalesced, ideas that were ultimately captured in *Common Sense*. In Fast's depiction, Paine noted, "Believe me, I hate no man for what he is, not even that fat German bastard, George the Third. But I've seen man nailed to a cross, nailed there for God knows how many thousands of years, nailed with lies, oppression, gunpowder, swords. Now someone puts an ax in my hand, and I have a chance to help cut down that cross. I don't pass that chance by" (45–46).

Fast's most powerful critique of American oppression was in his *Freedom Road*, a historical novel about the Reconstruction period. Originally published in 1944, *Freedom Road* was republished as part of *The Howard Fast Reader* in 1960, with W. E. B. DuBois writing the foreword for the 1960 edition of the novel. Making note of the falsehoods surrounding Reconstruction in the American mind, DuBois stated that "this distortion of history and apology for crime is what Howard Fast sought to begin to counteract in 1944. ... His story is fiction, but his basic historical accuracy is indisputable; its psychological insight is profound; and thousands of readers can testify to its literary charm" (Fast 1960, 394). The novel focused on Gideon Jackson, a recently emancipated man in South Carolina who had fought with the Union Army. Although uneducated, Jackson was thoughtful and highly respected in his community, and thus elected as a representative to the Constitutional Convention. Jackson educated himself—working from primers initially, then moving on to sophisticated readings—and became quite politically savvy, eventually winning a seat in the State Senate and, ultimately, the U.S. Congress. Jackson's political platform was a three-pronged effort at civil rights: protect suffrage, ensure public schooling for all, and distribute land to the freedmen. With regard to education, Jackson noted to fellow convention members, "A man with a gun is not a slave, depending on one thing, his gun. Before he come like other men, you got to take away gun. Now with education—that you cannot take away from a man who has learned, and I believe a man who has learned truly cannot be a slave. In one way, it like a gun, in another way, it is better than the gun" (Fast 1960, 455).

In the culmination of the book, Gideon Jackson and other poor black and white families had collectively purchased large tracts of land that used to comprise the "Carwell" plantation on which Jackson had once been enslaved. Living in relative racial harmony throughout the Reconstruction era, Jackson made a desperate plea for the lame-duck president, Ulysses Grant, to retain a federal military presence in the South:

> Out of that terrible war came reconstruction—essentially a test for democracy, a test of whether freed Negroes and freed whites—for the poor white was as much a slave before the war as the black—could live and work and build together. I say the test was taken and proven. ... For the first time in the history of this nation, black men and white men together built a democracy in the south. You have the proof, the schools, the farms, the just courts, a whole literate, eager generation. But this was not done easily and never done completely; the planters organized their army, white-shirted scum by the thousands. ... I tell you, the day Rutherford B. Hayes takes office, those troops will be withdrawn—and the Klan will strike. (Fast 1960, 534–535)

Jackson's prediction came true; the Ku Klux Klan, the elite southerners, and the "law" came together and killed many of the men, women, and children of Carwell and, with the federal military gone, restored the southern system of apartheid (Fast 1960).

As a card-carrying member of the Communist Party, the oppression and exploitation of industrial workers also was a prominent theme in Fast's Cold War work, especially in *The American: A Middle Western Legend*. In 1948, two years after its publication, H. L. Menken told Fast that "if he had written *The American* ... he would have put down his pen with pleasure" (Fast 1994, 192). Fast's (1946) *The American* chronicled the life and radicalization of German-born John Peter Altgeld, from his boyhood to his term as the governor of Illinois in the 1890s. For Fast, place of birth mattered little; the true "Americans" and "citizens," such as Altgeld and Thomas Paine— both of whom were European—fought against authoritarian tendencies (Fast 1943, 1946). According to Fast, Altgeld initially began to consider the persecution of leftist workers when, as a judge, his socialist friend asked him to speak out against the looming execution of the first group of supposed anarchists in the Haymarket bombing. Although he did not intervene at that time, the Haymarket affair forced Altgeld to consider the evidence against the defendants—of which there was little pointing to their direct involvement—and, more importantly, to contemplate the plight of laborers; as governor, Altgeld pardoned those remaining in prison for the Haymarket bombing. After developing some level of class consciousness— although never coming to socialism—Altgeld became more dedicated to labor issues, a dedication that was dramatically captured in the novel when his friend spoke of him to the socialist leader Eugene Debs:

"I tell you he's for the people, for the workingmen. He believes in the people."

"Maybe he believes in them—" [Debs conceded.]

"You could say that Lincoln was one of them [politicians] too. But Lincoln was different. Lincoln fought for us, for the people."

"There were four million black slaves then. There are twenty million wage slaves today."

"The working man supports Altgeld, I tell you, things will change. There will be no more shooting and clubbing of workers. The courts will be ours as well as the millionaires.'" (Fast 1946, 194)

Although remaining skeptical, Debs did come to support, at least partially, Altgeld's political agenda, an agenda that tried, unsuccessfully, to push the Democratic Party in a much more progressive and populist direction during the 1896 presidential primary.

ECONOMIC REFORM

Of course, for Debs the solution to the oppression in the United States was socialism, a sentiment shared by Fast (1946, 1994). In *The American*, Fast (1946) depicted Debs debating the plausibility of a socialist revolution in the United States with a worker:

"This isn't a country for socialism. Even the workers don't want socialism."

"They don't know [Debs responded]. They live in a pit. Do you want sunshine, if you've never felt it on your skin?"

"Socialism is a theory, an idea. Sometimes I think it's a crazy idea, put forward by people out of their minds. It never worked anywhere."

"It was never tried." (193)

Despite the McCarthyism of the era, many of Fast's novels during the Cold War subtly advocated for a socialist type of economic reform. In order to remain somewhat protected from the witch hunts, Fast and other writers used historical fiction (and fantasy) as a means of introducing leftist economic visions to their American audiences in an indirect and, thus, relatively safe manner.

While Fast railed against class-based economies in a number of historical novels—in *The Unvanquished*, for instance, Fast ([1942] 1997) criticized the aristocratic tendencies during the American Revolution—this criticism was particularly acute in *Spartacus*. Fast (1951) detailed the splendor of the vast plantations, their reliance upon slave labor, and the Roman aristocracy's inability to see the slaves' humanity. In the novel, Gracchus discussed the Roman caste system with Cicero, noting:

> We live in a republic. That means that there are a great many people who have nothing and a handful who have a great deal. And those who have a great deal must be defended and protected by those who have nothing... [T]he many, many people who have no slaves at all must be willing to die in order for us to have our slaves (304).

The great irony was that the masses who joined the army to defend the wealthy had "nothing" because they were pushed off their land to make room for the great slave plantations. According to Fast (1951), this inequality was precisely what drove Spartacus and his armies to war, a war against the economic order of "Roman law." "Our law is simple," Spartacus stated. "Whatever we take, we hold in common, and no man shall own anything but his weapons and his clothes. ... And we will take no woman, except as wife ... [and] [j]ustice will be equal between them" (166–167).

While not quite the communal ownership of Spartacus' band, Fast (1960) explored land redistribution during the Reconstruction period in *Freedom Road*. Gideon Jackson, the former slave turned political leader, developed a plan to break up the large plantations in order to provide an amount of security to poor whites and blacks in the South, as well as to foster racial and economic justice. "When we get the land," Jackson noted, "when we parcel it out, when we set up a nation of free farmers down there ... then we stand on our own feet and talk loud and sure. Once that land's our own, we are not going to give it up, never" (509). Of course, Jackson was unable to implement his plan throughout the South, but he, other former slaves, and a handful of white tenant farmers were able to collectively purchase the old Carwell plantation. In Fast's depiction, the poor whites and blacks managed to divide the vast tract of land equitably and live peacefully as yeoman farmers for a time. That peace, however, came to an end as the former slaveowners came back into political power after Reconstruction, utilizing the Ku Klux Klan as their henchmen to undo the social, political, and economic gains of the freedmen and sympathetic whites. Fast concludes the book by noting the relative historical accuracy of the account: "All that I have told about as being done at Carwell was duplicated in many other places. White men and Black men lived together, worked together, and built together, much as I have described here. In many, many places, they died together, in defense of what they had built" (616).

MILITARISM, VIOLENCE, AND BRUTALITY

In Fast's best-selling *April Morning*, New England colonists feared, on the eve of the American Revolution, that their beloved land would become a stratocracy. The protagonist's father "hated all things military" and was deeply worried that the English and the revolutionaries would "turn us into a garrison state," concerns that Fast himself had about the Cold War (Fast 1962, 52; Fast 1994). Yet, Fast was no pacifist. Although he had no bloodlust, he was more than willing to engage in physical confrontations to defend his beliefs. In 1949, for instance, he was on the front lines of the Peekskill riots as anti-communists and racists tried to shut down the African-American singer Paul Robeson's concert in rural New York (Fast 1994). In a sense, Fast was a proponent of what Slavoj Žižek (2008) has called "divine violence," the willingness to aggressively confront oppression in order to achieve or restore justice. Fast (1957, 1994), it should be noted, willingly joined the war effort—and the Communist Party—to end the fascist menace, by all means necessary. In many of his novels, his characters fought for just causes: to end slavery in *Spartacus* (1951); to overthrow British tyranny in *The Unvanquished* ([1942] 1997); and to defend the civil rights of southern blacks in *Freedom Road* (1960). Although no stranger to violence in his real life—he was a tough Jewish street kid after all—or in his fiction, Fast abhorred militarism, brutality, and the perception that violence and war were psychologically uncomplicated and valorous endeavors.

Like other critical writers of his generation, Fast refused to portray war as a simplistic act of patriotism. Akin to Norman Mailer's ([1948] 1998) depiction of war and its participants in *The Naked and the Dead*, Fast's characters were not monolithic and heroic soldiers; they were fully human, afraid of being killed and wishing for an end to the fighting. In the conclusion of *The Unvanquished*, for example, Fast ([1942] 1997) noted that his goal in the book was not to portray George Washington and his army "as tin gods, but in some measure as I believed them to have been, as human beings" (314). This rejection of patriotic heroism is quite vivid in *April Morning*. In the novel, the teenage protagonist Adam Cooper's initiation into the battle of Lexington was not gallant; instead he "was nauseated with apprehension and fear," stating that "my hands were soaking wet where they held my gun." The young Cooper, having seen men killed—including his father— vomited and, as the battle began, lost control of his bladder (Fast 1962, 101, 142). Similar sentiments were detailed in *The Unvanquished*, in which Fast ([1942] 1997) described the weathered cod fisherman in Washington's army. As the intense fighting began, Fast ([1942] 1997) noted of them that "they were hard, as their fathers and grandfathers had been hard, but they were not hard enough for this, not hard enough to keep the blood in their faces and not hard enough to keep from retching" (172).

While the Revolutionary War was presumably a just war in Fast's mind, it was a war nonetheless, and, as such, the American soldiers—typically ordinary men and boys—sometimes lost the will to participate. Adam Cooper noted, "I put a lot more trust in my two legs than in the gun, because the most important thing I had learned about war was that you could run away and survive to talk about it" (Fast 1962, 142). For the soldiers in Washington's army, "They were bewildered and frightened, each of them immersed in his own personal catastrophe, each of them certain that the whole thin dream of revolution was done with, that nothing remained except to save his own skin" (Fast [1942] 1997, 30). In Fast's portrayals, even the Revolutionary leaders expressed their grave concerns about the conflict. On the eve of war, Thomas Paine stated, "I hate war…. Of all the ways to hold man in contempt and make a beast of him, war is the worst. There is nothing on earth I hate more than war" (Fast 1943, 83). Yet, the war came, and, as an officer relayed to Washington about the day's battle, "it was hell, just hell, just bloody, bloody hell" (Fast [1942] 1997, 23).

In addition to the realistic characterizations of war, Fast and other writers of his generation tried to foster more progressive attitudes among their readers by demonstrating the consequences of militarism and violence through detailed and gruesome depictions of brutality. In *Spartacus*, the product of Roman militarism was "six thousand, four hundred and seventy-two corpses hanging from crucifixes … along the Appian Way" during the aftermath of the slave revolt (Fast 1951, 9). To emphasize the cruelty of the Roman military, Fast (1951) provided a detailed description of the crucifixion of a gladiator:

> Three more blows buried the spike five inches into the wood, and a final blow bent the head, so that the hand could not slip off. Then the same process was repeated with the other hand. … Now the rope around his chest was cut, so that he hung entirely by his hands, with only the support of the cord around each wrist to lessen the weight on the spikes. … Then the gladiator fainted. (243–244)

Like Fast, Thomas Pynchon ([1963] 1964) vividly portrayed the ruthlessness of colonial militarism in Africa in his first book *V.*, a novel that partially brought together both science fiction and historical fiction. Describing the German colonial army's treatment of the indigenous population, Pynchon noted that after one soldier, "with the tip of his sjambok, had had the obligatory sport with the black's genitals, [the Germans] clubbed him to death … and tossed what was left behind a rock for the vultures and flies" (245). In the same flashback to colonial Africa, Pynchon recounted the experience of "natives already exterminated—sleeping and lame burned en masse in their pontoks, babies tossed in the air and caught on bayonets, girls approached with organ at the ready … only to be shot through the head first and then ravished" (245). Pynchon and Fast's messages to their readers could not have been more obvious: the brutality of militarism was evil.

CONCLUSIONS: LEARNING AND THE LEFT

The themes of Fast's historical fiction during the Cold War—the ugliness of tyranny and oppression; the call for a more socialistic economic system; and the brutality of militarism—were learned by readers. By the late 1940s, between three and four million people had read *Citizen Tom Paine*, despite it having been banned by New York City's public schools in 1947 (Sorin 2012, 133-134). After *Spartacus* had been rejected by many of the major publishing houses and, thus, was self-published, Fast (1994) "discovered through the years—often from the children of those who had bought the book—that reading it became an act of defiance by people who loathed the climate of the time" (294). The book sold well and later became a motion picture. Not long after the publication of *Spartacus*, the Canadian writer Ted Allan told Fast in a personal correspondence that he had heard the book had already "sold over 37,000 copies." Allan concluded the letter by stating: "How wonderful that you don't need the bastards [the mainstream publishing industry]!" (Allan to Fast 1952).

In his fictionalized—although highly accurate—account of the era, Philip Roth (1999) portrayed the teenage Jewish protagonist as an avid reader of Howard Fast's books as he moved toward the Left, *Citizen Tom Paine* being a particular favorite. Although a novel, Roth's account paralleled the experiences of many young people and adults in America; fellow writers and fans sent Fast letters discussing their appreciation for his work. Allan, for instance, told Fast he considered "Freedom Road the most exciting book I've ever read" (Allan to Fast 1952). Educator William L. Patterson also noted his fondness for the book:

> At present words with which to express the depth of my admiration for your great book "Freedom Road," fail me. I should like you to know, however, that I regard it as one of the greatest offensive weapons yet forged for the struggle on the cultural front, with repercussions in the political and economic life of our country. (Patterson to Fast 1944a)

Patterson concluded his letter to Fast by stating that "what Harriet Beecher Stowe did with 'Uncle Tom's Cabin' you have made possible in this period of 150 years of a people's revolution with 'Freedom Road'" (Patterson to Fast 1944a). Others noted that Fast was "a champion in the cause of human liberty" (Melvin to Fast 1957). Besides promoting the Left in America, Fast's writings found eager audiences abroad (Fast 1994; Sorin 2012) and may have helped energize some of the participants in the Hungarian Revolution of 1956. Mrs. John Santo, an American admirer of Fast who had been living in Hungary, "circulate[d Fast's articles] ... among the intellectuals" of Budapest. As she told Fast in 1958, "There is little doubt in anyone's mind that these articles had great impetus and were used to springboard much of the propaganda that ignited the revolution" (Santo to Fast 1958).

In addition to the personal correspondence that hailed his books and articles, Fast also received numerous invitations to speak about his books and ideas from student groups and schools. The Abraham Lincoln School in Chicago, of which Patterson was the assistant director, hosted a symposium on civil rights and Fast's work in 1944, an event that the author attended and at which he was well received (Barrows to Fast 1944; Patterson to Fast 1944b). Between 1956 and 1961, student groups at Brandies University, the University of Michigan, the University of Chicago, and Sarah Lawrence College also sent Fast invitations to talk at their institutions, sometimes expressing an interest not only in his fiction but also in his political worldview (Larner to Fast 1956; Young to Fast 1957; Adelman to Fast 1958; Krasnow to Fast 1958). Similarly, North Carolina State College booked Fast to speak in its series on the arts in 1961; previous presenters included literary figures such as John Dos Passos and Lawrence Ferlinghetti (Knowles to Fast 1961). Clearly, young people and adults in the United States and abroad were fascinated with Fast's work and, at times, were moved to action; as one admirer stated to Fast, "I was sure you would want to know how you played TOM PAYNE [*sic*] yourself" (Santo to Fast 1958). In 1956, Fast wrote, "I think that a new day is at hand for the forces of the left, and the sky looks a little brighter than it has for a long time" (Fast to O'Connor 1956). The events of the coming decade certainly demonstrated the prescience of Fast's statement.

NOTE

1. Although not fiction, John Hersey's *Hiroshima* (1946) also brought to life the dangers of nuclear weapons for a young readership.

REFERENCES

Adelman, Lois to Howard Fast. 1958. Correspondence, Howard Fast Collection. University of Pennsylvania.

Alger, Jr., Horatio. (1868) 1990. *Ragged Dick: Or, Street Life in New York with the Bootblacks*. New York: Signet Classic.

Allan, Ted to Howard Fast. 1952. Correspondence, Howard Fast Collection. University of Pennsylvania.

Amis, Kingsley. 1960. *New Maps of Hell: A Survey of Science Fiction*. New York: Harcourt, Brace.

Ashby, LeRoy. 2006. *With Amusement for All: A History of American Popular Culture since 1830*. Lexington: University Press of Kentucky.

Barrows, Alice to Howard Fast. 1944. Correspondence, Howard Fast Collection. University of Pennsylvania.

Bradbury, Ray. (1953) 1991. *Fahrenheit 451*. New York: Ballantine Books.

Brians, Paul. 1984. "Nuclear War in Science Fiction." *Science Fiction Studies* 11 (3): 253–263.

Cart, Michael. 2001. "From Insider to Outsider: The Evolution of Young Adult Literature." *Voices from the Middle* 9 (2): 95–97.

Dos Passos, John. 1932. *1919*. New York: Harcourt Brace.

Dreiser, Theodore. 1931. *Dawn*. New York: Horace Liveright.

Fast, Howard to Harvey O'Connor. 1956. Correspondence, Howard Fast Collection. University of Pennsylvania.

Fast, Howard. (1942) 1997. *The Unvanquished*. Armonk, NY: M.E. Sharpe.

———. 1943. *Citizen Tom Paine*. New York: Duell, Sloan and Pearce.

———. 1946. *The American: A Middle Western Legend*. New York: Duell, Sloan and Pearce.

———. 1947. "An Author's Defense." *The English Journal* 36 (6): 323–324.

———. 1951. *Spartacus*. New York: Howard Fast.

———. 1954. *Silas Timberman*. New York: The Blue Heron.

———. 1957. *The Naked God: The Writer and the Communist Party*. New York: Frederick A. Praeger.

———. 1960. *The Howard Fast Reader: A Collection of Stories and Novels*. New York: Crown Publishers.

———. 1962. *April Morning*. New York: Bantam Books.

———. 1994. *Being Red: A Memoir*. New York: M. E. Sharpe.

Hartman, Andrew. 2008. *Education and the Cold War: The Battle for the American School*. New York: Palgrave Macmillan.

Hersey, John. 1946. *Hiroshima*. New York: Alfred A. Knopf.

Hicks, Granville. 1945. "Howard Fast's One-Man Reformation." *College English* 7 (1): 1–6.

Jenkins, Christine. 2001. "International Harmony: Threat or Menace? Youth Services Librarians and Cold War Censorship, 1946–1955." *Libraries and Culture* 36 (1): 116–130.

Kaestle, Carl F. 1988. "Literacy and Diversity: Themes from a Social History of the American Reading Public." *History of Education Quarterly* 28 (4): 523–549.

Knowles, A. Sidney to Howard Fast. 1961. Correspondence, Howard Fast Collection. University of Pennsylvania.

Krasnow, Stephanie to Howard Fast. 1958. Correspondence, Howard Fast Collection. University of Pennsylvania.

Larner, Jeremy to Howard Fast. 1956. Correspondence, Howard Fast Collection. University of Pennsylvania.

Leonard, Andrew. 2005. " 'The Bradbury Chronicles': The Sci-Fi Writer Who Could Write." *New York Times*, July 24.

Lewis, Sinclair. (1922) 2003. *Babbitt*. Mineola, NY: Dover.

———. (1920) 1963. *Main Street*. New York: New American Library.

London, Jack. (1908) 1957. *Martin Eden*. New York: Macmillan.

Mailer, Norman. 1991. *Harlot's Ghost*. New York: Random House.

———. (1948) 1998. *The Naked and the Dead*. New York: Picador.

Melvin, Bruce L. to Howard Fast. 1957. Correspondence, Howard Fast Collection. University of Pennsylvania.

Mickenberg, Julia L. 2006. *Learning from the Left: Children's Literature, the Cold War, and Radical Politics in the United States*. New York: Oxford University Press.

Mills, C. Wright. (1956) 2000. *The Power Elite*. New York: Oxford University Press.

Mintz, Steven. 2004. *Huck's Raft: A History of American Childhood*. Cambridge, MA: Belknap.

Mishler, Paul C. 1999. *Raising Reds: The Young Pioneers, Radical Summer Camps, and Communist Political Culture in the United States*. New York: Columbia University Press.

Mookerjee, R. N. 1974. *Theodore Dreiser: His Thought and Social Criticism*. Delhi, India: National Publishing House.

Niebuhr, Reinhold to Howard Fast. 1957. Correspondence, Howard Fast Collection. University of Pennsylvania.

Ohmann, Richard. 1997. "English and the Cold War." In *The Cold War and the University: Toward an Intellectual History of the Postwar Years*, edited by Andre Schiffrin, 73–105. New York: The New Press.

Patterson, Wm. L. to Howard Fast 1944a. Correspondence, Howard Fast Collection. University of Pennsylvania.

———. to Howard Fast 1944b. Correspondence, Howard Fast Collection. University of Pennsylvania.

Peabody, Richard, and Lucinda Ebersole. 2005. *Conversations with Gore Vidal*. Jackson: University Press of Mississippi.

Pells, Richard H. 1989. *The Liberal Mind in a Conservative Age: American Intellectuals in the 1940s and 1950s*. New York: Harper and Row.

Pynchon, Thomas. (1963) 1964. *V.* New York: Bantam Books.

Ramsey, Paul J. 2009a. "The Dark Ages Haven't Ended Yet: Kurt Vonnegut and the Cold War." *American Educational History Journal* 36 (1): 99–114.

———. 2009b. "Plato and the Modern American 'Right': Agendas, Assumptions, and the Culture of Fear." *Educational Studies* 45: 572–588

Rodgers, Daniel T. 2011. *Age of Fracture*. Cambridge, MA: Belknap.

Roth, Philip. 1999. *I Married a Communist*. New York: Vintage International.

Santo, Mrs. John to Howard Fast. 1958. Correspondence, Howard Fast Collection. University of Pennsylvania.

Scribner, Campbell F. 2012. " 'Make Your Voice Heard': Communism in the High School Curriculum, 1958–1968." *History of Education Quarterly* 52 (3): 351–369.

Sinclair, Upton. (1906) 1986. *The Jungle*. New York: Penguin.

Sorin, Gerald. 2012. *Howard Fast: Life and Literature in the Left Lane*. Bloomington: Indiana University Press.

Vidal, Gore. (1948) 1965. *The City and the Pillar*. London: Heinemann.
———. (1962) 1964. *Julian*. London: Heinemann.
Vonnegut, Kurt. 2000. *Bagombo Snuff Box*. New York: Berkley Books.
———. (1952) 2006. *Player Piano*. New York: Dial Press.
———. (1968) 2006. *Welcome to the Monkey House*. New York: Dial Press.
Young, Donald S. to Howard Fast. 1957. Correspondence, Howard Fast Collection. University of Pennsylvania.
Zinn, Howard. 1997. "The Politics of History in the Era of the Cold War: Repression and Resistance." In *The Cold War and the University: Toward an Intellectual History of the Postwar Years*, edited by Andre Schiffrin, 35–72. New York: The New Press.
Žižek, Slavoj. 2008. *Violence*. New York: Picador.

ABOUT THE AUTHOR

Paul J. Ramsey is an associate professor in the Department of Teacher Education at Eastern Michigan University. "Joe" Ramsey completed his Ph.d. degree in the history of education at Indiana University and is the author of *Bilingual Public Schooling in the United States: A History of America's "Polyglot Boardinghouse"* (Palgrave Macmillan, 2010) and editior of *The Bilingual School in the United States: A Documentary History* (Information Age Publishing, 2012). His historical interests include bilingual education, immigration, childhood, popular culture, and globalization. Joe would like to thank the wonderful folks at the University of Pennsylvania archives for their assitance with this project.

CHAPTER 6

PEDAGOGY OF THE
RADICAL BLACK PRESS

Khuram Hussain

> *As a child I would get a Black Panther Paper*
> *and we would have political church on the front*
> *porch, in the lunchroom, in the back of study hall*
> *the Panther Paper was our bible{/EPI}*

> —Melvin Lewis (1990, 534)

"In practically a single breath" Malcolm Little's seventh-grade teacher summarized the entire history of black people: slaves who "were freed" and, in turn, "were usually lazy and dumb and shiftless" (X and Haley 1992, 114). To this his schoolbooks added "just one paragraph" that reduced four centuries of black American history to a story of bondage followed by emancipation. As a young man, unlearning these lessons was central to his political and personal transformation into Malcolm X—chief minister of the Nation of Islam. Throughout his activism, his formal schooling was a reminder that his "miseducation" was akin to that suffered by generations of black children. Further, he was convinced that the political and spiritual fate of black Americans was inextricably connected to the kind of education they received.

Learning the Left: Popular Culture, Liberal Politics, and Informal Education from 1900 to the Present, pp. 89–110
Copyright © 2015 by Information Age Publishing
All rights of reproduction in any form reserved.

89

Minister Malcolm X made the reeducation of black Americans a priority—expanding the Nation of Islam's adult education classes and parochial elementary schools, known as the "University of Islam." Beyond the classroom, his most accessible educational initiative was the newspaper *Muhammad Speaks*, which circulated thousands of weekly copies on street corners in every major city in the United States. The paper served as a distinct voice, foregrounding black perspectives on a range of social issues that received little coverage in the mainstream media (Streitmatter 2001). The substance and style of *Muhammad Speaks* influenced other underground media, most prominently the *Black Panther Intercommunal News*. The paper's founders carefully studied the content of *Muhammad Speaks* and mirrored its approach to reeducating readers (Newton 2009; Brown 1993).

Despite being known for their sensational rhetoric and calls for radical social reform, *Muhammad Speaks* and the *Black Panther* also served to reframe public discourse and public knowledge around a range of historical, political, and cultural issues. Within the context of education, this reframing involved protest against inequitable schooling and the articulation of progressive alternatives to improve educational opportunity for children of color. It also entailed a re-education of readers through the publication of culturally inclusive historical content and political perspectives that contended with dominant political thought.

The papers' educational function resonated with young people. As one college student described *Muhammad Speaks*, it was "an education in itself" (Lassier 1973). This chapter examines the role of *Muhammad Speaks* and the *Black Panther* in educating youth throughout the 1960s and 1970s. The radical black press was alive in the world of young people, functioning as a link to activism, a source of communal pride, and a body of knowledge that supplemented and subverted the public school curriculum. Ultimately, progressive teachers and students regarded the radical black press as alternative curricular content, and they employed it in their classrooms to instigate critical thinking and a deeper analysis of politics and history.

This chapter illustrates how the radical black press' counterpoint to mainstream racist narratives operated as a kind of a counter pedagogy and counter curriculum. The radical black press assailed the Eurocentric design of public education as indicative of institutional racism and state repression. Conversely, the papers' first-hand coverage of underrepresented content served as evidence that oppressed people can construct their own knowledge and participate differently in the world of ideas. The papers' critique and creativity provided students and educators with a reparative rejoinder to dominant ideology *and* a framework for democratizing knowledge. Ultimately the radical black press facilitated a process of education that pointed toward the liberatory possibilities of learning.

This chapter begins with a brief history of the radical black press as a community-oriented site of "counterpublic" knowledge construction—that analyzed dominant social doctrine from the perspective of under-represented voices and produced original and sophisticated ideas in the process (Fraser 1989). Next, the chapter will examine the dynamic presence of the radical black press in the lives of young people, who engaged with the papers as readers of its content and special contributors to its pages. Dionne Danns (2003) observes that black high-school students in the late 1960s developed an agenda for activism that was uniquely rooted in an understanding of the oppressive character of their schools. The radical black press served to cultivate youth activism. Students used the press to protest against injustices in schools, and read the papers to better understand how their experiences fit into the wider arrangements of power. Lastly, the chapter will explore how radical educators used the press to teach young people to liberate themselves. Teachers employed the papers to provide students with a sense of personal empowerment, and to cultivate a critical consciousness about the political nature of knowledge. In the end, they wanted students to see that a liberating education required the transformation of political and cultural systems through which learning occurred; therefore, education should be a revolutionary activity. The unique character of the radical black press made it well suited to help teach this lesson.

MILITANT WEEKLIES "DEDICATED TO JUSTICE"

The distinct tone, style, and content of the 1960s radical black press was largely an outgrowth of the vision and structure established by Malcolm X. Throughout his years in the Nation of Islam (NOI), Malcolm X held a firm belief in the power of an independent black press as the only medium for "voicing the true plight of our oppressed people to the world" (X and Haley 1992, 247). After several proto-journalistic endeavors, he settled on a formula for a 1960 city paper, titled *Mr. Muhammad Speaks*, which proved to be strikingly effective at appealing to black "Harlemites." The tabloid-sized city paper's banner read: "A Militant Monthly Dedicated to Justice for the Black Man." The paper included the religious teachings of NOI leader Elijah Muhammad, and stood out in its professional layout, quality of writing, and coverage of news events pertinent to black communities. Malcolm X went outside his organization to hire renowned professional black journalists and writers. He directed them to produce a protest-oriented paper that used stirring language to stage news of the day within a narrative of racial justice (Sales 1994). All male members of the NOI were required to sell a quota of papers each week, and they did so largely on foot, peddling outside churches, storefronts, and community centers. The triple threat of quality journalism, a racially charged approach to current events, and an aggressive grassroots sales campaign earned it notoriety throughout New York City. In 1961, the paper moved to Chicago and replaced Malcolm X with Dan Burley as chief editor. By 1964 it grew from a monthly to a weekly national publication (Lincoln 1994).

The co-founders of the Black Panther Party, Bobby Seale and Huey Newton, borrowed the tabloid format and tone of *Muhammad Speaks* and also required their male members to hawk the paper. Both papers also took a militant approach to current affairs, oriented themselves around community concerns, and staffed their offices with activist editors. *Muhammad Speaks'* editors had a record of civil rights and social justice activism that preceded their work at the paper. Dick Durham was a CIO labor organizer; Leon Forrest participated in the March on Washington; and Dan Burley, John Woodford, Askia Muhammad, and Lonnie Smith had strong records of anti-racist, advocacy journalism (Rusinack 2003; Woodford 1993; Forrest 1972b). With the exception of David Du Bois, editors of *Black Panther* were all active participants in the organization's racial justice activities. Eldridge Cleaver and Elaine Brown helped organize the Black Panther's protest activities against police violence, housing discrimination, and school segregation. Jo Nina Abron taught children at the Panther's Oakland Community School, and each of them directly or indirectly supported the party's relief programs, such as the free breakfast program for children, the liberation schools, clothing distribution, and first-aid training (Abron-Ervin 2011; Hilliard and Cole 1993; Brown 1993).

The radical press served as an extension of the editors' effort to win rights and opportunities for blacks and the working class. They articulated a commitment to improve the lives of black Americans through excellence in journalism and by covering stories they regarded as significant to their readers and "often unreported by the white press" (Forrest 1972a, 8). The publications proudly offered themselves up as a counterpoint to the failures of the mainstream press to get at the complex, lived realities of communities of color. Leon Forrest assailed the "Neighborhood News" section of major dailies that printed special sections for inner-city readers. He saw this as a shallow attempt to absorb and isolate under-represented voices "while the suburbs remained purely untouched. This means that the newspapers in question don't have to change their basic editorial policy and the paucity of blacks informing decision making on [e]ditorial boards" (Forrest, 1972a). By contrast, Forrest argued that newspapers "are not autonomous agents unto themselves, but rather nourished and accredited by the community" (Forrest, 1972b).

Muhammad Speaks and the *Black Panther* embodied Forrest's sentiments, developing and sustaining relationships with black communities. The

Chicago-based *Muhammad Speaks* had bureaus in New York, Los Angeles, Atlanta, and Washington, D.C. and had scores of correspondents nationwide. The Oakland-based *Black Panther* published news reports from members in every major city on the East and West coasts. The papers worked to maintain relevance among local patrons by dispatching journalists to cover regionally pertinent issues. The viability of *Muhammad Speaks* rested on its capacity to serve and be relevant to the interests of black consumers in black communities; the paper built its reputation on it.

Complementing the grassroots approach of the editors, the vendors ensured the papers' salient presence in black communities. Their parent organizations relied on the revenue, resulting in a flood of NOI and black Panther members selling papers in front of black churches, NAACP headquarters, and on the street corners of black commercial centers across the country. Pedestrians and motorists alike became accustomed to hearing "Salaam Alaikam, come back to your own, read *Muhammad Speaks!*" and "We're the Panthers, want to see? Buy the paper!" (Lincoln 1994, 218; Hilliard and Cole 1993, 123).

As other black papers steadily declined, *Muhammad Speaks* and *Black Panther* laid claim to hundreds of thousands of purchases every week. Expansive and aggressive salesmanship, along with quality coverage of issues of interest to black readers, propelled the papers' circulation (Clegg 1997). David Hilliard, who helped establish *Black Panther*, recalled that it "didn't take much to sell those papers even then" because black Americans "wanted that newspaper because it gave a different counterpoint to the establishment media that was so biased and racist as a matter of fact" (Hilliard 2007).

A LIVING PRESS IN THE WORLD OF YOUNG PEOPLE

Young people made up a substantial percentage of the radical black press' readership. For a variety of reasons, the radical black press was alive in the world of young people throughout the 1960s. It functioned as a link to activism, a source of communal pride, and a body of knowledge that served to supplement or subvert public knowledge—including the public school curriculum. Passing through the hands of teenage members of the Nation of Islam and the Black Panther Party, the papers found their way into the hands of young people not affiliated with the organizations and, ultimately, onto high-school campuses.

Given their status as minors, many teenage members of both organizations were not permitted to participate in a variety of activities, but they were encouraged to sell papers (Abu-Jamal 2008). When the first edition of the *Black Panther* came out, Bobby Seale and Huey Newton distributed stacks to hundreds of youth "on bicycles" to circulate in their neighbor-hoods (Seale 1996, 147).

Advertisements in the newspapers used incentives to encourage teenag-ers to distribute the papers. A half-page advertisement in the March 16, 1969, edition of the *Black Panther* read "YOUNG PEOPLE WANTED to sell THE BLACK PANTHER." The ad included a photograph of a teenager on a bicycle, holding the unfurled newspaper. The caption read: "The young man in the picture earned enough money in 3 weeks to buy the bike on which he is sitting. You can do the same or better." The Nation of Islam also instituted a rewards system that included a free dinner for the entire family at Salaam, the popular NOI owned restaurant (Tate 1997).

Teenage sellers were also motivated by a pride of association with older members of their respective organizations. Vilbert White recalled that during his boyhood in the Nation of Islam, he felt a deep sense of pride seeing the diligence of "handsome, strong, well-dressed men" selling the papers (White 2001, 43). Darren Tate joined the Nation of Islam as a teen-ager and was thrilled by the opportunity to sell *Muhammad Speaks* alongside older members. He felt a sense of "personal accomplishment" moving the paper in his community (Tate 1997, 79).

Given their access to high-school campuses, young members actively sold the paper in and around their schools. In Philadelphia, Black Panther Captain Mumia Abu-Jamal was accustomed to teenage visitors at Party headquarters "who wanted to sell the paper in their schools." Their enthu-siasm prompted Abu-Jamal to caution them to "be careful, to only take as many as they were fairly certain [to sell]" (Abu-Jamal 2008, 197). A Berkeley High School student wrote the editors to share her interest in selling the *Black Panther* in her high school and inquired "if it is against the school laws to sell the paper on a High School campus." She planned to "call the [district] office" to find out. In response, editor Raymond Lewis informed the "black and beautiful revolutionary sister" that "now, the PANTHER LAW is the law of the land" and lauded her interest in selling the paper on campus (Wyse 1968a, 5).

Subsequently, high-school students bought and read the papers, regard-ing them as alternative sources of knowledge that helped reframe their worldview. High schooler Kevin Murphy told the editors of the *Black Panther* that "your weekly news reports have increased the consciousness of me and my friends by continually revealing the hypocrisy, the racism and malice that those in high places exhibit in their endless drive to drain human and natural resources while they line their own pockets." Murphy predicted that "the white middle class will come to the realization that they have been deceived and robbed by their leaders: they will see that their American dream is as plastic and artificial as Disneyland and that the only real truth lies in the pages of newspapers such as this one" (Murphy 1973,

16). After dropping out of high school, Flores Forbes turned to the *Black Panther* where he "discovered a new world" that "spoke volumes to my lost little soul" (Forbes 2007, 19). Mikal Shabbaz recalls reading *Muhammad Speaks* "cover to cover" as a teenager, appreciating the scope and depth of a paper that let him "know what was happening in the world and why things were the way they were and how come they couldn't be different and how they got that way" (Shabbaz 2014).

DIALOGUE BETWEEN YOUTH AND TEXT

Along with being an illuminating source of alternative information, the radical press served as an interactive text, intimately engaged with the lived realities of young people. As an elementary school student, Qur'an Shakir recalled *Muhammad Speaks* "felt like it was our paper. We felt like we could contribute to it" (Shakir 2013). The papers published student poetry, used students as investigative journalists, and aggressively advocated for students' perspectives on a range of social policy issues. Editors centered those student voices that bolstered their wider social critique, and subsequently young people employed the radical black press as a platform for engaging the politics of their everyday lives. This dialogical relationship is vividly illustrated in the youth-oriented character of the press' news coverage.

The *Black Panther* and *Muhammad Speaks* quoted young people at length, used students as reporters, and made their stories news when the mainstream press ignored them. When, for example, black students in High Point, North Carolina, were suspended for formally requesting the school board to add black studies, the *Black Panther* covered the story while the local press made no mention of the incident (Streitmatter 2001). The *Black Panther* and *Muhammad Speaks* published dozens of such stories about the abuse and criminalization of black students at the hands of teachers and officers in what the *Black Panther* described as "maximum security" schools ("Maximum Security High" 1970, 26). The papers placed a national spotlight on the issue of police violence against children and adolescents. Students' direct reports were often published, which offered unique perspectives on the lived oppression of high schoolers. In a April 1970 edition of the *Black Panther*, two 15-year-old black students explicated an encounter outside of school, where police officers struck one student ...

> ... with his billy club; he was standing in front of me so it bashed my cheek bone. I fell down and the next one snatched me up and hit me with his club, he struck the other side of my face in the same place. I fell again and the third police snatched me by my collar and stood me up. He didn't use a club, he smashed my jaw with his right fist. (Powe 1970, 6)

The other student's injuries required hospitalization because, "there is damage to the brain, enough so that he cannot get a solid night's sleep without quite possibly never waking up again" (Powe 1970, 6). This incident went unreported in the local and national press, let alone from the perspective of the victims.

Such graphic first-person narratives were not treated as isolated, as was conventional in the mainstream press, but were mined for deeper meaning. Stories of school-sponsored violence and repression were framed as part of concurrent racial and socioeconomic disparities in law enforcement and education. The papers identified a linear relationship between the two. In doing so, they highlighted the interplay between school and police oppression that not only countered popular media narratives about black youth criminality, but offered structural analysis in place of cursory mainstream news coverage of "youth incidents." In doing so, they demonstrated how student journalism, backed by professional editors, produced multidimensional news stories that raised readers' consciousness about structural inequalities in the lives of youth of color.

Youth encounters with the radical black press were spurred on by the rising tide of late 1960s black student activism on high-school and college campuses. By 1968, unprecedented levels of mass protest by students of color spread to college and high-school campuses nationwide. Frustrated with the limited pace of legislated education reform and trained in organized protest, black students put their energies toward demanding greater authority over educational curriculum. The protests were remarkable for their impact on school operations, often slowing or stopping administrative functions for weeks or months, and winning important concessions for curricular reform (Rojas 2007).

The radical black press took assertive measures to give voice to university and high-school protestors. *Muhammad Speaks* described student activists as the "vanguard of revolution" ("Wilkins Goes All-Out Against Black Studies" 1969, 6) and ran a regular series between 1968 and 1973 titled "Inside Black Revolts on Campus." The series included investigative reporting by embedded journalists at various campuses, and it focused on the demands of protestors. Further, *Muhammad Speaks* did not merely talk about the students, but *through* them; editors reprinted student writing and ran special reports, honing in on student demands, interviewing protestors, and publishing their vision for substantive school reform.

Concurrently, the *Black Panther* intimately collaborated with high-school activists. The paper served as a platform for organizing high-school students—advertising events, publishing student demands, and providing student journalists with an opportunity to contribute to the paper. Black student unions (BSU) were especially well supported by the press. A January 25, 1969, advertisement stated that "Black Student Unions have formed a state wide Union of B.S.U.'s and are in the process of organizing on a national level. We call upon all BLACK STUDENTS to unite." The ad went on to admonish students to become "part of a united movement" and "stop moving on an individual basis" ("Important' Black Student Unions" 1969, 19). Other ads in the paper notified readers about upcoming national and regional BSU conventions ("H.S. Convention" 1968). *The Black Panther* served as a national staging ground for students to share their activities. Students reprinted the detailed demands and resolutions of black student groups from around the country. Such demands were often submitted to boards of education and school administrators and reprinted in the *Black Panther*. A 1968 edition of the paper published a list of 12 BSU demands, which included "student initiated courses, … in service training … in Black history and culture for all teachers," and a "Black Curriculum Committee" consisting of both student and teachers of color ("BSU Voices Demands" 1969). BSU students from Berkeley High had previously submitted the demands at a regular meeting of the Berkeley Unified Board of Education (Minutes 1968).

One of the student participants in Berkeley BSU's action was Iris Wyse, who also played a pivotal role in the *Black Panther* ("BSU Voices Demands" 1969). Wyse was a core member of Berkeley's BSU and helped forward the organization's political activities. She was also a loyal reader and contributor to the *Black Panther*. In early 1968, Wyse had begun submitting poetry and writing op-eds in the paper. By the end of the year, she was brought on as the official "student editor" of the *Black Panther*. As editor, Wyse reported on the activities of black student unions nationwide, while bolstering "that beautiful and truthful paper," the *Black Panther*, as a vital source of "all the happenings of our black community" (Wyse 1968a). In her dual role as BSU member and contributor to the *Black Panther*, Wyse concurrently reported on the activities of the BSU in the newspaper and promoted the paper as an educational resource. It was therefore unlikely a coincidence that among Berkeley BSU's demands to the board of education was a call for courses on "Black Journalism" and a call for literature like the *Black Panther* to be stocked in the school library (Minutes 1968). Her work illustrated the dual role of the *Black Panther* as both a subject *and* object of student-driven curricular reforms.

The demands of Wyse and the Berkeley BSU pointed to the growing assertion by students that the radical black press be regarded as curricular content. For instance, one month after Berkeley BSU's action, students from the BSU at McClymonds High in Oakland put forth demands at the annual California BSU conference that their school library carry subscriptions of the *Black Panther* and *Muhammad Speaks* (Wyse 1968b). In the Bay Area, high-school students used the *Black Panther* to complete research reports (KQED 1970). Of particular interest to student activists was the value of the radical Black press as supplemental text to the burgeoning corpus of black-oriented social studies school curriculums, which included the study of history, politics, and culture. A student from Chicago's Saint Paul High School wrote to *Muhammad Speaks* to request a copy of the newspaper because the school "recently instituted a course in Afro-American History and Culture" and he wished to "include all aspects and persons in this curriculum" (Baringer 1969, 10).

The student's call to include the radical press in high-school history and social studies curriculum was notable given the degree to which the papers, particularly *Muhammad Speaks*, included multicultural history and international current events content in their pages. *Muhammad Speaks* regularly carried a one or two-page spread spotlighting prominent black American or African historical achievements. Each week readers were treated to biographies and accomplishments of ancient African kings, inventers, and adventurers, as well as black American freedom fighters like Frederick Douglass, intellectuals like Du Bois, and scientists like Benjamin Banneker. These stories bridged space and time, connecting the past to the present and Africa to America. For instance, a 1962 story about Timbuktu told of "a society where university life was highly regarded and scholars were beheld with reverence" (Clarke 1962). The story circled back to the present day to illustrate the living legacy of learning among peoples of African descent.

The *Black Panther* included a weekly sidebar series titled "This Week in Black History," adjacent to education related news stories. The series detailed a sequence of historical events from the 1700s to the 1970s, highlighting black agency. For example, a May 1974 edition of "This Week" reported the "daring and courageous" events of May 13, 1862, when a "black steamship pilot, sailed an armed Confederate steamer ... out of Charleston, S.C. harbor and presented it to the Union Navy." The sequence ended with the story of a black female candidate for Oakland city council in 1974 ("This Week" 1974). Each week the sidebar presented histories that were invisible in mainstream history books. From the historic negotiations between Roosevelt and A. Philip Randolph, to the black security guard who arrested intruders at the Watergate Hotel, the *Black Panther* provided readers with an alternative picture of American history ("This Week" 1974). Taken together, the historical content in the papers offered readers a rich corpus of historical content that was responsive to the growing demands of student activists for culturally relevant materials.

Muhammad Speaks' historical content was intended to be a direct response to the mono-cultural curriculum of most high schools. The paper's first chief editor, Richard Durham, understood textbook reform as an extension of the black struggle for racial justice:

Today when at least the more "moderate" elements in the freedom struggle in the country are concentrating on desegregation in education, it is particularly urgent that we demand equal treatment in the school books as well as in the school rooms. (Durham 1962)

Muhammad Speaks editor John Woodford described the historical content of the paper as a way to "fill in the gaps" of mainstream history curriculum (Woodford 2009) and provide readers with content they could not access otherwise.

"A JUMPING OFF POINT" FOR RADICAL TEACHING

Progressive and activist teachers exploited the radical press' reframing of historical and political agency around the lives of people of color. Educators used the papers to provide students with a counter narrative that would prompt them to think differently about the dynamics of their world. In particular, the papers played a distinct educational role as sources of multicultural history and models of critical thinking.

There is substantial evidence that educators used the papers as a teaching resource in various contexts. The most illustrative body of evidence comes from the educational programs affiliated with the Nation of Islam and the Black Panther Party. Since the late 1950s, the Nation of Islam ran a set of fulltime nationwide parochial elementary schools known as the "University of Islam" (UOI), which primarily served organization members' children (Lincoln 1994). Beginning in 1969, the Black Panthers instituted "Liberation Schools" as supplementary education programs for children and later "Intercommunal Youth Institutes" (IYI) as full-time schools (Hilliard 2007).

The *Black Panther* and *Muhammad Speaks* often published photographs of educators in IYI and UOI classrooms teaching with the respective papers. The images depicted multiple modalities of teaching with the radical press—in small discussion groups, whole classroom direct instruction, and individual tutorial work. An August 9, 1969, photo in the *Black Panther* showed an IYI elementary student seated with two teachers, working intimately through the pages of the paper. Another August edition of the paper included a photo of IYI students seated forward in rows, each with the *Black Panther* open and a caption that read "The Youth Make the Revolution" (1969, 19). An October 1, 1965, photo in *Muhammad Speaks* captured two elementary-age children leaning over the newspaper. The caption read: "They will not grow into adults thinking all the worthwhile progress in America and the world was wrought through the skill of only white hands and brains" ("Young Sons" 1965). The images conveyed to readers that these papers were vibrant texts in the learning lives of students.

While both organizations' education programs commonly used their schools as a space to dogmatically articulate organizational doctrine (Perlstein 2002), their classrooms were also spaces where a broader set of educational ideals were counter posed to dominant curricular content. Herein, the radical press played a supportive role, particularly in regard to fields of study commonly identified as "social studies"—history, social science, and current events. In other words, the newspapers served as "counterpublics." So did classrooms. Educators used the papers to instigate cognitive dissonance, forcing students to rethink dominant social narratives, to take a more international perspective on current events, and to gain exposure to a more multicultural history. In so doing, they used the radical press in the classroom to frame black liberation struggles in terms of critical thinking and multicultural curriculum.

For liberation school educators like Seattle's Garry Owens, the *Black Panther* served as a "jumping off point" for teaching literacy skills and conducting deeper discussions about history, politics, and culture (Zane and Jefferies 2010, 71). Liberation schools nationwide were run in conjunction with the black Panther's free breakfast program for children. Neighborhood children arrived at the Panther's center before school to eat a healthy breakfast, and, while their food was served, party members would lead short lessons (Owens 2013). According to educator Anthony Ware, teaching focused largely on reading, writing, and discussion (Zane and Jefferies 2010).

The *Black Panther* was used as a reading resource in liberation and IYI schools. Students were asked to "read something from one of the articles" to their peers and collectively identify important terms and language (Owens 2013). Liberation school educators built deeper discussions into these literacy lessons. In Oakland, Akua Njeri's students at the liberation school were provided papers to take home and return with questions to discuss (Njeri 1991). Panther educator Melvin Dickson asserted that "once you get kids reading, they enter an entirely different realm" (Zane and Jefferies 2010, 71). The *Black Panther* was useful in tapping into "different realms" of understanding. Teachers were particularly interested in directing students to examine the paper's historical and political conceptualization. Owens and others used articles to "bring to light the fact that people of color all over the world had some dignity, they had a history that predated Europe." The history of Africa and black Americans aimed to counter dominant narratives that framed black history as having "started with slavery" and to affirm that the antecedents of black children "came from … civilization" (Owens 2013).

The use of the *Black Panther* to redress misrepresented and underrepresented histories, fit into the broad educational vision of both the Black Panther Party and the Nation of Islam leadership. Bobby Seale demanded educators teach students "about themselves, about black history ... not the same bullshit they get now" (quoted in Zane and Jefferies 2010, 71). Likewise the director of the University of Islam schools, Christine Johnson, called upon educators to help children of color "realize early that they have a history with meaning, and not a meaningless, nebulous something about Negro history and how much progress we have made since slavery" (Johnson 1961). The rich and unique historical content in the radical black press was distinctly useful in this regard.

The radical black press provided teachers with stories that illuminated new insights and alternative readings of the past, which expanded the historical imagination of students and teachers alike. For instance, the *Black Panther*'s detailed discussion of Louis Leakey's 1950s discovery of the earliest humans in Africa brought to light the anthropologist's research in an accessible language. For many liberation school teachers and students, this was their first insight into the full significance of Leakey's study of African premodern history (Owens 2013). Similarly, a *Muhammad Speaks'* article captured the imagination of students and teachers with their story of an imposing Mexican stone sculpture that was, "100 years older than 1492, when Columbus is said to have discovered America. The thick lips and broad nose indicate a definite African strain, thus refuting the belief that the first Africans came to America only as slaves." ("100 Years Before Columbus" 1964)

Such stories were used to draw students' attention to new social science research that was impacting the landscape of historical knowledge. It also provided an opportunity to address historical knowledge in terms of power and liberation.

Educators and editors worked in tandem to frame historical knowledge within a wider conversation about structural power and personal empowerment amid disempowering structural inequalities. The *Black Panther* asserted that despite the gravity of Leakey's research, mainstream sources had "bowed" to the prevailing sensibilities of "Western thought and culture," which refused to "make available to the people" an accurate account of the African side of human history ("In Search of Man" 1973). Liberation school educator Akua Njeri conveyed the character of this critique to her students, telling them, "You came from a rich culture. You came from a place where you were kings and queens. You are brilliant children. This government has placed you in an educational situation that constantly tells you [otherwise]" (Njeri 1991, 15–16).

Teachers used the radical press to motivate students to inquire into the past and inspire news way of approaching history. In liberation schools, the *Black Panther*'s vignettes on historical figures like John Brown and Harriet Tubman were pointed out to students who were directed to do more research on their own (Owens 2013). Njeri's students at the Oakland Liberation School were provided papers as homework (Njeri 1991). Students at the UOI and liberation schools followed up initial discoveries in the newspapers with further inquiry through encyclopedia or library research (Shakir 2013). This approach aimed to cultivate an ethic of curiosity about the world. According to Garry Owens, the *Black Panther* was a great resource for educators, because it "would come out on a weekly basis" providing teachers an opportunity to draw students into the "front end of a much longer story" that they could pursue in greater depth (Owens 2014). Collectively, teachers, students, and editors critiqued dominant modes of knowledge construction, while constructing and giving value to new kinds of knowledge.

At the heart of this approach to social studies education, was an effort to motivate students to think beyond their assumptions and drive their own learning. Leaders of both UOI and Panther schools articulated an educational vision rooted in critical thinking and student-directed learning. Black Panther leader Huey Newton argued that the primary task of education was not "to transmit a received doctrine from past experience," but "to provide the young with the ability and technical training that will make it possible for them to evaluate their heritage for themselves" and to "translate what is known into their own experiences and thus discover more readily their own" (Newton 2009). UOI director Christine Johnson asserted that education was too often limited to an interest in " 'Why can't Johnny read' and not 'What does Johnny read.' " If students were "permitted to read and believe everything they are taught in school" without critical inquiry, they would proceed through life unable to "separate the truth from the lie" (Johnson 1961, 16)

Coverage of the Intercommunal Youth Institutes in the *Black Panther* illustrated a student-centered approach to history education built on the progressive ideal of democratic classrooms. The paper covered stories of students acquiring historical knowledge through hands-on experiential modes of learning within interdisciplinary contexts. A 1974 story presented students learning the "historical development of black people" through the exploration and creation of art. An IYI instructor told the paper that the "works of famous black artists are discussed on the merits of the art, not on the personality of the artist" ("Art in the Service" 1974). This approach to history embodied the progressive education vision of organizing learning around student-driven problem solving and historical inquiry, as opposed to isolating the discipline of history or focusing primarily on historical facts.

Stories in the press emphasized learning that facilitated a relationship between historical knowledge and personal meaning. The *Black Panther* highlighted lessons that used autobiographies like *Black Boy* and *The Autobiography of Malcolm X* in conjunction with the study of events in black history. The paper highlighted the development of students' personal connections with events such as Nat Turner's revolt, the March on Washington, and Cesar Chavez's farm workers' march. An assistant teacher at a liberation school told the *Black Panther* that "they are eager to learn and exchange ideas because the curriculum is based on true experiences of revolutionaries and everyday people who the children can relate to." Progressive education was described as an ideal method for cultivating political consciousness among students "simply because they can relate to what is being taught" (Douglas 1969, 19).

Educators interested in student-directed learning found the radical black press uniquely situated to promote inquiry in their classrooms. Former IYI instructor Steve McCutchen saw the *Black Panther* as a resource for self-directed learners "willing to understand a different side of the question" (McCutchen 2014). As a student in the UOI, Qur'an Shakir experienced *Muhammad Speaks* within the context of self-directed learning. "We were different kinds of thinkers," Shakir recalled. She and her classmates moved beyond the general directives of their instructors, toward creative explorations of texts, individually researching information that had initially been introduced in class (Shakir 2013).

Student-directed classes used the radical press to examine popular assumptions about "truth" and the practice of privileging some perspectives over others. In the process, students were provided self-directed opportunities to assess, analyze, and reconstruct knowledge. For Garry Owens, "part of the value of the paper was ... that we could 'de-educate,' ... minds to ... go back to square one and [address] even the whole issue about who discovered America and all that" (Owens 2013). An editorial in *Muhammad Speaks* echoed this sentiment, asking educators and parents, "When your child comes to you with a question such as 'Did Columbus really discover America?' What will you answer? 'No the Indians were here long before Columbus.' We must take an active part in the affairs of our children and the schools which they attend" (Wilma 1962). Confronting the myth of "America's first great hero" was representative of the kind of popular historical narrative that educators, as well as the newspaper editors, aimed to disrupt (Loewen 2007, 31).

The juxtaposition of "official" state history with the multiracial history presented in the radical press allowed educators, in Akua Njeri's words, to "heighten the contradictions" between the two (Njeri 1991, 16). In general, the Black Panther Party employed "heightening contradictions" as a Marxist rhetorical tactic, aimed at accelerating the apparentness of capitalist exploitation (e.g. police violence against civilians the state claimed to serve, wars for "freedom" that expanded American economic supremacy, or public education that helped reproduce racial and social-class inequality). In the classroom Panthers contrasted the dominant narratives of black cultural and intellectual deficiency with historical evidence of blacks as socially responsible and intellectually productive. In Njeri's classroom, students could learn that while the "government says we're shiftless and lazy, we're showing we work the hardest." In her classroom, the fact that students were reading the *Black Panther* served to illustrate the contradictions: "We would give them papers to read ... [and] would come back asking questions. We would explain to them that if they were dumb, they wouldn't have been able to read this stuff" (Njeri 1991, 16).

As a teaching strategy, heightening contractions served what Paul Gorski (2009) described as a pedagogy of cognitive dissonance. According to Gorski, providing students with an alternative frame of reference served not only to disrupt students' untested assumptions about American history and culture, it facilitated an environment in which students "grapple with new ideas without accepting them blindly" (2). For educators, cultivating curiosity worked in tandem with the actual content. Garry Owens gave "kids enough information" to prick "their imagination or intellect" and spark a "cycle of inquiry" and curiosity they could carry throughout their education. Beyond simply gaining a more complex understanding of history, students were being instructed to think differently—through comparative analysis and a reconciliation of opposing narratives (Owens 2014).

For educators in Nation of Islam and Black Panther Party schools, lessons in contradiction were not disembodied intellectual exercises. Instead, they were rooted in lived realities of young people of color. Njeri's literacy lesson evidencing that students were not "dumb," was a rejoinder to the underlying assumptions of dominant social discourse and policy regarding black learning "deficiencies." Policy iterations, such as the 1965 Moynihan report and subsequent mainstream media coverage, served to reinforce popular 1960s perceptions of black cultural and social deficiency. The report's tone was appropriated by federal school policy makers, who focused on the need to correct, because of black children's social deficiencies in order to advance their educational opportunities (Patterson 2001). In response, educators like Njeri and Owens focused on the creative and productive lives of people of color, nationally, internationally, and historically—as well as in the classroom. They aimed to let students see for themselves the contradictions in the dominant social narrative that operated in their lives.

In so doing, teachers facilitated a learning process akin to Paulo Freire's "praxis." Freire believed that when learners activate intrinsically motivated critical inquiry, and educators facilitate creative reflections on that inquiry, learners can cultivate the kind of inventiveness necessary to transform oppressive conditions (Freire 1984). Like Freire, educators in the black Panther and NOI schools argued that state institutions historically repressed this kind of dialectical inquiry in order to miseducate and ultimately dominate people of color. Consequently educators and their allies in the radical press saw critical thinking as a weapon to contest the institutional and cultural arrangements of power that reproduced social inequality through education.

KNOWLEDGE AS AN ARRANGEMENT OF POWER

Educators in Black Panther and NOI schools seated their critique of popular historical narratives in a discussion of power and privilege. In the words of IYI educator Steve McCutchen, teachers helped students see that those who "control the institution are the ones who write the history of a particular social period" (McCutchen 2014). The radical black press echoed this sentiment through editorials and news stories on the systemic relationship between knowledge and power. A 1962 article in *Muhammad Speaks* by a black educator suggested that "we must consider the proper treatment of Negro history, especially in public education as a political rather than cultural or educational problem, to be solved by political means" (Bevridge 1962). Misrepresentations of black Americans were seen as endemic to a wider problem of inaccurate and inequitable representations of black Americans in public life. As historian Lerone Bennett notes, *Muhammad Speaks* told readers:

> History is used in America to undergird the whole superstructure of prejudice and race hatred. This is why there is a deep-seated resistance on the part of millions of whites against a complete revelation of the role of black people in the building of this country. (Bennett 1965, 17)

This problem struck at a core journalistic agenda of editors who were committed to telling a fuller, richer, and more empowering story of black experiences nationally and globally. One editor opined in 1962 that schoolbooks "participated in a cultural lobotomy" engineered "to make the American Negro a rootless person." The editor argued that publishers, authors, and artists in the field of children's books were part of a longstanding white-supremacist program to "defraud, dehumanize and demoralize black Americans into quiet submission of this country's unreal whites-only philosophy" (Durham 1962). It was in the context of this conceptualization of knowledge and power that editors attempted to counterbalance the absence of black contributions in textbooks by highlighting them in the paper (Woodford 2009).

The *Black Panther* also directed readers to consider the political nature of knowledge. They took an indirect, but pointed, approach to critiquing the public school history curriculum by placing it within the discussion of institutional racism, colonialism, and state repression. The paper's approach was illustrated in a 1968 story of a high-school mural in San Francisco that depicted a Eurocentric version of American history. The *Black Panther* described a "full-walled mural of George Washington shown in numerous guises portraying black slaves and scenes of other, so-called historic shootings and killing of Indians." The story covered the efforts of students to remove the mural and promote interracial dialogue. Throughout the piece, students of color and working-class white students were described as members of the "third world," and their struggle for racially inclusive history was framed as a contestation of power between the establishment elites and the organizing power of youth (Boston 1968).

The *Black Panther*'s discussion of historical knowledge was essentially a conversation about power and privilege. The paper identified Eurocentric history as a reflection of the structural inequalities that plagued American schools. An April 21, 1970, story titled "Parents Move on Conditions in Dearborn School" demonstrated this approach. The story detailed a poorly maintained school building, and the corresponding illustration on the same page depicted students standing in a rat-infested hallway gripping a textbook titled "pig history" (Robertson 1970). The image linked the capacity to control the resources in a school community to the capacity to construct and disseminate knowledge. Black Panther Eddie Joseph took this idea further, arguing that a school's history curriculum should be "planned by the community and those that work there would be employees of the people. In this way knowledge will not be an alien thing to the student" (Joseph 1970, 21). In other words, for knowledge to be authentic, black communities must be agents in its production, dissemination, and legitimation. Ultimately, curriculum and instruction involve arrangements of power that largely determine the capacity of an education to liberate or oppress.

CONCLUSION: THE IRONY AND
WONDER OF RADICAL PEDAGOGY

One of the great ironies of the pedagogy of the radical black press is that it directed students to read critically as a means of liberation and simultaneously pointed to the inherent limitations of critical reading within wider systems of structural oppression. So as students "wake up" from dominant white ideology's supremacy over knowledge to a richer understanding of history and politics—and develop analytical skills in the process—they realize they are still caught in "the American nightmare" (X and Haley 1992). Even the messengers of radical thinking and learning were soon subsumed by wider systems of domination. The early 1970s witnessed the state-sponsored implosion of both parent organizations and the decline of their newspapers and schooling systems (Marable 2011; Bloom and Martin 2013). The end of the 1960s also marked the dawn of systemic reversals of progressive social policy, especially in education (Hall 2005). The movement for multicultural curriculum fared no better, as major textbook companies collectively made superficial changes while retaining the fundamental character of white supremacy (Loewen 2007; Fitzgerald 1980).

Yet, embedded in the irony of the radical black press' pedagogy is a cultural and intellectual strand of the black freedom struggle: hope. William Grier and Price Cobbs (1968) contend that black Americans' fervent interest in education as a means of liberation required an act of hope: it is "a source of wonder where such unending faith had its origins" (61). Even under conditions of utterly unambiguous oppression, black educators, activists and students have historically pursued a critical and democratic education. For instance, Patrice Preston-Grimes' (2007) history of Jim Crow-era Georgia schools illustrates how black teachers developed civic-minded pedagogy in their classrooms. Despite having virtually no opportunity to participate in democratic life, students grappled with questions like, "What existing practices operate against realizing the ideals of democracy" and "What … steps can the Negro take to improve these conditions?"(15). The radical classrooms and texts of the 1960s and 1970s carried on a pedagogical tradition of hope amid hopelessness; a tradition which predated emancipation (Anderson 1988). Therefore, it is not surprising that the radical media's ceaseless resistance to intellectual hegemony and faith in transformational learning resonated at the grassroots, even at the nadir of post-*Brown* education reform. Despite its marginal status in mainstream thought, the radical black press amplified a populist "counterpublic" faith among black Americans that a liberating education was achievable, even amid the half-hearted commitments of dominant society.

REFERENCES

"100 Years Before Columbus." 1964. *Muhammad Speaks*, January 3.
Abron-Ervin, JoNina. 2011. *Driven by the Movement: Activists of the Black Power Era* Denver, CO: P & L Press.
Abu-Jamal, Mumia. 2008. *We Want Freedom: A Life in the Black Panther Party*. Cambridge, MA: South End Press.
Anderson, James D. 1988. *The Education of Blacks in the South, 1860–1935*. Chapel Hill: University of North Carolina Press.
"Art in the Service of People." 1974. *Black Panther Intercommunal News*, June 22.
Baringer, David. 1969. "Student Asks for Muslim Paper." *Muhammad Speaks*, February 23.

Bennett, Lerone. 1965. "Parents Now Want Children To Know More Negro History." *Muhammad Speaks,* September 16.

Bevridge, Lowell P. 1962. "Are Millions Being Brainwashed by White Supremacy Poison in Books for Children? Why Are They Always White Children?" *Muhammad Speaks.* July.

Bloom, Joshua, and Waldo Martin, E. 2013. *Black Against Empire: The History and Politics of the Black Panther Party.* Berkeley: University of California Press.

Boston, Linda. 1968. "Racist S.F. School Shows Its Mural." *Black Panther Intercommunal News,* October 27.

"BSU Voices Demands" 1969. *Berkeley High School Yearbook.*

Brown, Elaine. 1993. *A Taste of Power: A Black Woman's Story.* New York: Doubleday.

Clarke, John Henrik. 1962. "The Story of Timbuktoo's Astounding Civilization."*Muhammad Speaks*, October 31.

Clegg, Claude. 1997. *An Original Man: The Life and Times of Elijah Muhammad.* New York: St. Martins Press, 1997.

Danns, Dionne. 2003. "Chicago High School Students' Movement for Quality-Public Education, 1966–1971." *The Journal of African American History* 88 (2): 138–150

Douglas, Val. 1969. "The Youth Make the Revolution." *Black Panther Intercommunal News,* August 2.

Durham, Richard. 1962. "School Textbooks Buttress 'White Supremacy' Theory." *Muhammad Speaks,* July.

Fitzgerald, Francis. 1980. *America Revised: History Schoolbooks in the 20th Century.* New York: Vintage Books.

Forbes, Florence. 2007. *Will You Die with Me?: My Life and the Black Panther Party.* New York: Washington Square Press.

Forrest, Leon. 1972a. "Surging Community Newspapers." *Muhammad Speaks,* September 15.

———. 1972b. "A Journalist Discusses Craft." *Muhammad Speaks,* October 27.

Fraser, Nancy. 1989. *Unruly Practices: Power, Discourse and Gender in Contemporary Social Theory.* Minneapolis: Polity Press.

Freire. Paulo. 1984. *The Politics of Education: Culture, Power and Liberation.* South Hadley MA: Bergin and Garvey.

Gorski, Paul C. 2009. "Cognitive Dissonance: A Critical Tool in Social Justice Teaching." *EdChange.org.* October.

Grier, William, and Price Cobbs. 1968. *Black Rage.* New York: Basic Books.

Hall, Jacquelyn Dowd. 2005. "The Long Civil Rights Movement and the Political Uses of the Past." *The Journal of American History* 91 (4): 1233–1263.

Hilliard, David. 2007. Interview by Farai Chideya, *News and Notes,* NPR, December 5.

Hilliard, David, and Lewis Cole. 1993. *This Side of Glory: The Autobiography of David Hilliard and the Story of the Black Panther Party.* Boston: Little Brown.

"H.S. Convention" 1968. *Black Panther Intercommunal News,* October 12.

"'Important' Black Student Unions" 1969. *Black Panther Intercommunal News.* January 25.

"'In Search of Man' Leaky Symposium Ignored in Bay Area Press." *The Black Panther,* December 22.

Johnson, Christine. 1961. "Self Help or Oblivion for the Negro." *Muhammad Speaks*, October/November.

Joseph, Eddie Jamal. 1970. "Education from Jamal (N.Y. 21)." *Black Panther Intercommunal News*, February 28.

KQED. 1970. "Black Panther Newspaper." KQED Public Media Archives.Retrieved July 1, 2014, from https://diva.sfsu.edu/collections/sfbatv/bundles/188923

Lassier, Eugene. 1973. [Letter to the editor]. *Black Panther Intercommunal News*, January 1.

Lewis, Melvin E. 1990. "Once I Was a Panther." *Black American Literature Forum* 24 (3): 534–538.

Lincoln, Charles Eric. 1994. *The Black Muslims in America*. Grand Rapids, MI: William B. Eerdmans.

Loewen, James. 2007. *Lies My Teacher Told Me: Everything Your American History Textbook Got Wrong*. New York: Simon & Schuster.

Marable, Manning. 2011. *Malcolm X: A Life of Reinvention*. New York: Viking Press.

"Maximum Security High." 1970. *Black Panther Intercommunal News*, December 26.

McCutchen, Steve. 2014. Personal telephone conversation with author. July 3.

"Minutes: Berkeley Unified School District Regular Board Meeting." 1968. October 1.

Murphy, Kevin. 1973. "Canadian H.S. Student." *Black Panther Intercommunal News*, June 16.

Newton, Huey P. 2009. *Revolutionary Suicide*. New York: Penguin.

Njeri, Akua. 1991. *My Life with the Black Panther Party*. Oakland: Burning Spear Publications.

Owens, Garry. 2013. Personal telephone conversation with author. October 1.

Patterson, James. 2001. *Brown v. Board of Education: A Civil Rights Milestone and Its Troubled Legacy*. New York: Oxford University Press.

Perlstein, Daniel. 2002. "Minds Stayed on Freedom: Politics and Pedagogy in the African-American Freedom Struggle." *American Educational Research* 39 (2): 249–277.

Powe, Wilbur. 1970. "The Parents of Everett Junior High School Students Demand: No More Pigs Brutalizing Our Youth." *Black Panther Intercommunal News*, April 6.

Preston-Grimes, Patrice. 2007. "Teaching Democracy before Brown: Civic Education in Georgia's African American Schools, 1930-1954." *Theory and Research in Social Education* 35 (1): 9–31.

Robertson, Diane. 1970. "Parents Move on Conditions at Dearborn School." *Black Panther Intercommunal News*, May 21.

Rojas, Fabio. 2007. *From Black Power to Black Studies: How a Radical Social Movement Became an Academic Discipline*. Baltimore: The Johns Hopkins University Press.

Rusinack, Kelly E. 2003. "Dan Burley." In *Dictionary of Literary Biography: American Sportswriters and Writers on Sport*, edited by Richard Orodenker, 43–49. Abington, PA: Layman Book.

Sales, William. 1994. *From Civil Rights to Black Liberation: Malcolm X and the Organization of Afro-American Unity*. Boston: South End Press.

Seale, Bobby. 1996. *Seize the Time: The Story of the Black Panther Party and Huey P. Newton*. Baltimore, MD: Black Classic Press

Shabbaz, Mikal. 2014. Personal telephone conversation with author. July 1.

Shakir, Qur'an. 2013. Personal telephone conversation with author. October 3.

Streitmatter, Rodger. 2001. *Voices of Revolution: The Dissident Press in America.* New York: Columbia University Press

Tate, Sonyrea. 1997. *Little X: Growing Up in the Nation of Islam.* New York: Harper Collins.

"This Week in Black History." 1974. *Black Panther Intercommunal News*, June 22.

White, Vilbert L., Jr. 2001. *Inside the Nation of Islam: A Historical and Personal Testimony by a Black Muslim.* Gainesville: University Press of Florida.

"Wilkins Goes All-Out Against Black Studies." 1969. *Muhammad Speaks*, January 24.

Wilma, Ann. 1962. "What Have You Taught Your Child Today." *Muhammad Speaks*, February.

Woodford, John. 1993. "Messaging the Black Man." In *Voices from the Underground: Insider Histories of the Vietnam Era Underground Press*, edited by Ken L. Wachsberger, 191–198. Tempe, AZ.: Mica Press.

Woodford, John. 2009. Personal correspondence with author, May 22. Ann Arbor, MI.

Wyse, Iris. 1968a. "Letter to the Editor." *Black Panther Intercommunal News*, September 14.

———. 1968b. "Black Students Union's Statewide Convention." *Black Panther Intercommunal News*, November 2

X, Malcolm, and Alex Haley. 1992. *Autobiography of Malcolm X: As Told to Alex Haley.* New York: Ballantine.

"Young Sons of Minister Karriem Hassan and Rochman, Pick Out Words in Muhammad Speaks newspaper." 1965. *Muhammad Speaks*, October 1.

"Youth Make the Revolution." 1969. *Black Panther Intercommunal News*, August 9.

Zane, Jeffrey, and Judson Jeffries. 2010. "A Panther Sighting in the Pacific Northwest." In *On the Ground: The Black Panther Party in Communities Across America*, edited by Judson Jeffries, 41–95. Jackson: University Press of Mississippi.

ABOUT THE AUTHOR

Khuram Hussain is an assistant professor in the Department of Education at Hobart and William Smith Colleges. Hussain completed his doctoral degree in the cultural foundations of education at Syracuse University. His recent publications include "On the Charter Question: Black Marxism and Black Nationalism" in *Race, Ethnicity and Education* (2014) and "Against the 'Primers of White Supremacy': The Radical Black Press in the Cause of Multicultural History" in *American Educational History Journal* (2014). His current scholarship explores the radical origins of multicultural education and the contemporary grassroots resistance to neoliberal school reform. Hussain would like to thank Hobart and William Smith Colleges for their generous research support and research assistant Jennifer Abrams for her patient aid in scouring the archives.

CHAPTER 7

LEARNING THE UNDERGROUND

Plastic Childhood and Popular Culture

Marek Tesar

INTRODUCTION

This chapter argues for the importance of considering childhood resistance against the hegemonic discourse through popular culture. It argues that not only the documented adult underground movement resisted the Communist system in Czechoslovakia in the 1970s and 1980s, copying and working with ideas and popular culture that were recognized as mainstream in the West, but also childhood undergrounds, arising through connections with childhoods and childhood popular culture. This Western, in particular American and British, popular culture, strongly embodied in music, influenced the construction of a social, cultural, and political underground in Communist Czechoslovakia. Music had a productive power that infused the underground movement. Underlying this chapter is the infamous story of the Czechoslovak underground band Plastic People of the Universe (which played music inspired by Lou Reed, The Fugs, and Frank

Learning the Left: Popular Culture, Liberal Politics, and Informal Education from 1900 to the Present, pp. 111–127
Copyright © 2015 by Information Age Publishing

Zappa) and its artistic director Ivan Martin Jirous, who was known in dissident circles by the name of Psycho (Magor in the original, translated as Psycho by Vaughan 2009). Psycho's story of being "political" was performed through "disturbing the peace" of the quiet life in Czechoslovakia in the 1970s and 1980s, both through underground music and through texts for children. The Plastic People of The Universe were one of the most important proponents of the underground, challenging the system's stability by not conforming to the established ways, but at the same time producing and elevating a certain culture. This group, alongside others, was punished by the system for undermining the social contract and the status quo pursued by the Communist government. At the heart of the Plastic People of the Universe's existence lies the embodiment of American rock and roll and anti-establishment sentiments, while their cultural and political importance lies in the premise that the underground culture became important to intellectuals and philosophers. In a *Foucauldian* sense (Foucault 2003), this underground was responsible for the ascendance of subjugated knowledges. In the 1970s it became clear to dissident intellectuals that citizens were imprisoned not for challenging communism per se, but for challenging its performance—for "disturbing the peace" of the system. Such disturbance was caused by those who were different: for performing a certain culture, singing in English, having long hair, and confronting the desired notions and ideals of the Communist society. Therefore, this movement became an inspiration for the establishment and signing of Charter 77, a seminal act of resistance and underground political opposition to the Communist governance in Czechoslovakia, led by Vaclav Havel and Jan Patocka (and overseas it inspired charter 88 in Britain, charter 97 in Belarus, and charter 08 in China).

The theoretical grounding of this chapter is located within Jirous' (2006) seminal text that depicted a "third culture" and that theorized about the importance of pop culture such as the infusion and transformation of Western music into the Czechoslovak underground movement. Through this lens, this chapter will follow the tensions between the dominant and subjugated discourses, as the once forbidden underground band Plastic People of the Universe created a space and place of possibilities for a political underground in Czechoslovakia. In 1990, after the fall of the Berlin Wall, the story of this band culminates in then-Czechoslovak president Havel naming Frank Zappa as the consultant for the government on trade, cultural matters, and tourism, and later on as a cultural attaché. The Plastic People of the Universe became part of the dominant discourse. The messages of this chapter are thus multifaceted. They include a recognition of: the importance of popular culture in forming political thought; the complexities of youth and childhoods in relation to popular culture; problematizing what it means to be political and enacting notions of resistance through popular culture; and the importance of recognizing the subjugated discourse of resistant culture and its transformation into the dominant discourse in the course of historical development.

However, the core of this chapter follows the less-known aspect of this historic genealogical performance and story: Communist childhoods. Much has been written about the importance of American popular culture in Czechoslovakia and of the art of resistance (Blažek and Pospíšil 2010; Juzl 1996; Mitchell 1992; Rakova 2010; Ramet 1994; Vanicek 1997). This chapter's original contribution is the trickle-down effect of these stories and of the imprisonment of Jirous (Magor/Psycho) and his writing of children's stories that became the subjugated knowledge of the childhood underground. Psycho wrote these stories from prison and they became some of the most important *samizdat* (underground) publications for children. Similarly, his band was the most influential underground musical performance of resistance to the brutal Communist system. The link between the adult and child is particularly important. What was happening in the gatherings of adults, was in a certain way mirrored in childhood activities, where resistance to the prescribed stories represented the performance of childhood rebel subjectivities.

THE PRAGUE SPRING AND THE DISCOURSE OF NORMALIZATION

To set the scene, this chapter will firstly contextualize how the social and political situation in Czechoslovakia changed in the late 1960s. This period is referred to as the Prague Spring and is often portrayed by citizens as a romantic period of change and hope (Měchýř 1999; Williams 1997). The Prague Spring was important because during a short period of time different conditions for citizens arose through shifts in government agencies and edicts (Albright 1976; Karabel 1995). For example, censorship was lifted, foreign thinkers were published, and new ideas, books, and films were drafted and produced. In schools and universities, themes and topics that had previously been unimaginable and kept in silence were being openly discussed. Topics that had been added to curricula in the 1950s as part of direct Communist government propaganda were removed or ignored, including items in children's texts and magazines. It became easier for students to get scholarships for overseas study in Western countries, and newspapers openly criticized the governing agencies (Friday 2010; Renner 1989; Šimečka 1984; Windsor and Roberts 1969). Citizens recall this period as very romantic, colorful, and hopeful. They experienced freedom of the press, free expressions in art forms, and the freedom to travel. Students were part of public discussions, and the country was no longer isolated from its traditional influences, such as from countries like West Germany or France. For students, and all citizens, Western destinations like London, Vienna, Switzerland, and West Germany were suddenly closer than they had thought.

The Communist government and its public figures attempted to shift the country toward the so-called "socialism with a human face" (Ekiert 1996). Some academics claim that reforms by the Communist Party in the late 1960s that further loosened the grip of Stalinism and led to the Prague Spring did not intend to change the leading position of the party (Alan and Petrusek 1996; Měchýř 1999). Nevertheless, the party made some substantial changes in the way the country was run, one of the most critical being the abandonment of the censorship law (Gruša 1992; Tomášek 1994). To give up censorship meant to give up a form of control over citizens, over what they could read, see and experience. Once censorship was abandoned, people felt free to discuss and challenge the hegemonic ideas that formed the system. With state censorship gone, it seemed that anything could happen.

This anomaly of freedom in a totalitarian country did not last long, and the consequences for citizens and children were severe. The reaction to the Prague Spring from the Eastern Bloc (led by the Soviet Union) was harsh, brutal, and it shattered Czechoslovak society's idealism about the recent changes. When the armies of the Warsaw Pact, fronted by Soviet tanks, arrived in Prague in late August 1968, it shocked all citizens, including Communist Party officials, army representatives, teachers, artists, and workers. Citizens, such as my parents, often reflect on those late summer days, and how there was nothing their generation could have done differently. Purges in the party and society followed the 1968 events. Citizens' places and spaces changed, as Timothy Ash satirically notes:

> That window cleaner over there—his thesis was on Wittgenstein. Ask your waiter about Kafka—before his trial, he lectured on *The Trial*. Yes, the night watchman is reading Aristotle. Your coal will be delivered by the ordained priest of the Czech brethren. Kiss the milkman's ring: he is your bishop. (Ash 1991, 56–57)

For Ash, a scholar studying Central-Eastern Europe under Communist governance, Czechoslovakia became like a "lake permanently covered by a thick layer of ice ... politics, and indeed the whole of public life, is a matter of such supreme indifference" (Ash 1991, 57). But under this metaphorical ice, within the lake, everything and everybody moved in a certain form of resistance, while above, on the surface, there was peace and quiet. So as the Prague Spring was crushed, so was the whole nation: the system changed, life became distorted, relationships were altered, and the country slowly transformed into what became known as a post-totalitarian society (Havel 1985).

Havel's philosophical term "post-totalitarianism" represented the multitudes of power relations within the system, while acknowledging the complexities of all citizens' and children's living conditions under the control of the government agencies in the 1970s and 1980s. However, in scholarly and academic texts, this era is often referred to as an "era of normalization," which is used as more of an historical concept than a philosophical one, as it refers to the effect of the invasion by Warsaw Pact countries on Czechoslovakia during the Prague Spring (for example, see Ash 1991; Bren 2008; Žižek 2001). This event pushed citizens' lives to return to the so-called "normality" of life before the Prague Spring. Citizens lost their jobs because of the way they behaved during the Prague Spring or at the beginning of normalization, and often unskilled but loyal party members took on leadership positions (Kalinová 1999; Vančura 1999). Similarly, the education system changed, and childhoods were produced under conditions that attempted to return to the "normality" of the pre-Prague Spring era (Měchýř 1999). The developments during the Prague Spring were complex, multiple, and free of censorship; they created a threat, a deviation in the form of a resistance to the governance of the political system. The term normalization thus suggested that the Prague Spring was not a viable option for the governing agencies in the post-totalitarian era. Purges, tightened regulations, and censorship were the main techniques of a government that attempted to maintain a state of what normalization required—a return to the era prior to the Prague Spring (Gruša 1992).

The term normalization thus points to the 1970s and 1980s as the time of returning to what was considered to be the norm by governing agencies, before the Prague Spring. This chapter does not argue against using the term normalization per se, as it is an important label representing the vein of government agencies in the 1970s, and the desperation behind the use of power to turn relationships, developments, and peoples' lives back by a decade. In this time citizens and children removed themselves from public life. This opting out of public participation, and therefore withdrawing into private life, removed the need for intervention by government agencies and educational institutions. On the surface, these seemed to be less complicated times, where one could retreat into the private sphere to ignore so-called Socialist political, educational, and cultural developments.

So while the term normalization conceptualizes the essence of how government agencies behaved in all areas of public life, including education, it does not capture the shift in power relations, spheres of influence, and the subversiveness of the new system (Kusý 1985). For this reason, this chapter follows Havel and refers to this period as "post-totalitarianism," while the mainstream historical, political, and public discourse refers to it as normalization (Šimečka 1984).

DISTURBING THE PEACE

Some citizens opposed the post-totalitarian hegemony both in public and private forums. Those citizens who did so in public, and therefore actively engaged in the resistance—in the sense of parrhesia (Foucault 2001)—risked punishment from the governing agencies (Alan 2001; Pilař 1999). Dissidents thus opposed the post-totalitarian system intending to produce cracks in its everyday panorama. Havel argued that one does not become a dissident …

> … just because you decide one day to take up this most unusual career. You are thrown into it by your personal sense of responsibility, combined with a complex set of external circumstances. You are cast out of the existing structures and placed in a position of conflict with them. It begins as an attempt to do your work well, and ends with being branded an enemy of society. (Havel 1985, 63)

To follow Havel's argument, resistant discourses created cracks in the post-totalitarian panorama, and disturbed the peace of everyday life. "Disturbing the peace" was an offense, equaling in its mildest forms what in Western countries was labeled as hooliganism, and in its stronger forms, the equivalent of treason. If found guilty of committing this offense, the citizen was arrested and imprisoned for disturbing "the artificial peace of the post-totalitarian construct" (Wilson 1990, viii). The offense of disturbing the peace was considered to be any action that directly challenged the government's attempt to restore order in Czechoslovakia after the Prague Spring. This disturbance took many forms, such as distributing information, literature, music or news through radio broadcasts from and into Czechoslovakia. One of the most powerful ways that a counterculture or literary parallel polis operated was through the dissemination and circulation of self-published literature among citizens (Machovec 2005, 2008). Such "underground" publications were often referred to as *samizdats*. Cory Taylor (2009) portrayed how citizens reflected on their desire to read samizdats, stating that they felt that they must represent something of interest and of a subversive quality if some citizens went to such a dangerous effort to produce and distribute these texts.

What it meant to be a dissident distributing samizdat was extensively discussed by the Soviet dissident Vladimir Bukovsky (1978), as he outlined the experience of being a samizdat author: writing it, editing it, censoring it, publishing it, and getting arrested and imprisoned for it. To publish, distribute, and engage with samizdats, therefore, contained a certain element of danger. Citizens partaking in any aspects of the creation, distribution and possession of this homemade unofficial literature were severely punished. In the Czechoslovak context, Milan Šimečka describes the concept of how government agencies labeled samizdat:

> When they carry out house searches in Czechoslovakia, they are not looking for weapons, secret printing presses, duplicators, membership lists of secret societies, plans for overthrowing the government, or suchlike. You will not find anything of that sort in [a] Czechoslovak intellectual's home. What they are looking for is what they call "offensive literature." (Šimečka 1984, 96)

Children became everyday dissidents in their private lives. They were not dissidents in the sense of disseminating a counterculture in order to undermine the post-totalitarian system, like adult dissidents. In the private domain children experienced being everyday dissidents through their specific play, toys, experiences, and the stories within their "childhood underground." The private domains of childhoods were produced as dissident rebel subjectivities through the stories they shared about their experiences outside of the hegemonic space of the kindergarten.

The notion that there are spaces of childhood, with their own play, rules, and experiences, which challenge the dominant discourse, was not exclusive to the post-totalitarian context. Children's cultures have been observed across societies, cultures, and ideologies (Christensen and James 2008; James and Prout 1997). Furthermore, Henry Jenkins' (1993) research illustrated children's play was based on television that challenged adults, while others directly referred to childhood undergrounds (Knapp and Knapp 1976; Tucker 1995). Seminal work in this area was carried out by Max Van Manen and Bas Levering (1996), who argued that there are many forms of secrets in childhood, and other studies also referred to the importance of secrets in children's lives (Haynes 2005; Sturm 2008). Similarly, William A. Corsaro (2005) uses the terms peer culture and subculture to outline organized childhoods, mainly as they challenge adult authority. Therefore, stories and fairy tales that help form the childhood underground had a power that subverted the dominant discourse (Zipes 2006).

What constituted subversion in the post-totalitarian era was not that different from what it meant in Western countries, or within a neo-liberal ideology, but it was specific within its manifestations. Perhaps the best example was portrayed in literature, television shows, and plays that were considered as mainstream in Western childhoods. In the post-totalitarian context they fell into such categories as secret play, subversive notions, counter culture, and childhood undergrounds. These stories and experiences in post-totalitarian childhoods were governed by desires for alternative stories and games.

PSYCHO FOR KIDS

Samizdats for children were a specific genre of underground literature. Many studies have categorized these publications for children and explored their role in the literary and cultural discourse of Czechoslovakia (for instance, see Kovalčík 1993; Kubešová 1998; Prečan 1992; Přibáň 1993; Urbanová 1993). One of the most distinctive writers of children's stories was Ivan Jirous known under his pseudonym "Psycho." As mentioned above, Psycho was the artistic director of the underground art-rock band Plastic People of the Universe, who collaborated with the philosopher Egon Bondy. The band's famous work was released as an almost 60-page, LP sized booklet for the album *Egon Bondy's Happy Hearts Club Banned*. Due to his activities Psycho spent much of the late 1970s and 1980s in prison, and was one of the figures that inspired Havel to draft the dissident manifesto, Charter 77 (Palouš 1993).

Psycho's collection of poetry for children, *Psycho for Kids* (*Magor dětem* in the original), is currently considered to be an important piece of literature and was recently republished in the Czech Republic, both as a book and as an audio book. While it is extremely popular with some children and adults, others question its appropriateness due to its allegedly inappropriate themes. It was originally intended for children of preschool age; however, it is now considered more appropriate for older children at a primary school level (Vaughan 2009).

Psycho's book of poetry was conceptualized under extremely difficult conditions. Psycho was charged with crimes of subversion and disturbing the peace and was imprisoned for almost eight years in total. When Psycho went to jail, his daughter Františka was 18 months old and his other daughter Marta was only six months old. In the high-security prison where he was incarcerated, visitors were allowed only once every 10 months for 1-hour conversations, with no physical contact was allowed. Psycho's inability to hold and hug his daughters pushed him to write stories and poetry in his letters to his wife, Juliana, and he asked her to read them to Františka and Marta (Mlejnek 2005). These poems were intended to stay private, as correspondence from a parent to a child. They were not intended for public consumption, and they would never have been officially published in the post-totalitarian era, since they expressed values and ideas that were incompatible with the policies of socialist realism (Čáslavová 2006; Šámal 2009). The task of sending his letters from prison to his family was not easy:

The whole time [in prison] I did not have any other contact with my daughters than poems and fairy tales. And even that was extremely hard. I've written a long poem about ghosts, but it was censored and I was not allowed to send it. ... Finally I reached agreement with the prison censors. I was allowed to write three verses per letter. (Mlejnek 2005)

Psycho was allowed to send one letter every three weeks, and he found a way to smuggle more writing for his children out to them. Psycho's wife Juliana read each one of them to their children as stories to be continued, until the next letter arrived. At that time, Psycho experienced himself as a mythological creature, unable to have any relationship with his daughters, not knowing who they were or what they liked to do or not do (Rulf 1999). Psycho's poetry from this long period spent in prison (1982–1986) fulfilled a spiritual, educational, and absurd role in his relationship with his children. Prison rules stated that one could only write about private and not public matters, and Psycho commented on this rule of censorship in prison:

Can there be something more private than talking with your own children? Maybe I would have written more poetry or fairy tales, if I could have sent more at once. As it was it took a very long time before Františka and Marta could hear these stories in their entirety. It was concrete writing for concrete children. It was funny when these stories started to spread amongst dissidents. When parents came with their children to my place, they were looking at my daughters Františka and Marta with their eyes on stalks, as for them they were like Cinderella or Little Red Riding Hood. (Rulf 1999)

Scary Creatures and Super Creeps

Some of Psycho's stories were intimate goodnight lullabies that he wrote to his daughters, while others openly represented spiritual beliefs that were absent from public publications in the post-totalitarian society. For example, in the poem "The Clouds Asked the Sky," Psycho's clumsily rhyming verses, using his own children as main characters, state: "Ask Františka/why do cats have a moustache/and Františka will answer/God created them like that" (Jirous 2009, 9). The direct reference to God was allowed to pass in this private letter as the prison censors would treat this as a private matter, but these stories, captured in these letters, would most likely not have been published officially because of these references to God. In another poem "Good Night Lullaby," Psycho writes the following lines to his children:

Good night my beloved Františka, let's cover your tummy with your duvet/ the hens are already all asleep, the wind is silent, the clouds are asleep/little beetles are hidden under the leaves/only angels are up, to guide you in the night/on breath-inhaled cloud, good night, my darling. (Jirous 2009, 6)

The purely private story from a father to his children resonated among other children and their families and became increasingly popular in the underground of the post-totalitarian society. Spirituality and mythical creatures were not encouraged in public children's publications, which were guided by Socialist realism. Psycho's stories represented the personal and the individual, and did not relate to the collective, shining and happy outcomes of public childhoods. The texts outlined the everyday melancholy of a father missing his children, such as in the poem "Trees Are Undressing," where Psycho creates metaphorical connections that were not commonly present in public children's magazines such as *Little Bee*: "Trees are undressing, like you, Františka, before you go to bed" (Jirous 2009, 19). These stories were very attractive for children and their parents as they contained traces of the absurdity represented by fanciful content not present in the usual everyday stories that children faced. The realism of stories in the Communist system contained writing that was expected to be clear, explicit, non-elitist, and, therefore, understandable for everyone, while children enjoyed the nonsense in samizdat stories.

These fairy tales and poems were different from the stories published in *Little Bee* in a number of ways. There were no workers, no collective or bright and positive future childhoods as in the official literature. These stories were about individual relationships, which represented the stories parents would share with a child in the privacy of their home. There were clumsy rhymes, supernatural beings, and adult-like language, such as in the poem about two (not so) scary creatures: Tululum and Šmudle. These supernatural beings talked with each other: "When you were very young, we were planting egg shells/Now we should check if the eggs are ready to harvest" (Jirous 2009, 38). The absurd sense of humor and education that children gained about life from Psycho was evident in a poem where "Roosters are stuck in the bottlenecks, they look out through the hole in the grate/whether they are naughty or shy, Františka sees them all/ Františka will put all the roosters into the cone" (Jirous, 8). While in another, Psycho proudly connects himself with the movement of absurdity and word-play, as he concludes "Little girls will think/that their dad has written them only nonsense" (Jirous, 30). The private resistant discourse of these notions in Psycho's poems, challenged the hegemonic public discourse of safe official published stories for children in the Communist system.

The story "Marta Was Asking Františka" presented horror themes based on folk traditions as a pedagogical tool to educate his children from a distance. In the story, as Marta and Františka were falling asleep, they wondered: "Do we have the door closed? Won't the ghosts come in? Outside there is a thick darkness" (Jirous 2009, 21). Both little girls were afraid of ghosts and scary creatures and feared that they might appear and surprise them: "And doesn't some sneaky ghost want to appear from the well?" (Jirous). The girls first thought they would have so much fun instead of sleeping, but then the ghost appeared and "with claws blue from the smalt, it reaches over the girls/girls did not make a 'peep', they closed their eyes and slept straight away/the Ghost said: 'Lucky you', and disappeared like a raindrop" (Jirous 2009, 24). The story of a father that could not be with or teach his children was dispersed through these private stories.

Unlike official stories published in preschool magazines, Psycho's writing included witches, ghosts, and scary creatures, although they were not necessarily portrayed as negative or malicious beings. In these private stories, such characters often played roles representing neither the good nor the bad; were occasionally funny and sometimes scary; and were seen as normal, everyday, and important parts of life. Psycho's stories did not bring promises of happy endings, but analyzed and emphasized the fragility of relationships within the private discourse. Such ambiguous characters, as those which Psycho assigned to the protagonists in his stories, were important, as the official, dominant discourse for children of preschool age represented them only scarcely, and from a narrow, negative perspective. Svatava Urbanová (2003) interpreted this presence of scary creatures in Psycho's writings, saying that "children of dissidents were led to overcome the fear, because more than to fear the fairy tales creatures, they learnt to fear the impacts of the power of the government" (113). Psycho's fairy tales in which ghosts or dwarfs appear while children are asleep, were the most popular among children (Jirous 1997).

The Bottle of Rum

Psycho's samizdat fairy tales dealt with other subversive subjects that preschool children were not exposed to through official stories, such as alcohol. In the plot of "Another Fairy Tale for Františka," Psycho tells of an old witch living in a bottle, cooking pea soup, who invites the Evening Star for dinner. The Evening Star advises the witch that the soup would be much better if it contained more rum. They add rum to the soup, and then drink some more before dinner, and both happily sing together: "The whole house can be empty, but always have rum on the shelf! / You can live without flour, you can live without pepper / but the bottle from the shelf must always stare at you, believe me!" (Jirous 2009, 16). Then they eat the pea soup, but they do not realize that scary creatures are not allowed to eat anything green, or round, and they start to blow up, until the bottle breaks and the fairy tale is over. Psycho added the moral for his children at the very end: "So remember Františka, that what is good for ladybugs, like aphids, is not necessarily good for little girls, and what is good for little girls, like a pea, is not good for scary creatures. Good night!" (16). When this story first reached Psycho's family in his letter from prison, Juliana, Psycho's wife, said that after she had read this story to Františka and Marta, she had to go to the store to buy rum, because the children refused to be at home unless it was there (Rulf 1999).

The samizdat edition of the children's book *Psycho for Kids* was released as a collection of his poems and stories from prison, and Psycho's stories circulated among the children of his fellow dissidents and friends, who were used to being among adults who drank alcohol, smoked, and behaved in a way that government agencies warned children about. These adults and parents read the book with their children, or they read it to groups of children. Such stories produced a discourse where children could think about themselves and their childhoods in different ways than those produced by *Little Bee* and the public images of childhood. The private discourse provided them with fresh ideas that they did not otherwise think about, such as what might happen to naughty children: "Naughty dog gets to be tied up, naughty roosters get their beaks twisted/and the cats will put noses of naughty kittens into smelly pee/but the worst I will tell last/naughty children will be put into the pot!" (Jirous 2009, 27). Stories like these produced the rebel childhood subjectivities, of children imagining themselves beyond the dichotomy of a victim and a supporter of the post-totalitarian system (Havel 1985).

In addition to Psycho's stories for children that subverted the texts that children experienced (in kindergartens and in the official literature, in the themes they pursued and in text structures), the illustrations and their overarching messages were also subversive. The title illustration of *Psycho for Kids* was frightening and its childish drawing evoked an image of something between the silhouette of a child, a tree, and a ghost. Psycho's fairy tales carried themes of a strong spiritual connection to Czechoslovakia, to folk tales and to nature, contesting the dominant discourse in which children lived and grew up. In kindergartens and schools, children learned how to desire to become faithful young citizens and to have an unconditional love for the Socialist homeland and its governing rationalities. Psycho's stories challenged these desires through the use of language that children did not hear publicly, through clumsy but attractive verse structures, and through the scary, but sincerely caring nature of his stories. Another difference between these stories and the official ones was the element of unpredictability. By listening to the topics and themes of Psycho's stories, such as alcohol and separation from the family, children were confronted with different experiences that challenged the way they thought about themselves, and their childhoods. Hegemonic and resistant discourses contained stories that carried moral messages aimed at shaping positive, orderly childhoods. Resistant stories, however, encouraged positions of rebellion and possibility.

CONCLUDING COMMENTS: PSYCHO'S LEGACY

The censorship department of the prison considered Psycho's letters containing poems and fairy tales and determined that they could be sent out to his family only under certain conditions. As these stories were intended to stay private, they did not concern the government agency, and they therefore had relatively limited sanctions imposed on them. Psycho would never be able to have his poetry for children published in the official, post-totalitarian publishing house, as he was already labeled as an unsuitable writer or, as an official government agency stated, a writer of offensive literature (Jirous 1997). Moreover, from the perspective of the hegemonic literary discourse of Socialist realism, Psycho's stories contained incorrect rhymes, spiritual connotations, horror, absurdity, and silly humor, all of which were not accepted as appropriate themes for children's literature. They were not part of the official Socialist realism in which all official literature had to be placed (Marčok 2004; Stanislavová 2010).

To analyze the importance of Psycho's stories on the way children experienced their own childhoods, it is necessary to briefly explore Psycho's relationship with the dominant discourse. Psycho presented the following argument in the 1970s, outlining the tension between public and private spaces, and between the dominant and the resistant discourse, along similar lines to Vaclav Benda's (1991) parallel polis:

> The purpose of the underground in our country is to create a second culture. A culture that is independent of the official communistic channels, public appreciation and hierarchy of values, and of how the establishment rules with it. A culture, which cannot have the destruction of the establishment as an aim, because that would mean becoming part of the establishment. (Jirous 1997, 197)

The government agencies were concerned with Psycho's radical ideas published in the samizdat. The tension caused by Psycho's writing in post-totalitarian Czechoslovakia, where the government agencies allowed a certain amount of private autonomy, but controlled and carefully policed the public domain, peaked when his personal stories were published as samizdats at home and abroad, creating a crack in the panorama of everyday life.

Therefore, whether by an underground rock band or a private lullaby, childhoods are shaped by the political public culture as well as by private experiences of resistant culture. This chapter is an analysis of the importance of the culture influenced by the music that was popular in America in the late 1960s and 1970s through a trickle-down effect, and the way that its expansion behind the Iron Curtain influenced the formation of resistant political movements. It has uncovered unexpected historical and cultural connections between pop culture, politics, and childhoods. Children became "the youngest Plastics," following the trickle-down theory, and were the embodiment of rebellious acts inspired by the popular culture. Most importantly, Psycho's stories for children were shared among families, and the children who listened to these stories and other tales that subverted the officially produced and disseminated stories, became the students of 1989. They had their turn at contesting the post-totalitarian governing agencies at that time.

REFERENCES

Alan, Jozef. 2001. "Alternativní kultura jako sociologické téma" [Alternative culture as a sociological topic]. In *Alternativní kultura. Příběh české společnosti 1945–1989*, edited by Jozef Alan, 9–59. Prague, Czech Republic: Nakladatelství Lidové noviny.

Alan, Jozef, and Miloslav Petrusek. 1996. "*Sociologie, literatura a politika*" [Sociology, literature and politics]. Prague, Czech Republic: Karolinum.

Albright, Madeleine K. 1976. "The Role of the Press in Political Change: Czechoslovakia 1968." PhD diss., Columbia University.

Ash, Timothy G. 1991. *The Uses of Adversity*. Cambridge, England: Granta Books.

Benda, Vaclav. 1991. "The Parallel '*Polis.*'" In *Civic Freedom in Central Europe: Voices from Czechoslovakia*, edited by Gordon H. Skilling and Paul Wilson, 35–41. London: Macmillan.

Blažek, Petr, and Filip Pospíšil. 2010. " '*Vraťte nám vlasy!*': První máničky, vlasatci a hippies v komunistickém Československu." Prague, Czech Republic: Academia.

Bren, Paula. 2008. "Mirror, Mirror, on the Wall ... Is the West the Fairest of Them All?: Czechoslovak Normalization and Its (Dis)contents." *Kritika: Explorations in Russian and Eurasian History* 9 (4): 831–854.

Bukovsky, Vladimir. 1978. "*To Build a Castle: My Life as a Dissenter.*" New York: Viking.

Čáslavová, Petra. 2006. "Básnické dílo Ivana M. Jirouse: Vývoj poetiky" [Poetic work, Ivan M. Jirous: evolution of poetics]. BA diss., Masarykova University.

Christensen, Pia H., and Alison James, eds. 2008. *Research with Children: Perspectives and Practices*. New York: Routledge.

Corsaro, William A. 2005. *The Sociology of Childhood*. London: Sage.

Ekiert, Grzegorz. 1996. *The State Against Society: Political Crises and Their Aftermath in East Central Europe*. Princeton, NJ: Princeton University Press.

Foucault, Michel. 2001. *Fearless Speech*. Los Angeles: MIT Press.

———. 2003. *Society Must Be Defended: Lectures at the Collège de France (1975–1976)*. New York: Picador.

Friday, Julia. 2010. "Czechoslovakia from the Prague Spring to the Velvet Revolution: The Composition of Memory, Public Record and Archive." PhD diss., State University of New York.

Gruša, Jiri. 1992. *Cenzura a literární* život *mimo masmédia* (Censorship and literary life outside the mass media). Prague, Czechoslovakia: Ústav pro soudobé dějiny ČSAV [The institute for contemporary history of the Czech academy of sciences].

Havel, Vaclav. 1985. "The Power of the Powerless." In *The Power of the Powerless: Citizens Against the State in Central-Eastern Europe*, edited by John Keane, 23–96. London: Hutchinson.

Haynes, Joanna. 2005. "Secrets and Boundaries in Classroom Dialogues with Children: From Critical Episode to Social Enquiry." *Childhood and Philosophy* 1 (2).

James, Alison, and Alan Prout, eds. 1997. *Constructing and Reconstructing Childhood: Contemporary Issues in the Sociological Study of Childhood*. London: Falmer Press.

Jenkins, Henry. 1993. " 'Going Bonkers!': Children, Play and Pee-wee." In *Male Trouble*, edited by Constance Penly and Sharon Willis, 157–182. Minneapolis: University of Minnesota Press.

Jirous, Ivan. 1997. *Magorův zápisník* (Magorův Notebook). Prague, Czech Republic: Torst.

———. 2006. "Report on the Third Czech Musical Revival." In *Views from the Inside— Czech Underground Literature and Culture 1948–1989: Manifestoes, Testimonies, Documents*, edited by Martin Machovec, 7–31. Prague, Czech Republic: University Karlovy.

———. 2009. *Magor dětem* (Crazy kids). Prague, Czech Republic: Torst.

Juzl, Milos. 1996. "Music and the Totalitarian Regime in Czechoslovakia." *International Review of the Aesthetics and Sociology of Music* 27 (1).

Kalinová, Lenka. 1999. *K sociálním dějinám Československa v letech 1969-1989*. Prague, Czech Republic: Vysoká škola Ekonomická.

Karabel, Jerome. 1995. "The Revolt of the Intellectuals: The Prague Spring and the Politics of Reform Communism." *Research in Social Movements, Conflicts and Change* 18: 93–143.

Knapp, Mary, and Herbert Knapp. 1976. *One Potato, Two Potato: The Secret Education of American Children*. New York: W.W. Norton.

Kovalčík, Zdenek. 1993. "Biblické adaptace pro děti" [Bibilical adaptation for children]. In *Literatura pro děti a mládež v samizdatu a exilu*, edited by Vera Vařejková, 15–21. Brno, Czech Republic: Masarykova University.

Kubešová, Martina. 1998. "Literatura pro děti a mládež v samizdatu a exilu v letech 1948–1989." MA diss., Karlova University.

Kusý, Miroslav. 1985. "Chartism and 'Real Socialism.' " In *The Power of the Powerless: Citizens against the State in Central-Eastern Europe*, edited by John Keane, 152–178. London: Hutchinson.

Machovec, Martin. 2005. "The Types and Functions of Samizdat Publications in Czechoslovakia in 1948–1989." Paper presented at The Slavic Department Spring Research Symposium, University of Pennsylvania.

————. 2008. *Pohledy zevnitř: Česká undergroundová kultura ve svědectvích, dokumentech a interpretacích* [Views from the inside: an underground culture in the Czech Repulbic reports, documents, and interpretations]. Prague, Czech Republic: Pistorius & Olšanská.

Marčok, Viliam. 2004. *Dejiny slovenskej literatúry III* [History of Slovak literature III]. Bratislava, Slovakia: Literary Information Centre.

Měchýř, Jan. 1999. "Proměny společnosti v letech 1960–1989" [Transformation of Society in the Years 1960–1989]. In *Proč jsme v Listopadu vyšli do ulic*, edited by Jiri Vančura, 35–52. Brno, Czech Republic: Doplněk.

Mitchell, Tony. 1992. "Mixing Pop and Politics: Rock Music in Czechoslovakia before and after the Velvet Revolution." *Popular Music* 11 (2): 187–203.

Mlejnek, Josef. 2005. "Ivan Martin Jirous: Zmoudření dona Magora." *Týdeník Rozhlas*, (23). Retrieved from http://www.radioservis-as.cz/archiv05/2305/23titul.htm

Palouš, Martin. 1993. "Poznámky ke generačním sporům v Chartě 77 v druhé polovině osmdesátých let" [Comments to the disputes in the Charter 77 in the second half of the 1980s]. In *Dvě desetiletí před listopadem 89*, edited by Emanuel Mandler, 35–44. Prague, Czech Republic: Maxdorf.

Pilař, Martin. 1999. *Underground*. Brno, Czech Republic: Horst.

Prečan, Vilem. 1992. *Nezávislá literatura a samizdat v Československu 70. a 80.* [Independent literature and samizdat in Czechoslovakia]. Prague, Czechoslovakia: Ústav pro Soudobé Dějiny ČSAV.

Přibáň, Michal. 1993. "České exilové časopisy pro děti a mládež" [The Czech exile magazines for children and youth]. In *Literatura pro děti a mládež v samizdatu a exilu*, edited by Vera Vařejková, 25–27. Brno, Czech Republic: Masarykova University.

Rakova, Iva. 2010. "Czech Alternative Culture under Communism: Unofficial Music during the Period of 'Normalization.'" MA diss., University Palackeho.

Ramet, Sabrina P. 1994. *Rocking the State*. Boulder, CO: Westview Press.

Renner, Hans. 1989. *A History of Czechoslovakia since 1945*. London: Routledge.

Rulf, Jiri. 1999. "I labuť, i lúna: Magorova zimní meditace" [And swan, and lúna: Magorova winter meditation]. *Reflex* 10 (51): 20–23.

Šámal, Petr. 2009. "Jak se stát socialistickým realistou: Přepracované vydání sebe sama" [The literature of Socialist realism: the basis, structures and contexts of the totalitarian art]. In *Literatura socialistického realismu: Východiska, struktury a kontexty totalitního umění*, edited by Petr Šámal. Prague, 43–70. Czech Republic: Ústav pro Českou Literaturu AV ČR.

Šimečka, Milan. 1984. *The Restoration of Order the Normalization of Czechoslovakia*. London: Verso.

Stanislavová, Zuzana. 2010. *Dejiny slovenskej literatúry pre deti a mládež po roku 1960* [History of Czech literature for children and youth after 1960]. Bratislava, Slovakia: Literárne Informačné Centrum.

Sturm, Brian W. 2008. "Imaginary 'Geographies' of Childhood: School Library Media Centers as Secret Spaces." *Knowledge Quest* 36 (4): 46–53.

Taylor, Cory, director. 2009. *The Power of the Powerless*. Agora Productions.

Tomášek, Dusan. 1994. *Pozor, cenzurováno!: Aneb ze života soudružky cenzury* [Watch censored!: or the life of sisters of censorship]. Prague, Czech Republic: MV ČR.

Tucker, Elizabeth. 1995. "Tales and Legends." In *Children's Folklore: A Source Book*, edited by Brian Sutton-Smith, Jay Mechling, Thomas W. Johnson, and Felicia R. McMahon, 193–212. New York: Garland Publishing.

Urbanová, Svatava. 1993. "Literatura pro děti v samizdatu a exilu" [Literature for children in samizdat and exile]. In *Literatura pro děti a mládež v samizdatu a exilu*, edited by Vera Vařejková, 7–14. Brno, Czech Republic: Masarykova University.

Urbanová, Svatava. 2003. *Meandry a metamorfózy dětské literatury* [Meanders and metamorphosis of children's literature]. Olomouc, Czech Republic: Votobia.

Vanicek, Anna. 1997. "Passion Play: Underground Rock Music in Czechoslovakia, 1968-1989." MA diss., York University.

Vančura, Jiri. 1999. "Občan a totalitní stát" [Citizen and a totalitarian state]. In *Proč jsme v listopadu vyšli do ulic*, edited by Jiri Vančura, 77–96. Brno, Czech Republic: Doplněk.

Van Manen, Max, and Levering, Bas. 1996. *Childhood's Secrets: Intimacy, Privacy and the Self Reconsidered*. New York, NY: Columbia University.

Vaughan, David. 2009. "Psycho for Kids and Baby Punk: Czech Children's Writing since 1989." Retrieved from http://www.radio.cz/en/section/books/psycho-for-kids-and-baby-punk-czech-childrens-writing-since-1989.

Williams, Kieran. 1997. *The Prague Spring and Its Aftermath: Czechoslovak Politics, 1968-1970*. Cambridge, England: Cambridge University Press.

Wilson, Paul. 1990. "Introduction." In *Disturbing the Peace: A Conversation with Karel Hvížďala*, edited by Vaclav Havel, xi–xvii. New York: Random House.

Windsor, Philip, and Adam Roberts. 1969. *Czechoslovakia, 1968: Reform, Repression and Resistance*. London: Chatto and Windus.

Zipes, Jack D. 2006. *Fairy Tales and the Art of Subversion*. New York: Taylor and Francis.

Žižek, Slavoj. 2001. *Did Somebody Say Totalitarianism?: Five Interventions in the (Mis) use of a Notion*. London, UK: Verso.

ABOUT THE AUTHOR

Marek Tesar is a lecturer in childhood studies and early childhood education at the Faculty of Education at the University of Auckland. His focus is on the history, philosophy, and sociology of childhood. His research is concerned with the construction of childhoods and notions of the place and space of childhoods. He has published journal articles and book chapters in this area, and his doctorate on this topic received prestigious national and international awards.

CHAPTER 8

BOOKS ARE WEAPONS IN THE WAR OF IDEAS

Educational Reform in Popular Texts

Richard Ognibene

In 1942, the U.S. Office of War Information created a poster proclaiming that "Books are Weapons in the War of Ideas;" its purpose was to promote the publication and distribution of books representing American ideals as expressed in that era (Jenyum 2010). The central image of the poster was a drawing of a Nazi book burning activity next to a Franklin Delano Roosevelt quote noting that ideals related to freedom of expression in books cannot be destroyed by fire; they are indestructible weapons in the war against tyranny. In recent years, there has been an education war raging in the United States, often evident through the medium of popular books. This chapter will examine three of those texts that could be viewed as weapons in that war. The discussion will begin with analyses of *Fire in the Ashes* by Jonathan Kozol (2012) and *How Children Succeed* by Paul Tough (2012). An assessment of the third book, *Reign of Error* by Diane Ravitch (2013), will conclude this chapter. I will show how Ravitch's book has played a significant role in launching and sustaining resistance to the strategies

Learning the Left: Popular Culture, Liberal Politics, and Informal Education from 1900 to the Present, pp. 129–151
Copyright © 2015 by Information Age Publishing
129

devised by corporate leaders to alter traditional American educational ideals and the institutions historically responsible for achieving them.

AN IDEOLOGICAL BATTLE:
JONATHAN KOZOL VERSUS PAUL TOUGH

Jonathan Kozol's *Fire in the Ashes* was published on August 28, 2012, and Paul Tough's *How Children Succeed* appeared one week later. In the book-selling world, Kozol's work had limited success. *Fire in the Ashes* was not reviewed in either the *New York Times* or the *Los Angeles Times*, and the *Washington Post* review was written by Wendy Kopp (2012), the founder of Teach for America whose views were known to be contrary to Kozol's. The absence of positive, influential reviews likely contributed to the less than robust sales. *Fire in the Ashes* never appeared on the *New York Times* bestseller list, which was also the fate of Kozol's previous book, *Letters to a Young Teacher*, published in 2007. Given Kozol's long history as a prominent social and educational reformer whose influential books won prizes, were bestsellers, and were connected to positive reform outcomes, his recent books in the education war were perhaps thought of as weapons that were firing blanks.

The contrast with Paul Tough's *How Children Succeed* is astonishing. Tough was a well-regarded journalist with the *New York Times* prior to the publication of this his second book. His first, *Whatever It Takes* (2009), was an account of Geoffrey Canada's Harlem Children's Zone. It was a thorough account of the problems and successes of Canada's work, but not a bestseller. Conversely, the hardcover version of *How Children Succeed* was on the bestselling/also-selling list for 30 weeks beginning in mid-September 2012 and was included on prominent notable booklists at the end of that year ("Hardcover Best Sellers" 2013; "100 Notable Books" 2013) The paperback version was released in July 2013 and remained on the bestselling list for nearly a year ("Paperback Best Sellers" 2014). It was no contest; in the 2012 battle of the books, Tough clearly had the upper hand. What accounts for Tough's commercial success compared to Kozol, and what does it reveal about the difficulty of transmitting liberal ideals to the general public?

Part of the answer must be that Kozol is old news. Between 1967 and 2007, Kozol published 12 books. *Fire in the Ashes*, his 13th, draws directly from his experiences and contacts originating in three of his prior books, *Rachel and Her Children* (1988), *Amazing Grace* (1995), and *Ordinary Resurrections* (2000). The goal of his new book was to address a question he says he was asked frequently: What happened to some of the families discussed in previous books? *Fire in the Ashes* is a book that tells extended and updated stories about a few of those families and a handful of those children. If one was a fan of Kozol's work, the themes of the new book were already familiar, and if not, there might have been disappointment that the stories lacked any sustained social analysis that attempted to explain the causes of the problematic circumstances in these people's lives. One should remember, however, that Kozol had previously documented and assessed the specific circumstances under which the children of the Mott Haven section of the South Bronx were educated. More generally, in *Savage Inequalities* (1991), he described and evaluated the educational consequences of underfunded schools, and in *The Shame of the Nation* (2005), he examined the negative consequence of classroom life for children enrolled in schools that were segregated by race, ethnicity, and class, compared to students living in affluent communities. Kozol was a gifted storyteller and wrote with what one commentator called a "lyrical outrage" (Olson 2008, 45), but the stories he told in *Fire in the Ashes* were insufficiently novel to generate substantial interest in the book.

Perhaps an even more significant explanation of Paul Tough's commercial success compared to Kozol was that the ideology that grounds Tough's book was related to the concepts and language that dominated contemporary educational debates. By way of contrast, Kozol transitioned from the life of a would-be novelist to that of a teacher, civil rights activist, and educational reformer in the mid-1960s and early 1970s, a time when dominant reform goals focused on creating equal opportunity for those oppressed by social class elites and the institutions they created to maintain the status quo. It was the era of civil rights, the war on poverty, feminism, multiculturalism, and efforts to mainstream those who were disabled. Kozol's notoriety after publishing *Death at an Early Age* in 1967, an expose of the racism he observed as a first-year teacher in a Boston public school, thrust him into the world of radical social and educational reform led by individuals like John Holt, Paul Goodman, Ivan Ilich, Paulo Freire, and others; it created a way of looking at the world that was different from the perspective one would ordinarily develop when living a privileged life, as he had during his youth. Kozol has fiercely held on to that 1960s perspective ever since.

Tough's book, on the other hand, was shaped by the prevailing conservative perspective that has grown in importance since the time of Ronald Reagan's presidency. It was a perspective that prefers private over public institutions and asserted that market-based choices would be the best ones for society as a whole. It also asserted that assuming personal responsibility was the key to overcoming unfavorable circumstances in one's life. In education, this translated into charter schools and teacher accountability so that citizens could freely choose to flee from public schools and their unionized teachers whose evaluations must be available for all to see to facilitate those choices. It meant that teaching character traits was a preferred solution to overcoming dysfunctional learning environments rather than spending money to eradicate the causes of the dysfunction. It meant starving public schools because they were too costly, even if it required using philanthropy to prop up private schools until the public ones became unsustainable because the taxes needed to support them were portrayed as wasteful and then withheld. These discussion parameters have become what Rebecca Goldstein, Sheila Macrine, and Nataly Chesky (2011) call the "new normal," that is, the way in which consolidated news media controlled by financial elites frame educational questions for the rest of the society to debate. In that context, Kozol's incessant clamoring for equity funding for public schools, his insistence that impoverished neighborhoods be helped to acquire the resources that enable residents to live dignified and productive lives, and his unwavering rejection of the use of standardized curriculum and testing to produce a competent workforce for the bottom rungs of the economic ladder, served to block his access to some venues that would enable him to proclaim his message beyond those people he had already convinced years ago.

A CRITIQUE OF TOUGH'S ANALYSIS

Without a doubt, Paul Tough's *How Children Succeed* was the major education book of the 2012–2013 school year. Tough's book tour included appearances before school groups, several of which indicated that they would examine the possibility of recasting their educational practices to include suggestions found in his book. Tough's thesis was that poor school performance was not primarily caused by unalterable cognitive deficits; it occured because students growing up in extreme poverty had many adverse childhood experiences that caused toxic stress resulting in neurological and chemical changes that crippled the area of the brain (prefrontal cortex) that controled their executive function capabilities. Executive function was necessary for short and long-term educational success, and included such elements as the ability to concentrate, to think abstractly, to focus for longer time periods, to follow directions, and to adapt to changing situations in pursuit of long-term goals. Tough's conclusions were that the effects of toxic stress could be lessened by a more secure attachment between the child and parent, and that efforts to develop positive character traits in learners could yield better educational and social outcomes. Examples of those traits included "persistence, self-control, curiosity, conscientiousness, grit, and self-confidence" (Tough 2012, xv). Tough argued that these crucial character traits could be taught if educational institutions made the effort and focused on the best methods for doing so. Indeed, "grit" has become the educational watchword of the day (Cepeda 2014; Gow 2014). The researcher who Tough cited frequently popularized the idea: Angela

Duckworth (2013), was invited to give a TED Talk in the spring of 2013 and was named a MacArthur Fellow (2013) in the fall of that year.

The above is a simplified summary, but Tough's extended analysis was drawn from an extensive array of neurological, biochemical, physiological, and psychological literatures. His book made a significant contribution by presenting that material in way that was accessible to educators, as one would expect from a long-time successful journalist and editor. Nevertheless, I view the book as duplicitous because, without explanation, Tough adopted a perspective that was contrary to the substantial investigative work he had done previously. The omitted information from that prior work weakens *How Children Succeed* considerably.

The omission, the complete absence of any mention of Geoffrey Canada and the Harlem Children's Zone (HCZ) in Tough's book, was shocking because he spent five years researching and observing Canada's program in order to write his *Whatever It Takes,* a positive analysis of that man and the central ideas behind the success of the comprehensive program he created (Tough 2009). Canada was single-minded in his determination to raise the test scores and academic achievement of the children connected to the HCZ, and his basic strategy was to replicate for poor children the supportive environment available to middle-class children, what he envisioned as "a cocoon of support—educational support, emotional support, medical support—that starts at birth and never stops" (Tough 2009, 279). To implement this vision, the list of services Canada made available through the HCZ was extensive and diverse: parenting classes; pre-K programs that began at age three; a peacemaker program for neighborhood safety; charter schools for elementary, middle, and secondary education; after-school programs; leadership training; a fitness and nutrition center; an employment and technology center; a college preparatory program; an arts and media program; asthma, obesity, and drug and alcohol programs; a crisis intervention center; and a single stop center that provided information to families in need of social services and/or legal and financial advice. The remedies offered in *How Children Succeed* (parental attachment training, character lessons with a character report card, and teaching in a way that encourages overcoming failure) paled in comparison to what Canada thought necessary. What would make anyone choose these limited responses to academic deficiencies instead of the comprehensive approach Tough supported previously?

There really was nothing new about Tough's suggested approach; in fact, B. Edward McClellan's (1999) history of American education focused on attempts by individuals, institutions, and organizations to shape character; Puritan schools, McGuffey's Readers, Lawrence Kohlberg and Carol Gilligan's cognitive moral development work, and William Bennett's book of virtues are just a few examples of the historical efforts to influence character development, often with limited success. Certainly in modern times, when imported into a classroom, character building activities generally satisfied adult goals, but didn't necessarily connect with students in a meaningful way. The never-ending search for the right character education program logically suggested that those that came before were ineffective. Moreover, there were several fundamental questions one could ask regarding the approach to character development that Tough promoted. Joan Goodman (2012), for example, argued that character traits can be viewed as situational, that there was a moral dimension to character, considerations that were absent in *How Children Succeed*. For example, was self-control always a laudable trait in the face of the outrageous social inequalities with which the intended recipients of Tough's proposals lived? Tough wrote sympathetically about a few community service programs like Dr. Nadine Burke Harris' pediatric center in San Francisco, but nowhere in his book was there even a hint of anger that the structural inequities that existed in the places he wrote about, had persisted with little organized effort to remedy the devastating educational and social consequences they produced. Urban schools were underfunded and the inequities relative to their suburban counterparts grew. As a result, the lessening of achievement gaps occurred at a slower pace in the decade after No Child Left Behind than in the decade before it, a factor that also had negative economic consequences for the entire nation (Dillon 2009; McKinsey and Company 2009). In the United States in 2012, 22% of children lived in poverty, a percentage that was larger among children who are black or Hispanic, and many of those lived in single-parent homes headed by a woman. Slightly more than 25% of people who were black or Hispanic lived in poverty compared to the 10% who were white (U.S. Census Bureau 2012). Can one honestly believe that self-control or grit is all that is needed to help individuals who live at the wrong end of these statistics? Is attachment training really the answer to the main parenting issues encountered by female householders living in poverty? Tough's silence in regard to deeply entrenched inequality and the devastating social consequences that followed showed how completely he was taken in by the "no excuses" mentality of the CEOs and venture capitalists who appeared as heroes in both of his books (Osgood 2012). Tough's book was clearly a weapon, one deployed to misdirect the forces for change that sought to reorder a social system that sustained rather than reduced inequalities that were evident everywhere.

The title of Tough's book, *How Children Succeed*, suggested a somewhat universal application of his findings in relation to a substantial number of subjects in a variety of settings. Instead, what we found primarily was a lengthy examination of the means by which leaders of two New York City schools cooperated in developing an approach to character building in their institutions. There was also a whole chapter regarding the work of a middle-school teacher in Brooklyn who urged members of her chess team to reflect on their mistakes and persevere in order to develop better thinking skills, which ultimately enabled them to become national chess champions. This data source was so negligible that it seemed purposely deceptive to claim it as a basis for a theory of success to be used to help children with low academic achievement.

One of the New York City schools covered extensively in Tough's book was the KIPP Academy in the South Bronx founded in 1995. When KIPP organizational leaders discovered that KIPP graduates did not persevere in college, the organization partnered with psychologists who were connected with the character development work Tough described and generated a list of qualities that would provide strengths to deal with college success and other issues. The selected qualities emphasized were zest, grit, self-control, optimism, gratitude, social intelligence, and curiosity. Then time was set aside to foster the development of those qualities through specific classroom activities. Unfortunately, in the hands of the novice teachers KIPP employed, these activities often fell quite short of their goals (Rubenstein 2013a).

Some KIPP schools have had success at increasing student achievement. One factor that contributed to the success of some KIPP schools was that their per-pupil expenditures were substantially higher than those in public schools (Miron, Urshel, and Saxton 2011). This increased amount of per pupil spending was possible because private corporate wealth had sustained the charter-school movement in a way that was unimaginable to public school educators. Two examples will suffice: in 2000, Doris and Donald Fisher, co-founders of Gap Inc, gave $15 million to establish the KIPP Foundation whose purpose was to support the expansion of KIPP schools (Fast Company 2000); in 2011, the Walton Family Foundation gave $25 million to continue that work, and increased the funds available to improve the college completion rate of KIPP graduates (Walton Family Foundation 2011). Moreover, KIPP academies were private schools (even though receiving public funds) and always had financially supportive boards of trustees drawn from the economic elite in whatever community they served. This was true of the KIPP Academy in New York City, the school that Paul Tough highlighted in *How Children Succeed* and that he suggested should serve as a model for America's public schools.

The other school Tough used to illustrate how children should be helped to form character traits that will support better chances for long lasting educational and social success, was the Riverdale Country School in the Bronx, a school that charged students $42,000 per year to attend its middle and upper school. I will simply say again that Paul Tough examined a very narrow subset of schools to illustrate his views about creating success-oriented students, and I can not imagine the relevance of Riverdale Country School to the needs of public schools a few miles away in the South Bronx, like the ones that Kozol had described with sorrow. Tough's choice of exemplars in *How Children Succeed,* and his favorable description of the substantial private capital that sustained the Harlem Children's Zone, clearly indicates his allegiance to corporate driven educational reform. There were other examples in the book, but they all shared the same characteristics; they had special funding and they represented a tiny percentage of the large numbers of American students who needed extra help to succeed.

In a review of *How Children Succeed* and *Fire in the Ashes,* Helen Epstein (2012) observes that some of the stories about young people "in Tough's book are inspiring, but missing from the narrative is a discussion of where all this brain-damaging stress came from in the first place" (33). In my view, reading Jonathan Kozol's prior books provides a clear but tragic depiction of the places and conditions that complete the narrative Epstein rightly demands. Tough may have defeated Kozol in the 2012 battle of the books, but the weapons he suggests will prove inadequate to overcome the social and educational dysfunction that Kozol described so vividly. Kozol's collected works remain influential and instructive. They are widely read in college courses and routinely inspire young people to become teachers. In so doing, they help keep alive the liberal ideals Kozol has proclaimed since his first book in 1967 (Ognibene 2012).

THE EVOLUTION OF DIANE RAVITCH: FROM CRITIC TO LEADER OF THE RESISTANCE

Diane Ravitch is an educational historian whose numerous books have made her a prominent figure in that discipline beginning with the publication of her first book, *The Great School Wars* in 1974. The book served as her dissertation at Columbia University and was done under the direction of Lawrence Cremin, easily the most prominent educational historian of the era. Cremin (1965) believed that the development of public schools to sustain democracy and build community was part of the genius of American society, but he also believed that schools were only one of the institutions that played an educative role in creating a social order relevant to the needs of a democratic society. Not surprisingly, Ravitch accepted this perspective as well.

Ravitch entered the field during a period in which opposition to traditional interpretations of educational history were commonplace. Historians such as Michael B. Katz, Joel Spring, Clarence Karier, and others, viewed many social institutions, including schools, as instruments used by elites to exert social control, to thwart efforts to promote equality, and to maintain the status quo, thus preserving their privileged position. Ravitch found that interpretation unbelievable and wrote a critique in the preface of *The Great School Wars* and then more comprehensively in her next book, *The Revisionists Revised: A Critique of the Radical Attack on the Schools* (1978). The schools were not, in her view (and Cremin's), instruments to reproduce social inequality or a mechanism of cultural repression. They were a primary mechanism to attain literacy, encourage social mobility, and promote the common good. Ravitch was an ardent defender of America's public schools, warts and all.

By her own admission, Ravitch's perspective began to shift when she was invited to serve as assistant secretary of education (1991–1993) in President George H. W. Bush's administration. In that context, and subsequently, she began to associate with conservative educational thinkers such as Chester Finn, Terry Moe, Caroline Hoxby, and Paul Peterson, and she helped to found conservative educational advocacy groups, like the Thomas B. Fordham Foundation and the Koret Task Force at the Hoover Institution. To overcome the presumed weakness of public schools, these people and organizations emphasized market-based ideas in their educational reform plans, ideas that would logically lead to a demand for school choice though the use of vouchers and the creation of charter schools. They argued that if the public schools had competition, it would force them to improve their overall performance. To improve public school academic offerings, these same players sought to create national curriculum standards patterned after the cultural literacy norms developed by another colleague, E. D. Hirsch (Ravitch 2010).

Ravitch's prior defense of America's community-controlled public schools, and her admiration of the curriculum and instructional ideals of John Dewey had been, to say the least, compromised. To promote her new educational views, Ravitch produced popular books: *National Standards in American Education* in 1995 and *New Schools for a New Century: The Redesign of Urban Education* (with Joseph Viteritti) in 1999.

Lawrence Cremin, Ravitch's mentor, wrote a prize-winning book in 1961 that argued that the decline of progressive educational ideals through the middle 1950s essentially ended the movement, but in *Left Back*, Ravitch (2000) disagreed with that assessment. While there were cycles of child-centered and back-to-basics educational reform for the remainder of the 20th century, the proliferation of courses and programs continued to minimize connections to the traditional curriculum and the social awareness and critical thinking that it produced. For Ravitch, the continuing effort to devise curriculum standards was the crucial task for twenty-first century education. The standards were important for all students, especially for those whose environments would least likely enable them to have any connection to traditional academic content and the benefits that emerge from that contact. Given her long and substantial criticism of America's public schools noted above, how was it possible that Ravitch in 2010 would publish a game-changing text entitled *The Death and Life of the Great American School System?* "Great?" For about 20 years, she had been saying something else. This change of heart required some explanation, especially since it made her a front-line defender of public schools in the face of unrelenting attacks by those who were once her conservative allies.

RAVITCH TO THE RESCUE

Ravitch (2010) did provide an explanation for her altered perspective, which she viewed as a normal reaction when a historian was faced with new evidence. While it appeared that the No Child Left Behind (NCLB) Act signed in 2002 by President George W. Bush contained many of the elements that Rativch favored, she concluded that in actual practice the policy did more harm than good. In Ravitch's view, the insistence that an unrealistic number of students should achieve improved math and language arts skills by a regimen of practice and then official tests, had "hijacked" the standards movement. The math and language arts emphasis diminished the importance of other subjects, and content standards being created for those and other disciplines tended to be bland in order to avoid the type of controversy that doomed the history standards developed in the mid 1990s. Ravitch could not support either of these trends.

Her next reversal was related to school choice, especially as she saw it operate in New York City, her hometown. Mayor Michael Bloomberg had achieved control of the school system in 2002, and with his school chancellor, Joel Klein, set out to create as many charter schools and small high schools as possible as a way to raise achievement levels. This was their signature reform, and it came at the cost of distressing parents in many communities where schools were closed and children were sent elsewhere. In reality, these reforms did not improve test scores when all the manipulations to show improved results were uncovered. The fact that the school choice and test score accountability movements neglected the character development and civic purpose of schools, was another reason Ravitch severed her connection to these movements.

Perhaps the best-known chapter in *The Death and Life of the Great American School System* was The Billionaires Boy's Club. Contrasting the purposes and *modus operandi* of older foundations created by Andrew Carnegie, Henry Ford, and Walter Annenberg that tended to support educational improvement efforts that were local and/or methodologically specific, newer philanthropists like Bill Gates, Eli Broad, and the Walton family set out to remake the whole American educational system. Identifying the vast amount of resources available to these billionaire venture philanthropists, Ravitch explained the obvious connection between their preference for unregulated entrepreneurial systems, including charter organizations and schools, and their insistence that teacher accountability and retention should be tied to improved student test scores, an approach that would substantially lessen the ability of teacher unions to protect members from capricious administrative behavior. In addition to this fierce anti-union mentality, deregulation made it possible to obtain unfettered access to the enormous education marketplace, and this new form of assessing teacher success though student performance created savings by pushing out higher-paid teachers, hiring less expensive ones, and shrinking the total number of teachers needed by putting more students in classes of teachers with the best record of success. The myriad of factors that contributed to or reduced the possibility of that success were not considered.

The influence of *The Death and Life of the Great American School System* made Ravitch a leader of the resistance movement to challenge and turn back the conservative campaign to remake the public school system based on the free market principles they favored. Her role was clearly visible at the Save Our Schools March in Washington on July 30, 2011. The Save Our Schools (SOS) coalition was created by a collection of teachers and organizations opposed to the practices resulting from NCLB and its successor, Race to the Top (RTTT). Included among the SOS speakers were a cadre of leading educators long associated with progressive educational views: Pedro Noguera, Linda Darling-Hammond, Deborah Meier, Jonathan Kozol, and Diane Ravitch. Valerie Strauss (2011), a *Washington Post* columnist who was present at the event, wrote the following:

> Ravitch, whose best-selling 2010 "The Death and Life of the Great American School System" helped galvanize teachers to publicly protesting their discontent with former president Bush's No Child Left Behind, and the current administration's Race to the Top, told the crowd that public schools are "not shoe stores" and shouldn't be managed as businesses.

During her remarks, Ravitch noted that our best schools, those with the least amount of poverty, had international testing results that were as high as any other nation. Echoing Jonathan Kozol, Ravitch said that "the shame of our nation is that we lead the developed world in childhood poverty." Strauss reported that Ravitch's "celebrity with people in the crowd was such that when she was done, they began to chant thank you." Ravitch received the prestigious 2014 Grawemeyer Award in Education for the *ideas* that flowed from the educational analysis offered in *The Death and Life of the Great American School System,* the book she published four years earlier (Grawemeyer Awards 2014).

ONWARDS TO VICTORY

Winston Churchill's *Onwards to Victory* speeches were notably more optimistic than earlier ones, because the tides of war were finally shifting in favor of the Allies. In the education wars that have been ongoing for more than two decades, it seems that in 2014, liberal views of education have resurfaced after more than two decades of assault from the Right. It is not too much to say that Diane Ravitch has led the forces that are helping to overcome the dominant conservative educational perspectives that appeared unstoppable only a short time ago. The *New York Times* characterized her as a "loud voice fighting [the] tide of [a] new trend in education" (Rich 2013). As one commentator noted, "after just six years of battle," Ravitch is "the single individual who most influenced the eventual outcome ... the restoration and renewal of public schools" (Horn 2013).

Ravitch's influence increased with the 2013 publication of her second anti-corporate reform book, *Reign of Error: The Hoax of the Privatization Movement and the Danger to America's Public Schools.* Unlike Jonathan Kozol's *Fire in the Ashes,* the *New York Times* reviewed Ravitch's book, and like the *Washington Post,* published a lengthy interview with the author. The *Los Angeles Times* published two news stories about *Reign of Error* in conjunction with Ravitch's appearance in the area shortly after the book was published. Other national outlets like the *Huffington Post, Salon,* the *New York Review of Books,* and *Commonweal* also reviewed or wrote laudatory essays about the book that helped to place it on the *New York Times* bestseller list for four weeks, but, as we shall see, its impact far outpaced its sales.

Reign of Error continued and extended the themes and criticisms present in *The Death and Life of the Great American School System,* though its format was substantially different. Many of the first 20 brief chapters presented data that refuted assertions made by public education critics about issues such the achievement gap (it is not increasing), graduation rates (they are increasing, not falling), and international test scores (which will have little effect on the strength of our economy). Additional chapters once again identified corporate reformers and examined the language they used to entice supporters, while others discussed and critiqued exemplars of the reform movement, such as Michelle Rhee and Teach for America, both of whom are heavily endowed by corporate foundations and other wealthy individuals from the entrepreneurial class. Much of the second half of the book offered information about specific educational practices and approaches that would improve educational outcomes if they were funded equitably (preschool education, smaller class size, full service schools, etc.). It also reiterated Ravitch's core belief in the democratic necessity of maintaining public control over the institution historically entrusted with the task of promoting our nation's social, political, economic, and moral development. She was emphatic that this could not be the work of private enterprise.

Reign of Error is essentially a fact book that provides information to a growing number of people opposed to corporate reform principles and practices. This opposition consists of a coalition of teachers, educational administrators, parents, educational researchers, leaders of independent educational organizations, and, most recently, legislators in states in which corporate reform activities are most evident and constituent opposition is loud enough to be heard. In addition to data, Ravitch's book also provides a critical interpretative lens to help members of the coalition present their arguments in ways that are both cogent and congruent with criticisms voiced in places beyond their local sphere of influence.

Commentators on *Reign on Error* often use language associated with conflict, in this case, the "war" between liberal and corporate educational reform perspectives. One commentator thought of the book as a handbook of resistance (Schmidt 2013). Motoko Rich (2013) in the *New York Times* said that Ravitch had created "an army of new backers," and a blogger wrote that she was "speaking to the growing and rumbling army of educators" (Horn 2013). In a reference to a well-known corporate reform public relations film, a Ravitch enthusiast wrote "the reformers can wait for Superman all they want. We've got Wonder Woman" (Rubinstein 2013b). A female second-grade teacher from Iowa identified the weapon she thought Wonder Woman should have:

> If I were to create art to decorate the cover of [her] new book ... it would include an illustration of Diane Ravitch, sledgehammer in hand, smashing a brick wall with the words 'Education Reform.' We would see bricks falling down with words on them such as Race to the Top, Arne Duncan, NCLB, vouchers, Gates Foundation, and standardized assessments. (Prime 2013)

Ravitch has been called a crusader, a fierce warrior, and, more gently, a folk hero to the Left. She is viewed as both a general and a cheerleader in the movement to oppose corporate educational reform, and her leadership and cheering have intensified as the coalition forces win victories here and there. Ravitch herself named the group opposed to corporate reform: "What do we call the millions of parents and teachers, principals, superintendents, school board members, and researchers who fight for democratic control of education? 'The Resistance'" (Ravitch 2014). Beyond her books, what other mechanisms has Ravitch used to spread her message so that others on the Left can understand and act on it?

NEW WEAPONS IN THE WAR OF IDEAS

Ravitch has used both Facebook and Twitter to promote her new book and the ideas contained therein. *Reign of Error* has 13,000 "likes" on Facebook, and Ravitch has 85,000 followers on Twitter. She has a homepage that has all the standard author features, but it also links to posts that appear on her blog everyday. In contrast, Jonathan Kozol, a perennial hero to the Left, has virtually no presence on Facebook or Twitter, nor are there any active links on his homepage. Ravitch's web presence has a personal feel; indeed, her homepage even has links to her recent speeches and interviews. Kozol's web presence is less than half hearted. His homepage is a publisher and speaker's bureau creation, but no more than that. These differences no doubt have contributed to the success of *Reign of Error* and the relative invisibility of *Fire in the Ashes*. A more powerful explanation of that success is the existence of Ravitch's blog and the evident affection it inspires for her as a person as well as the sustained enthusiasm for the ideas she promotes.

Ravitch's blog (www.dianeravitch.net) is like a perpetual motion device that does not take weekends or holidays off. The energy sources are Ravitch's determination to prevail in the education war, and the support of readers who provide an unending supply of personal stories and links to news items about corporate educational reform activities in their communities. Additional information comes from other bloggers, who have a smaller readership and whose messages reach a larger audience when posted on the Ravitch site, and from educational researchers who decode and demolish technical claims about such favorite reformer topics as value-added accountability measures, charter school achievement results, and the interpretation of international test data. These bloggers and researchers are experienced educators and/or outstanding scholars who add enormous detail to the themes developed in *Reign of Error*. In addition to the examples noted above, Ravitch's blog provides information on a wide range of activities that flow from corporate reform beliefs, many of which are quite contrary to past practices in American public education. Some of those examples relate to the imposition of the Common Core state standards, the crony capitalism exhibited in the awarding of charter school contracts, the unethical sale of technology and programs designed to meet Common Core requirements that the sellers were influential in creating, the efforts of governors and legislators to eliminate local control of schools, the granting of foundation funds to school board candidates who will support corporate reform practices if elected, the destruction of communities through arbitrary decisions to close schools, and the demonizing of teachers as a way to foster an environment that promotes privatization. The purpose of such information is to motivate her troops to continue the battle.

Ravitch's blog is impressive. Launched in April 2012, it had reached 12 million page views in May 2014. During 2013 there were 4,007 new posts on the blog bringing the total blog archive to 6,627 posts at the end of that year. In the beginning, the blog was almost oppressive, sending about 20 new posts every day, a number that was later reduced slightly. The blogging circle around Ravitch is unwaveringly loyal and often coordinated. *Reign of Error* was published on September 17, 2013; on that day, and on the day before and after, over 50 reviews were sent by bloggers to readers across the country. There was a buzz about the book that dominated posts on Ravitch's blog for about three months. Not only do bloggers send posts to Ravitch, many post hers on their sites daily.

None of these interactions would matter much if all this communication was simply an expression of personal opinion; instead, Ravitch and her blogger friends, and all those who are influenced by them, have mounted attacks against the Common Core state standards and their related tests, and, against all odds, they are winning some of those battles. A rare coming together of the Right and the Left has spurred opposition for different reasons: the Right believes the Common Core represents a federal over-reach and is unconstitutional; those on the Left don't disagree but are more concerned that the standards promote bad educational practice. The Left, Ravitch, and her army of followers believe that the standards are developmentally inappropriate, diminish opportunities to maintain a broad range of curriculum choices, abuse children through excessive testing, and destroy the creativity of both learners and teachers.

These themes have resonated with people all across the country. By the end of 2013, there was political pushback in 23 states from governors, legislators, and/or state education superintendants against the core itself, the testing it requires, or the speed of its implementation (Schneider 2013). In 2010 there were 45 states that agreed to implement the Common Core standards in order to have an opportunity to apply for grants from the Obama administration's Race to the Top education initiative; the current state-based opposition represents slightly more than half of the states that originally signed on. There are anti-Common Core Facebook groups in 41 states (Stop Common Core 2013). All these developments can be observed in New York state, where Diane Ravitch resides (Brooklyn). Opposition to the Common Core is especially emotional and vocal in New York because of the inexplicable decision of the state's board of regents to mandate testing in 2013 based on the core *before* the state curriculum was completely developed or teachers had been trained to implement it. Not surprisingly, across the state only 30% of students passed the language arts and math tests, but the passing rate of African American and Hispanic students was less than 20%. Parents and school leaders throughout the state went ballistic, especially since sustained efforts to convince State Education Commissioner John King and Regents' Chancellor Merryl Tisch to slow down the testing process were simply ignored. While these efforts were statewide, they were most vehemently pursued by parents and school leaders from Long Island and Westchester County, regions where Ravitch was invited to give keynote addresses to parents, to an ad hoc multi-district teacher group, and to a gathering of school administrators and school board members (Donnelly 2014; Gustavson 2014; Take Action 2013).

Ravitch regularly posts Westchester and Long Island protest news on her blog and identifies individual school administrators leading those protests as "education heroes." Parent groups against the Common Core and testing have been organized, such as the Long Island Parents for Education and Pencils Down Rockland County, which, among other things, supported and publicized the growing "opt-out" strategy to protect their children from excessive testing. In October 2013, three members of the New York State Assembly from Westchester County launched an effort to have the state abandon the testing program, and in December, the senate's education committee recommended a bill to ban all testing in the primary grades and to conduct an evaluation of the entire testing program (Savayan 2013; Flanagan 2013). In January 2014, New York Governor Andrew Cuomo concluded that the implementation of the Common Core was seriously "flawed" and created a special panel to recommend corrective action with a report due by June (Blain 2014). His Westchester Republican opponent in the forthcoming 2014 election has made opposition to the Common Core and testing part a prominent feature in his platform (Klepper 2014).

Opponents of Common Core and testing severely criticized John King, the commissioner of education and Merryl Tisch, chancellor of the New York State Board of Regents (Baker 2013). Their backgrounds reflect the interests and values of the corporate educational reform tradition. Each has distinguished personal educational credentials; what they do not have is anything resembling substantial teaching experiences or experience with public education. King worked for a charter school organization when he was appointed assistant commissioner in 2009. Tisch had a brief career as a primary teacher at a prominent Hebrew school in New York City. She became a regent in the mid 1990s due to her elite social status as the wife of the CEO of the Lowes Corporation, whose support the Republican then governor in Albany wanted to cultivate. Tisch was responsible for creating policies around the adoption of the Common Core, and King, who had been in the same doctoral program with her at Columbia University, was responsible for overseeing mechanisms by which the core was implemented and students tested in the schools. Because King and Tisch seriously botched the rollout of the Common Core and its testing component, and were unwilling to alter their plans in the face of unrelenting criticism, they were frequent targets in Ravitch's blog. The criticism also weakened the support of some of the other regents and encouraged the creation of anti-King groups such as the NYS Allies for Public Education (www.nysape.org), which lists as one of its primary activities the Campaign for the Resignation of Education Commissioner John King. The organization also serves as an information clearinghouse for parents and to enable them to arrange opt-out mechanisms (Baker 2013; Odato, 2013). Two members of the organization's steering committee are close associates of Ravitch.

Another organization created out of the anger over the core curriculum and testing is the Badass Teacher Association (www.badassteacher.org). Corporate reformers have a purposely naïve view of teaching, insisting that the only way to measure good teaching is to compare student test scores before and after they are placed with a specific teacher in any given year. The goal is to use this data to sort out the "great" teachers, to get rid of the rest thus increasing class size as a consequence, and to reinforce the "no excuses" mantra about learning outcomes without examining any other variables that contribute to those outcomes. This reasoning infuriated Mark Naison, professor and director of the Fordham Urban Studies Program, and Naison has become a frequent contributor to Ravitch's blog. In the summer of 2013, along with two teachers (one from Long Island), he formed the Badass Teacher Association (BAT), created a website and a blog, and invited teachers to join. Thousands of teachers accepted the invitation (including Ravitch) and formed BAT Facebook groups in almost every state. The website alerts members to educational events taking place in their area, ones which need teacher participation to counter whatever corporate reform plan is being proposed. The BAT blog lists eight "blogs we like." The first one listed is Diane Ravitch's blog, and *all* of the others are bloggers who frequently contribute to her blog. One of the things Ravitch has accomplished, was to create a circle of corporate reform critics who support each other's work and substantially magnify their anti-reform message through their individual blogs.

In March 2013, Ravitch and two frequent contributors to her blog announced the formation of a new organization, the Network for Public Education (NPE). The purpose of the organization is to bring together bloggers and grass roots organizations fighting to preserve public education in the face of the privatization initiatives of corporate education reformers (www.networkforpubliceducation.org). The NPE collects and distributes relevant news from members on its website, podcasts, and on Facebook and Twitter. Another important role it plays is the endorsement of board of education candidates who have views that are congruent with those of the NPE and articulated in *Reign of Error.* The endorsements help to raise money for poorly funded candidates and encourage others to help in their campaigns. There are about 75 bloggers and organizations that are members ("allies") of NPE, and Ravitch serves as president. NPE is sustained by donations from members and individuals connected to the blogging and grassroots groups that are the core of the organization. In March 2014, NPE held its first national conference at the University of Texas in Austin, at which participants issued a call for congressional hearings on the misuse of testing. To raise awareness of this demand, NPE members launched a Twitter *Storm* of 20,000 tweets that reached 400,000 supporters, the media, and the general public, who then flooded congressional offices with phone calls in support of holding those hearings.

CONCLUSION

Conservative critics of Jonathan Kozol often dismiss him as someone from the past who can safely be ignored, as if seeking social justice and democratic ideals can ever be out of fashion. Kozol's place as a hero to the Left was secured long ago. Indeed, some of his book titles have functioned as leftist-oriented code words and have provoked discussions about significant social and educational issues: death at an early age, savage inequalities, and the shame of the nation. As has been suggested, the last two of his 13 books have been overlooked, partly because they were repetitive, but also because traditional ways of calling attention to them were inadequate. Kozol's books were important weapons in wars waged by the Left, but his arsenal now appears to be empty.

Paul Tough's *How Children Succeed* had a remarkable run as a bestseller. The book appealed to those who supported the common-sense notion that certain positive character traits can enhance the potential for academic success, and to those who believed that pressing social and educational issues could be solved if people could be trained to try harder. While Tough also participated in newer social media forums to spread his message, his efforts were miniscule compared to those of Ravitch. Tough believed that his recommendations would help overcome educational deficits, and he offered them in the hope that they would be adopted and implemented successfully. Ravitch, by comparison, was a leader of the rebellion against the dominant ideas espoused by corporate educational reformers that adversely affected those same learners, and she seems determined to press on until the rebellion succeeds.

In an interview published in a Korean newspaper in December 2013, Tough was asked whether there had been meaningful changes in American education and society since the publication of his book. His reply was that "he was not aware of any major policy changes that 'How Children Succeed' has helped to bring about." He also thought that there was "interest" in his book from educational administrators, and that there were "conversations" about it around the dinner table and in teacher's lounges (Seon-ah 2013). These seem to be very modest outcomes. Sales data related to *How Children Succeed* suggest that in the ongoing education war, Tough assembled a book-buying army of followers that should be invincible. By his own admission, however, in terms of substantial accomplishments, his forces have seemed unable to advance, perhaps because, unlike Ravitch, he has not helped create a support staff of people and organizations with similar goals and a willingness to work together to achieve them.

Ravitch has been relentless in her efforts to combat corporate reform educational goals and restore a leftist perspective rooted in the belief that educational activities that promote individual growth and social cohesion are crucial to preserving and strengthening American democracy. Her books, her use of social media, and her organizational work all support ideals that are essential to the Left. Her views are almost always cited when opinion magazines publish educational articles, and YouTube videos capture her speaking at venues of every sort; all this exposure has had some good effect. The most obvious impact is that the Common Core, which was so readily adopted in 2010, is under scrutiny in many places, as are the tests designed to accompany them (Ujifusa 2014a; Ujifusa 2014b). In February 2014, the New York State Board of Regents voted to delay the full implementation of the Common Core graduation requirements until 2022, to halt the implementation of any new tests and allow for some flexibility in administering others, and to seek an easily obtained federal waiver from the unbelievable requirement that learning disabled students and English-language learners take the same tests as their classmates (Bakerman 2014; Karlin 2014).

A final example of Ravitch's influence has been in the field of politics. New York City's new mayor, Bill de Blasio, was sworn in on January 1, 2014, and began to make good on his promise to undo much of Bloomberg's corporate education agenda, (Hernandez and Baker 2013). Ravitch endorsed de Blasio over several others early in the primary process, encouraged her blog readers to support him, and served as his informal education advisor during the primary and regular elections. Ravitch's Network for Public Education (NPE) played a key role in supporting the election of Ras Baraka as mayor of Newark, NJ. New Jersey has a Republican governor who favors privatization, a recent education commissioner who trained at the Broad Urban Superintendents Academy and who appointed a Newark superintendant who used to work for Teach for America. This trio is attempting to end traditional public education in Newark via school closures, teacher layoffs, and the creation of charter schools staffed by Teach for America graduates. Baraka, a former Newark school principal, has offered an alternative plan to save and improve the public schools that mirror principles espoused by the NPE, which sent out pleas for financial support and other help for his campaign. NPE used a *Thunderclap* Twitter campaign to simultaneously reach their individual and group members to increase awareness of the importance of Baraka's election (Maxwell, 2014; Network for Public Education 2014). These efforts paid off, and despite the odds, Baraka won with 54% of the vote.

Publishing a well-received book is still an important weapon in the war of ideas. However, as has been shown, disseminating a book's ideas through social media and linking those ideas to activities that support left-leaning values and institutions, creates a weapon whose power is enhanced. Leaders on the Left should take notice.

REFERENCES

"100 Notable Books." 2012. *New York Times Book Review,* November 27.

Bakerman, Jessica. 2014. "Anti-Common Core Bandwagon Nears Capacity." January 23, http://www.capitalnewyork.com/article/albany/2014/01/8539167/anti-common-core-bandwagon-nears-capacity

Baker, Al. 2013. "At Forums, New York State Education Commissioner Faces A Barrage of Complaints." *New York Times,* November 17.

Blain, Glenn. 2014. "Common Core Needs 'Corrective action': Gov. Cuomo." *New York Daily News,* January 21.

Cepeda, Esther. 2014. "The Grit Factor in Success." *San Jose Mercury News,* February 8.

Cremin, Lawrence. 1961. *The Transformation of the School.* New York: Knopf.

———. 1965. *The Genius of American Education.* New York: Knopf.

Dillon, Sam. 2009. "No Child Law is not Closing Racial Gap." *New York Times,* April 29.

Donnelly, Brian. 2014. "Education Expert Rails against Standardized Testing in Bedford." *Bedford Daily Voice,* January 18.

Duckworth, Angela. 2013. "The Key to Success? Grit." http://www.capitalnewyork.com/article/albany/2014/01/8539167/anti-common-core-bandwagon-nears-capacity

Epstein, Helen. 2012. "Children of the Storm." *The Nation,* December 3.

Fast Company. 2000 "Social Capitalists: KIPP Foundation." Fast Company. http://www.fastcompany.com/social/2008/profiles/kipp-foundation.html

Flanagan, John. 2013. "NYS Education Chairman Flanagan Calls for Immediate SED Action on Common Core and Unveils a Package of Legislative Actions" December 12, http://www.capitalnewyork.com/article/albany/2014/01/8539167/anti-common-core-bandwagon-nears-capacity

Goldstein, Rebecca, Sheila Macrine, and Nataly Chesky. 2011. "Welcome to the 'New Normal'": The News Media and Neoliberal Reforming Education." *Journal of Inquiry and Action in Education* 4 (1): 112–131.

Goodman, Joan. 2012. "What Kind of Success Does 'Character' Predict?" *Education Week*, November 27.

Gow, Peter. 2014. "What's Dangerous About the Grit Narrative, and How to Fix It." *Education Week*, March 3.

Grawemeyer Adwards. 2014. "Ravitch Wins Grawemeyer Education Award." www.grawemeyer.org.

Gustavson, Jennifer. 2014. "Expert Calls for Protest on Standardized Testing." *Riverhead News-Review*, January 23.

"Hardcover Best Sellers." 2013. *New York Times Book Review*, April 13.

Hernandez, Javier and Al Baker. 2013. "De Blasio Recognizes Obstacles Standing=in Way of School Plans." *New York Times*, December 30.

Horn, Jim. 2013. "America's Education Whistleblower: Diane Ravitch and the Reign of Error. *Common Dreams*, September 25.

Jenyum. 2010. "Books are Weapons in the War of Ideas." *Daily Kos*, September 8.

Karlin, Rick. 2014. "Under Pressure, Regents Agree to Slow Common Core Rollout." *Times Union*, February 10.

Klepper, David. 2014. "Astorino and Moss Want to Party Like It's 1994." *Daily Gazette*, May 16.

Kopp, Wendy. 2012. "Fire in the Ashes: Twenty-Five Years among the Poorest Children in America." *Washington Post*, September 28.

Kozol, Jonathan. 1967. *Death at an Early Age: The Destruction of the Hearts and Minds of the Negro Children in the Boston Public Schools*. Boston; Houghton Mifflin.

———. 1988. *Rachel and Her Children: Homeless Families in America*. New York: Ballantine.

———. 1991. *Savage Inequalities: Children in America's Schools*. New York: Crown.

———. 1995. *Amazing Grace: The Lives of Children and the Conscience of a Nation*. New York: Crown.

———. 2000. *Ordinary Resurrections: Children in the Years of Hope*. New York: Crown.

———. 2005. *The Shame of the Nation: The Restoration of Apartheid Schooling in America*. New York: Crown.

———. 2007. *Letters to a Young Teacher*. New York: Three Rivers.

———. 2012. *Fire in the Ashes: Twenty-Five Years among the Poorest Children in America*. New York: Crown.

MacArthur Fellows Program. 2013. "Angela Duckworth." September 25, http://www.macfound.org/fellows/class/2013/

Maxwell, Lesli. 2014. "Newark's New Mayor Demands Return of Schools to Local Control." *Education Week*, May 17.

McClellan, B. Edward. 1999. *Moral Education in America*. New York: Teachers College Press.

McKinsey and Company. 2009. *The Economic Impact of the Achievement Gain America's Schools*. www.mackenseyonsociety.com

Miron, Gary, Jessica Urschel, and Nicholas Saxton. 2011. *What Makes KIPP Work? A Study of Student Characteristics, Attrition, and School Finance*. http://www.edweek.org/media/kippstudy.pdf

Network for Public Education. 2014. "A Local Election with National Implications: Ras Baraka for Mayor of Newark, NJ." May 10. Website: www.networkforpubliceducation.org

Odato, James. 2013. "Common Core Divides State's Regents Board." *Times Union*, December 15.

Olson, Kristen. 2008. *Schools as Colonizers*. Saarbrucken, Germany: VMD Verlag.

Ognibene, Richard, ed. 2012. *A Persistent Reformer: Jonathan Kozol's Work to Promote Equality in America*. New York: Peter Lang.

Osgood, Katie. 2012. "Paul Tough is Way Off-Base. And Stop Saying 'Grit.' " @ *The Chalk Face*, September 30.

"Paperback Best Sellers." 2014. *New York Times Book Review*, June 22.

Prime, Amy. 2013. "Prime: Diane Ravitch's New Book Takes Education Myths to Task." *Des Moines Register*, September 17.

Ravitch, Diane. 1974. *The Great School Wars: New York City, 1805–1973*. New York: Basic Books.

———. 1978. *The Revisionists Revised: A Critique of the Radical Attack on the Schools*. New York: Basic Books.

———. 1995. *National Standards in American Education*. Washington D.C.: The Brookings Institution.

———. 2000. *Left Back: A Century of Failed School Reforms*. New York: Simon & Schuster.

———. 2010. *The Death and Life of the Great American School System. How Testing and Choice Are Undermining Education*. New York: Basic Books.

———. 2013. *Reign of Error: The Hoax of the Privatization Movement And the Danger to America's Public Schools*. New York: Alfred A. Knopf.

———. 2014. "What Do We Call Our Side? The Resistance." April 7, http://dianeravitch.net/2014/04/07/what-do-we-call-our-side-the-resistance/

Ravitch, Diane, and Viteritti, Joseph, eds. 1999. *New Schools for a New Century: The Redesign of Urban Education*. New Haven: Yale University Press.

Rich, Motoko. 2013. "Loud Voice Fighting Tide of New Trend in Education." *New York Times*, September 10.

Rubinstein, Gary. 2013a. "Teacher Quality at KIPP." April 10, http://garyrubinstein.teachforus.org/2013/04/10/teacher-quality-at-kipp/

———. 2013b. "Let It Reign!" September 17, http://garyrubinstein.teachforus.org/2013/09/17/let-it-reign/

Savayan, Tania. 2013. "3 Westchester Assembly Members Seek to End New Core-Linked Tests." *The Journal News*, October 21.

Schmidt, George. 2013. "Reign of Error: Perhaps the Most Important American Book of the 21st Century: Putting 'Service' Back in its Proper Place of Dignity, Respect, and History." *Substance News*, September 19.

Schneider, Mercedes. 2013. "Is California Common Core Unrest State #29?" www.deutsch29,wordpress.com, December 21, https://deutsch29.wordpress.com/2013/12/21/is-california-common-core-unrest-state-23/

Seon-ah, Yang. 2013. "Interview: New Insight into How Children Succeed." *The Hankyoreh*, December 25.

Stop Common Core in Alabama. 2013. "States Which Oppose Common Core." http://www.auee.org/states-who-oppose-common-core.html

Strauss, Valerie. 2011. "The Save Our Schools March." *Washington Post*, July 30.

Take Action Long Island Newsletter. 2013. March, http://www.takeactionli.org/documents/newsletters/TALi_Newsletter-March2013.pdf

Tough, Paul. 2009. *Whatever It Takes*. Boston: Houghton Mifflin Harcourt.

———. 2012. *How Children Succeed: Grit, Curiosity, and the Hidden Power of Character.* Boston: Houghton Mifflin Harcourt.

Ujifusa, Andrew. 2014a. "Resistance to the Common Core Mounts." *Education Week*, April 21.

———. 2014b. "State Political Rifts Sap Support for Common-Core Tests." *Education Week*, May 6.

U.S. Census Bureau. 2012. *Income, Poverty, and Health Insurance Coverage in the United States: 2011*. U.S. Census Bureau: Washington D.C.

Walton Family Foundation. *Walton Family Foundation Invests $25 Million in KIPP to Serve 59,000 Students by 2015*. The Walton Family Foundation, http://www.waltonfamilyfoundation.org/mediacenter/educationreform/walton-family-foundation-invests-$25-million-in-kipp-to-serve-59,000-students-by-2015

ABOUT THE AUTHOR

Richard Ognibene was formerly professor and dean of the College of Education and Human Services at Seton Hall University and recently retired from Siena College, where he is professor of education emeritus. Ognibene completed his EdD degree in the history of education at the University of Rochester and is the editor of *A Persistent Reformer: Jonathan Kozol's Work to Promote Equality in America* (Peter Lang Publishing, 2012). His research interests include school choice and charter schools, religion and education, and the historical roots of contemporary educational issues. Ognibene would like to thank Joseph DeVitis for encouraging his recent academic work and providing opportunities to share it with a wider audience.

INDEX

CPSIA information can be obtained
at www.ICGtesting.com
Printed in the USA
FFOW02n1536050815
15698FF